Strategic Perspectives on Planning Practice

Politics of Planning Series

Barry Checkoway, Editor

Neighborhood Policy and Planning   Phillip L. Clay and
   Robert M. Hollister

The Politics of Public-Facility Planning   John E. Seley

Human Services at Risk   Felice Davidson Perlmutter

**Neighborhood Revitalization and the Postindustrial City:
   A Multinational Perspective**   Dennis E. Gale

Strategic Perspectives on Planning Practice   Barry Checkoway

Economic Development Planning   Edward M. Bergman

Strategic Perspectives on Planning Practice

Edited by
Barry Checkoway
The University of Michigan

Lexington Books
D.C. Heath and Company/Lexington, Massachusetts/Toronto

Library of Congress Cataloging-in-Publication Data

Strategic perspectives on planning practice.

  (Politics of planning series)
  Includes index.
  1. Planning. 2. Strategic planning. I. Checkoway,
Barry. II. Series.
HD30.28.S7337   1986   658.4'012   85–40011
ISBN 0–669.10366–7 (alk. paper)
ISBN 0–669–14227–1 (pbk. : alk. paper)

Published simultaneously in Canada
Printed in the United States of America
Casebound International Standard Book Number: 0–669–10366–7
Paperbound International Standard Book Number: 0–669–14227–1
Library of Congress Catalog Card Number: 85–40011

The paper used in this publication meets the minimum requirements of
American National Standard for Information Sciences—Permanence of
Paper for Printed Library Materials, ANSI Z39.48–1984. ∞™

86 87 88 89 90 8 7 6 5 4 3 2 1

Contents

Figures and Tables   vii

Preface   ix

1. Strategic Perspectives on Planning Practice:
    An Introduction   1
    Barry Checkoway

Part I   Contextual and Structural Perspectives   9

2. Planning Practice in an Age of Reaction   11
    John W. Dyckman

3. Politics in Planners' Practice   25
    Howell S. Baum

4. Usable Planning Theory: An Agenda for Research
    and Education   43
    Judith Innes de Neufville

Part II   Strategies and Skills in Practice   63

5. Strategic Planning in the Public Sector: Approaches
    and Directions   65
    John M. Bryson, R. Edward Freeman, and *William D. Roering*

6. Making Planners More Effective Strategists   87
    Jerome L. Kaufman

7. Policy Analysis with Implementation in Mind   105
    Carl V. Patton

8. **Participatory Research and Community Planning**   123
    L. David Brown

9. **Governing and Managing Public Organizations**   139
    John E. Tropman

10. **Developing Coalitions in the Face of Power: Lessons from the Human Services**   153
    Milan J. Dluhy

11. **Roles for Planners in Community Development**   165
    Neil S. Mayer

12. **Feminist Advocacy Planning in the 1980s**   181
    Jacqueline Leavitt

13. **Political Strategy for Social Planning**   195
    Barry Checkoway

Part III   Future Prospects   215

14. **The Institutional Focus of Planning Theory**   217
    Seymour J. Mandelbaum

15. **Toward a New Epistemology of Practice**   231
    Donald A. Schön

16. **Planning under Freedom: A New Experiment in Democracy**   251
    Bertram Gross and Kusum Singh

Index   271

About the Contributors 275

Figures and Tables

Figures

5–1. Strategic Planning Process   72

5–2. *Philadelphia Investment Portfolio* Proposed Portfolio Assessment Matrix   75

5–3. Hennepin County Strategic Planning Process   77

8–1. Two Phases of Community Planning   133

Tables

6–1. Position, Salience, and Power of Target Groups on Planning Issue   97

6–2. Relationships among Target Groups on Planning Issue   98

6–3. Position, Salience, and Power of Target Groups before and after Strategic Action   99

10–1. Characteristics of Four Coalitions in the Human Services   157

10–2. Typology of Coalitions Based on Stability and Structure   160

11–1. Ratios of Actual to Planned Outputs for Completed Projects   168

11–2. Staff Development Skills and Project Success   171

11–3. Staff Development Skills and Success in Leveraging Funds   171

11–4. Financial Marketing Skills and Project Success: Commercial and Economic Development Projects   173

11–5. Financial Marketing Skills and Project Success: Housing, Community Development, and Energy Projects   173

Preface

Planning operates in a changing political context. Private groups blame government for economic problems and planning agencies for a variety of ills, while planners face obstacles of implementation and struggle for survival in the face of power. Austerity policies and adversarial assaults on agencies have worsened conditions in many cities and neighborhoods. Federal budget reductions have affected many persons who had depended on agencies because they perceived few other possibilities. State budget deficits and tax revenue shortages have caused cuts in agencies and services that have affected the poor, minorities, and other disadvantaged groups at a time of increasing need. These conditions challenge planners to recognize change and develop capacity for the years ahead, but many lack knowledge, skills, and attitudes to respond effectively in the face of power. Some planners formulate strategy and build support for implementation, others retrench agencies or manage cutbacks, and others sit tight or retreat rather than play a more active strategic or political role.

This book presents strategic perspectives on planning practice. It examines contextual and structural issues, strategies and skills for practice, and prospects for the future. It draws on work in several fields and includes cases of planners and agencies that employ innovative or examplary methods to relate strategy and politics to practice. It does not suggest that these planners and agencies are typical in the field or that these methods alone are sufficient to alter the context of practice. It does suggest that planning operates in a changing context and that strategy can serve as a resource to influence implementation.

It is a pleasure to acknowledge some of those who contributed to this book. David Prosperi, editor of the *Journal of Planning Education and Research,* which included earlier versions of selected chapters, was a source of valuable and appreciated assistance throughout the project. Harold Johnson, dean of the School of Social Work at the University of Michigan, provided encouragement and support to help complete the work. Others who deserve special mention include Jeffrey Butts, Jay Chatterjee, Patricia Ellis,

Dan Madaj, and Jaime Welch-Donahue. Margie, Amy, and Laura Checko-way provide the patience, love and understanding that give meaning to my work.

The contributors to this book remember Paul Davidoff, advocate for equity in planning and a participant in this project before his death. We will donate our royalties to the fund established by the Association of Collegiate Schools of Planning in his memory.

1
Strategic Perspectives on Planning Practice: An Introduction

Barry Checkoway

Planning practice is changing. Previous years of economic growth stimulated development and contributed to an increase in planning initiatives. The number of federal, state, and local planning agencies increased in areas such as housing and community development, health and human services, land use and natural resources, environmental and transportation planning. In addition, regional and special purpose bodies with territorial or functional responsibilities became numerous.

In times of growth, planning was viewed by many as a type of urban engineering and applied social science characterized by objective fact-finding and the so-called rational model. The plan, as a statement of the general interest, was often considered a means of generating support throughout the community. Implementation was largely a matter of choice among technical alternatives. Planners were akin to technical experts who advised decision makers without promoting particular policy positions. Some planners who criticized contradictions between the rational model and actual practice, advocated minority interests and social justice ends, or used planning as a vehicle for power redistribution and social change were by no means typical in the field.

Today planning operates in a changing context. Economic recession has replaced growth and reduced development. This situation has exacerbated conditions in central cities and metropolitan areas, some of which are slowing, even declining, in population, employment, and other measures of urban activity. Private groups blame government for economic problems and planning agencies for a range of ills. They mobilize substantial resources, mount campaigns to shape public attitudes, and elect representatives who reduce government and cut planning agencies. Planners no longer expect to generate widespread support but instead may struggle for survival in the face of power.

Austerity policies and adversarial power challenge planners to recognize change and develop capacity for the years ahead. Some planners have applied skills to formulate strategy and mobilize resources for practice. However, other planners have opted to sit tight rather than to play a more strategic or political role. They may appear passive and withdrawn, although it would be a mistake to interpret passivity and withdrawal as symptoms of apathy rather than of alienation from a situation from which they were being displaced. Meanwhile, hardly a day passes when the media fail to report reductions and cutbacks.

This book provides strategic perspectives on planning practice. It recognizes that planning operates in a political context and that planners must think and act strategically to be effective. It deals with strategy and politics related to practice in diverse domains, in territories from neighborhood to nation, and in several functional fields. The contributors represent a range of individuals, each highly experienced, deeply committed, and anxious to communicate. Together they seem to share a belief that change is needed in planning, and they write as if it were possible.

John Dyckman (chapter 2) begins by arguing that the problems facing planners go deeper than recent austerity policies to the structural context in which planning operates. Although planners may have once been concerned with broad social policy and long-range plans, they subsequently became entrenched in government bureaucracies applying instrumental rationality and technical skills to projects shaped by authoritarian regimes and powerful private interests. When private interests turned hostile, elected conservative representatives, and began to dismantle bureaucracies, planners were vulnerable and lacked support. Dyckman challenges planners to learn lessons from the past and to use the present as a basis to reexamine theory and practice. He urges them to think critically, to open dialogue with society, and to act like political leaders in the community.

However, most planners perceive themselves as neither political nor community leaders. Howell Baum (chapter 3) reviews several studies of planners and finds only a minority who regard planning as properly or inevitably political, a majority of straightforward technicians who believe planning is or should be concerned with rational consideration of information, and a substantial group who are ambivalent about acting politically and who tend to emphasize technical planning as a result of this ambivalence. Others value political skills but do not use them in practice, or apply political skills but experience administrative controls and professional tensions that may prove fatal to them in the agency. There are exceptional planners who employ innovative methods to build support for agency plans, but they are not typical in the field.

This image has implications for planning research and education. First, most planners do not perceive themselves as political, a situation that could be a problem that research and education should address. Second, a minority of planners are political and their work could provide lessons for others. Third, a substantial group of planners are ambivalent but could be viewed as constituents or allies for developing new roles and changing the nature of practice. There is no a priori reason why planners could not develop knowledge, skills, and attitudes conducive to acting more politically or more like leaders. Planning research and education could find excellent opportunities here.

"Planning is in a state of crisis," Judith Innes de Neufville concludes in chapter 4. She contends that planning schools agree on no common literature, raise questions that have no answers or produce stale debate, and provide poor instruction in ways to make planning work. She argues that planning theory is inconsistent with experience, irrelevant to application, and frustrating to scholars and practitioners. She believes that educators have the responsibility "to explain the profession to itself, to make explicit the nature of practice, to develop theories of how and why certain modes of practice tend to produce one or another type of result." She advocates planning theory that would be grounded in practice, descriptive and predictive as well as normative, and based in empirical research and lessons from the field. But she cautions that "the void will not be filled until planning theory can make much more explicit what it is that planning is really about."

Several contributors employ empirical research and analyze strategy in practice. Strategy is a process that includes skills to set objectives, develop plans, build support, and mobilize resources toward goals. It involves choice and sequence, staging and timing, and a combination of roles and styles. It shows commitment to think ahead, anticipate alternatives, and consider what may result from current decisions. It thus deals with the future of the present and represents an effort to act in accordance with images of the future and implementation in mind. The strategic skills in this book are not the only ones available or needed, but they are among the most important.

John Bryson, Edward Freeman, and William Roering (chapter 5) argue that public agencies are strategically weak and could benefit from practices developed in business, where strategic planning has a long history of private uses. They describe private sector practice according to the Harvard policy, portfolio, industrial economics, stakeholder, and decision process models. They analyze applications to public sector agencies such as the Ramsey County Nursing Service, *Philadelphia Investment Portfolio,* and Hennepin County, which represents the case of an entire government engaged in strategic planning. They conclude that strategic planning can help revitalize and redirect government but also can have limitations in public practice.

Should planners formulate strategy? Some analysts warn against the application of corporate models to public, nonprofit, or voluntary agencies where strategy might violate norms or undermine trust on which public practice presumably depends. However, the issue is not whether planners should act more like business but whether they should develop strategy at all. Meanwhile, corporate groups will continue to formulate strategy and influence agencies.

Jerome Kaufman (chapter 6) argues that although planners apply strategy more often than conventional wisdom holds, and although knowledge is available for adaptation from business and politics, most planners appear neither trained nor skilled in formulating strategy, and the topic is hardly mentioned in the planning literature. He draws on interviews with planning agency directors and finds that most depend largely on intuition and give low priority to systematic strategic analysis. He reviews strategic analysis schemes that include developing skills to identify key actors, learn their interests, and get them to help implement plans. He presents an approach to analyze target groups systematically in terms of their basic position, specific concerns, likelihood of involvement, political resources, internal interactions, and external relationships as a basis to influence decisions, although he also recognizes that such analysis would require fundamental changes in role behavior of most planners.

Other contributors emphasize research and analysis in strategic practice. Carl Patton argues in chapter 7 that many policies do not have their intended impact because policy analyses are not conducted with implementation in mind. Earlier analysts have used population projections, cost-benefit analysis, and other technical methods but have given less attention to implementation analysis and political feasibility. He argues that implementation should be considered throughout the policy process, that policies should be both technically feasible and politically viable, and that practitioners should play a clearly defined role in strategic and political work for policy implementation. He presents practical tips to incorporate political factors into analysis of the policy process, analyze interests of key actors, test policies through demonstrations and experiments, and implement policy by developing strategy. "Above all," he concludes, "effective implementation requires attention to technical and political issues."

L. David Brown (chapter 8) emphasizes research and analysis with a focus on the direct participation of people who are traditionally excluded in the process. Many planners view themselves as technical experts who apply rational models and social science to community planning. They conduct research in relative isolation or in small teams of professionals and then deliver the results to decision makers. They often assess community conditions without leaving the office and contacting residents. Some consult with the public through social surveys and public hearings, but neither is particularly effective as a means of involving individuals or influencing implementation.

Brown advocates participatory research as a means to involve people in planning. This approach brings individuals together to assess common problems, analyze root causes, and formulate alternative actions. Brown analyzes participatory research with small farmers in India, citizen groups in Appalachia, and local residents in Urban Heights. These cases show that practice can increase information, involve individuals and groups, and improve decisions. He identifies obstacles to practice but concludes, "When planners successfully expand participation in planning, the resulting plans reflect the interests of a larger public, and the planning process mobilizes resources for effective implementation."

Other contributors examine internal and external organizational structures that influence implementation. Structure includes formal means to represent interests, generate ideas, make decisions, allocate resources, collaborate with others, and implement plans. It can involve established policies and procedures, roles and responsibilities, methods and skills to achieve ends. Structure is not strategy but can facilitate its practice.

John Tropman analyzes ways of governing and managing the internal structure of public organizations in chapter 9. Most public organizations emphasize money and people more than ideas as means for implementation. Tropman describes the policy manager as the person responsible for providing an adequate supply of ideas and facilitating implementation in a changing environment. He or she helps generate ideas, build structures for their consideration, assure ratification by an executive or authority, develop guidelines for operations, and make activities operational through boards of directors, committees, task groups, meetings, or other vehicles. Tropman argues that organizations should formalize this function because ideas are too important to be left to chance.

Milan Dluhy (chapter 10) emphasizes ways of collaborating and forming coalitions with other organizations. Coalitions are working relationships to mobilize interests, develop a common program, and generate power to fulfill the program that is developed. They help individuals or groups to influence issues far more than what each could accomplish alone.

Dluhy draws on data from participant observation of coalitions working to keep homeless persons off the streets, professionalize the treatment of troubled youth, involve the elderly in community projects, and return missing children to their families. He analyzes each coalition on a continuum according to structural characteristics and concludes that successful coalitions need adequate resources, sensitive leadership, effective communications, and means to influence public attitudes and motivate members around issues. "In the end," he concludes, "coalitions provide one of the most effective vehicles for planners to achieve their objectives when faced with the power configurations that might otherwise appear intimidating."

Other contributors relate strategy to particular territories, constituencies, and functional fields. Neil Mayer (chapter 11) analyzes roles for planners in community development at the neighborhood level. Although many urban neighborhoods have suffered a downgrading cycle of inadequate services, deteriorated infrastructure, and withdrawal of people and institutions, some residents have organized to overcome decline and redevelop their communities. Mayer reports on a national study of community development corporations that practice neighborhood revitalization in U.S. cities. He finds that each of the most successful organizations has formally incorporated itself, developed competence in specific projects, and expanded competence into other areas. Each has developed leadership by an effective director, employed expertise by development staff, involved community groups and outside actors, and dealt with the changing external environment. Mayer derives general propositions from empirically based practice in neighborhoods but with specific implications for agencies in other territorial areas. Is this what de Neufville means by theory from practice?

Jacqueline Leavitt relates strategy to women as a constituency for planning practice in chapter 12. Changing demographic, employment, income, and other factors are affecting urban areas and causing problems for women. Planners have responded to some of these problems but without always addressing the needs of women explicitly. Leavitt develops feminist advocacy planning as an approach to incorporate gender as a variable in practice and to evaluate reforms from a feminist perspective. She analyzes case studies and argues that "closing the gender gap can improve conditions for women and make planning more relevant to the larger society." Leavitt relates planning to gender, but does her approach have implications for class, race, age, and other constituencies in society?

Barry Checkoway (chapter 13) formulates political strategy for social planning as a field that operates against adversarial power at a time when social programs are more important and needed than ever. He draws on research and practice and includes cases of planners that apply strategy to influence implementation. He conceptualizes an approach with skills to identify issues, develop constituencies, build organizational structure, expand public awareness, and activate people in planning. There are obstacles to the expansion of political strategy, but exceptional agencies provide lessons nonetheless. Checkoway applies strategy to social planning, but could this approach also apply to other planning fields?

What are the prospects? Seymour Mandelbaum (chapter 14) helps conclude this book with perspectives on recent planning theory. Planning theoreticians sometimes take criticism because they have not replaced the so-called rational model with a consensual practice paradigm that coheres the field, or produced empirically based knowledge that explicates the nature of practice, or communicated effectively with practitioners in their own terms. The conventional image is that contextual conditions once contributed to an increase in planning initiatives and shaped a paradigm on which there was relative agreement in the field. But then conditions changed, adversarial power-holders attacked agencies, and competing intellectuals criticized the paradigm and exposed gaps between theory and practice.

Mandelbaum appreciates the work of recent theoreticians, but he questions some of the emergent emphasis and wonders about the desirability or possibility of the task. Will a shift in theory to empirical research on practitioners and their shortcomings divert theoreticians from a focus on structural relationships and institutional designs? Is it a mistake to expect theoreticians to produce a consensual paradigm when practitioners have neither disciplined themselves, dealt with their own fragmentation, nor applied much of the knowledge that is already available? Is a complete general theory of planning possible when many practitioners appear unwilling or unable to fulfill responsibilities as reflective professionals? Is the crisis of planning not one of theory but rather one of practice that blames theory for its own shortcomings? Mandelbaum criticizes the critics rather than takes them at face value and, in so doing, poses a challenge for the future.

Does the situation in planning reflect a general crisis of the professions in society? Donald Schön reflects on the crisis of professional knowledge and the search for a new epistemology of practice in chapter 15. Schön argues that knowledge has not necessarily kept up with changing social reality and that professional practice paradigms—particularly the positivist epistemology of technical rationality built into many agencies, professional schools, and research institutions—have been giving way to indeterminate zones of practice involving artistry and uncertainty rather than technical expertise and clear choice among alternatives. Some professionals have responded by confining themselves to a limited range of problems or by cutting reality to fit available techniques. Others, however, have reconsidered their work and sought an epistemology of practice that goes beyond previous paradigms to develop alternatives grounded in analysis of artistry that competent professionals bring to their practice. Schön describes professionals who are able to apply reflection in action in which they know what to do in uncertain situations. He challenges professional schools and research institutions to develop empirical knowledge based on analysis of competent practitioners. Is this what earlier contributors mean when they argue that planning education should teach theory grounded in practice and that research should focus on practitioners able to apply strategy and implement plans? And will a new epistemology of practice produce planners able to operate in the face of power?

Bertram Gross and Kusum Singh (chapter 16) conclude this book by taking up the challenge posed by Dyckman in chapter 2. Whereas Dyckman challenges planners to think critically, effect dialog with society, and act like political leaders in the community, Gross and Singh encourage planners to enter the political arena and adopt planning under freedom as a new experiment in democracy. They view planners as neither advocating the interests of others nor involving citizens in decisions made elsewhere but as active participants who espouse social values and work for political change. They urge planners to identify with a political party or party coalition, view party platforms as proposed plans, and participate in elections that present choices among competing plans. They advocate legislation based on full employment, economic rights, open politics, and comprehensive planning with local participation. They call for democratic management based on free flow of information and public involvement; bottom-sideways communication backed by national elections and interaction of individuals and groups; an innovative approach to bureaucracy with guidance by elected officials and public interest organizations; and community leadership with honeycomb organizational structure, leadership rotation, cooperative process, and mutual empowerment of members. Gross and Singh conclude that such ideas may seem highly improbable but that planning merely for what presently appears feasible is hardly planning at all, whereas their approach is "to practice the high morality of caring for ourselves and others at the same time."

Whatever the prospects, planning in the United States is in transition. Contextual conditions are causing change and challenging planners to reconsider earlier approaches. New initiatives are needed to relate strategic thought and action to implementation in diverse domains, territorial areas, and functional fields. There are obstacles to expanding strategic perspectives on planning practice, to be sure, but exceptional agencies show possibilities that may be considered for adaption from one area to another. If efforts to relate strategy to planning practice, and this book about them, help raise questions for future research and action, then an important objective will be served.

Part I
Contextual and
Structural Perspectives

2
Planning Practice in an Age of Reaction

John W. Dyckman

T he era of optimism in urban planning in the United States came up short with the disillusion of the Johnson presidency. A backlash descended on planners from the Right and the Left. The Great Society plans attracted the scorn of the new conservatism and were buffeted by the Viet Nam War and the critics on the Left. Over thirty years, U.S. city planning had pushed and struggled against the internal critique of its social blinders toward a measure of social planning competence, only to find ferocious political resistance to its efforts. By the mid-1970s, critics on the Right were advocating a retreat from social-science-based intervention, and critics on the Left were deploring the futility of official social planning. Many public planners found themselves enfiladed. If the early—friendlier—critics had attacked the social myopia of urban renewal, the class bias of physical plans, and the unjustified pretensions of public interest, they had at least ventured programs for redress in the form of more self-conscious sociology of the profession, advocacy for the underrepresented, citizen participation, and expanded social outlook. Utopianism was to be countered by a programmatic perspective and bold vision by careful accountability of costs and benefits. All this effort and adaptation, adjustment and critical reexamination, now appears to have availed the planners very little.

The triumph of Reagan and the Right, Propositions 13 and 2½, national social retreat and local fiscal austerity, and privatization and deregulation appear to be swamping the terrain staked out by planners. Thoughtful planners must be asking themselves, Were the past two decades abnormal in their level of public program support?, Were we victims of unwarranted optimism and innocence about the issues of real concern to Americans?, and Have we failed in a fundamental political analysis of planning in the United States? Since 1949, planners have been, in large measure, clients of a powerful state bureaucracy and, in particular, of the U.S. Department of Housing and Urban Development. Now that department is in the process of dismantling

Reprinted by permission from the *Journal of Planning Education and Research* 3:5–12. Copyright © 1983 Association of Collegiate Schools of Planning.

numerous functions, and the patron bureaucracy is in virtual dissolution. The guerrillas in the bureaucracy are in danger of losing their bases, and many may be out in the streets soon.

The fates of professions are subject to notorious booms and reversals, as the example of engineering teaches us. But the question of the activity's place in the society is less subject to fundamental doubts for many professions. Planning's difficulties are in part a function of its intimate relationship to politics, whose vagaries are notorious. Planners may be disposed to sit this period out, in the confidence that their political fortunes will eventually be reversed. This period, however well it is borne by planners, may at the same time be the occasion of a careful reexamination, and perhaps discovery, of their appropriate and most promising place in the U.S. political, economic, and social systems.

While I am not persuaded that planning practice in the United States has had much to do with planning theory, there is little doubt that the present difficulties afford an excellent occasion for theories that aid this reexamination. A good planning theory would be one that places in perspective the nature of the society and the state that delegates the planning powers, sets the planning tasks, and limits the exercise of technical discretion. It would also be a theory that analyzes and exposes the social forces and cultural traditions that give rise to the idea of planning and that limit its uses. Such theory could be more than consolation to planners; it could also provide both a critique and an agenda.

Los (1981, p. 63) has established several origins of a contemporary interest in planning theory. These are "the desire of practicing planners to give a meaning and some usefulness to their role in society," "the need felt by academic planners to understand the link between methodology and theories on the one hand and actual planning on the other hand," "the need felt by some planners to improve by means of planning the distribution of power in society," and "the need of the adepts of a critical or radical view of planning to give more theoretical foundation to their dissatisfaction with current practice and current methodology." These points are concerned with practice from one or another perspective, and all imply the recognition that practice is informed by theory. They differ in the domain of the theory they are seeking—as Los puts it, some seek how planning ought to be done, and others examine how it is actually practiced or the social nature of planning itself. In an activity such as planning, nonetheless, the distinction between *is* and *ought* is fragile because while positive studies of practice are useful, they are not by themselves a guide to planning action, given the purposive nature of planning.

The action orientation of planning places it in a position in which the activity can scarcely be neutral about *oughts* and in which the studies of the *is* are likely to be critical. Touraine's (1977, p. 307) comment about sociology is instructive:

Sociological analysis can never identify itself with the management of society and even less with the state. This is why power, whatever its form, is mistrustful of sociology, because it criticizes instead of justifying, distinguishes instead of integrating. However, power is only too glad to call upon sociology to help it combat deviancy, reinforce socialization, eliminate archaisms. And power will tolerate it more easily when it itself is not very integrated, subject to crises of change and adaptation.

Whatever one thinks of sociology in the United States, these remarks have a certain force for planners. It is telling that power will tolerate planning more easily when planning is not very integrated intellectually, when it justifies instead of criticizes, when it helps power combat social irregularities—in short, when the intellectual house of planning is not well in order. Are we then to conclude that the present mistrust of planning is a measure of its critical intellectual coherence, or are we to judge that it is a reflection of its failure to serve adequately the social tasks assigned by power?

The Liberal Ideology of Planning

The attack on planning in the United States preceded the Reagan victory. It is to be found in publications such as *The Public Interest* throughout the 1970s, as noted earlier. In one such attack, Shuck (1976, p. 9) contended that "it seems more plausible to conclude that we simply do not know how to build urban communities, fashion a national transportation system, or eliminate social disintegration, much less accomplish all of these objectives simultaneously through an integrated strategy or plan." This argument, which is reminiscent of the attacks on social engineering of Karl Popper, seems to be dismissing planning because it cannot work and is therefore a poor servant of power. While the record of planning accomplishments provides some ammunition for this view, other critics of a less market-favoring persuasion would find the difficulty not in the inherent intellectual limitations of the idea of planning but in the structure of the society in which planning is asked to operate. If one accepts the latter view, he or she is drawn to the question, Do the practitioners of planning have a clear view of that society? If so, what is their view?

A review of the planning literature since the 1960s, shows a variety of views, but the dominant view appears to be that of a pluralistic, interest group image of the society in which the planner is variously a mediator of interests in some broader public interest, is at times a defender of the underrepresented interests, and at other times is a frank advocate for his or her agency's position.

Given this orientation, planning liberals might be satisfied with a rule of conduct based on Rawls's (1971) theory of justice. In this theory he recommends a social contract ensuring each person's equal right to equal basic liberties and the reduction of inequalities (social and economic) by deciding in favor of the greatest expected benefits for the least advantaged, while maintaining positions open to all under a fair equality of opportunity. The position of Rawls promises to reconcile egalitarianism with utilitarianism, or at least utilitarianism as tempered by social welfare considerations. While the rule is rather idealistic—idealistic because Rawls assumes, for logical reasons, that we are all ignorant of our place in society, our class position and social status, our place in the distribution of natural assets and abilities, and our deeper aims and interests and that no one is disadvantaged by natural chance or social contingencies—it appears to give an operational guide to liberal planners.

At the same time, these assumptions may be too much for practicing planners and other liberals to make because they abolish much of the traditional agenda. In any event, this position either assumes away or ignores the structural problems of our society. Class, race, and sex do not enter the analysis, other than through income. There is no history of domination, oppression, or hopelessness. Of course, the rule is purely normative and does not attempt a positive analysis. How the rule should be applied, and by whom, is left aside. In that sense the rule is in the true spirit of utilitarianism, from Mill to Pigou.

Nonetheless, the rule has a certain appeal. The American Institute of Planners (1973) Code of Professional Responsibility contains a canon which states that:

> A planner shall seek to expand the choice and opportunities for all persons, recognizing a special responsibility to plan for the needs of disadvantaged groups and persons, and shall urge alteration of policies, institutions and decisions which militate against such objectives.

Like Rawls's rule, this is a process rule. It tells us what to do at the margin of action. It is reformist in force, whatever its eventual intention. But it tells us nothing of what to expect from the society in which we live, except that we have, as intellectuals, bought a large part of the baggage of utilitarianism.[1] Still, whatever the difficulties in the behavioral rules and axiomatics, the difficulty that concerns us is a real world one. What are the realities that confront us in the society and state in which we live? Does the politics of parties illuminate or obscure the social forces of our time? Is there a future for liberal reform, or has it foundered on reaction?

In a number of writings, Theodore Lowi has incisively sketched the location and contradictions of the liberal tradition in the United States. Putting liberalism in historical perspective, Lowi (1969, p. 55) notes that "the decline of capitalist ideology as the American public philosophy took the form of a dialogue against a more public view of society, . . . [and] the dialogue between the new liberalism and the old liberalism, or new conservatism, comprises the constitutional epoch immediately preceding our own, ending in 1937." What the Reagan administration represents is the resuscitation of the debate that Lowi sees ending in 1937. The new conservatism, or the old liberalism, however, is situated in a world situation in which government power, whatever the rhetoric, has been greatly enhanced. The new conservatism takes advantage of the liberals' ambivalence toward power, so well marked by Lowi.

For planners, the recent abandonment by the liberals was in part, at least, a dialectic outcome of the difficulties of liberalism. In this, the liberals have been a victim, along with the planners, of their preoccupation with process. Their joint concern with functional, rather than substantive, accountability left both open to attack on the score of results. This concern, as Lowi (1969, p. 67) noted, means a focus on "questions of equity, balance and equilibrium to the exclusion of questions of whether or not the program should be maintained or discontinued. It also means accountability to experts first and amateurs last; and an expert is a man trained and skilled in the mysteries and technologies of the program." This, he concludes, is "the final victory of functional over substantive considerations."

Lowi (1969, p. 97) continues that "interest-group liberalism seeks pluralistic government, in which there is no formal specification of the means or ends. In pluralistic government, there is therefore no substance. Neither is there procedure. There is only process." Some will find in this a caricature of pluralistic liberalism. Nonetheless, the tendency to put the emphasis on program goals at the expense of social outcomes, to push accountability to experts, and to favor process over substance is recognizable as a shortcoming of much U.S. planning. In large measure, this tendency is defensive; that is, the planner who sees his or her environment as a pluralistic competition of interests also sees protection of professional turf and emphasis on process as adaptive behavior.

However, deeply ingrained cultural forces favor this stance along with the purely adaptive ones. Ramos (1981) observed that Americans are wholly acculturated to instrumental reason. As he puts it, we are "calculating instrumentalists" who have, since the time of Hobbes, held to a doctrine of primitive individual self-interest, have treated reason as a reckoning of consequences, have embraced the fact-value dichotomy of empirical science, and have accepted the "whip of economic forces" as the spur to action. In this culture the ethics of responsibility are ethics of process rather than of ultimate ends. The notion of reason that pre-Enlightenment philosophers believed would provide substantive foundations for visions of the good life has been reduced to an individual concern, inappropriate to political dialogue. Birnbaum (1977) has also emphasized the fragmentation of contemporary reason, relating its reduction to instrumentalism to the breakdown of a once-unified sensibility. It is ironic that planning, which is historically associated with notions of community, with its substantive, unifying content, and with more or less utopian visions of the good life, has become, in the West, a part of the technocratic apparatus with its commitment to instrumental rationality and to process goals.

Utopianism and Critical Theory: The Search for Substance

In the concluding section of *The Origins of Modern Town Planning* (1967, p. 106) Benevolo observed that "a systematic study of the relationship between politics and town-planning does not yet exist. . . . But even the little documentation that there is is sufficient to reveal the vital importance of the 1848 crisis in this field as in all others." He is referring here to the attack on Utopian Socialism in the *Manifesto* of Marx and Engels in that year and their subsequent criticism of Proudhon, the ateliers proposals of Louis Blanc, and other communitarian socialists elaborated in the First International in 1864. For Benevolo, these criticisms drove a wedge between the substantive reconstructionist ideas of the Left and the mainstream parties of the International. These criticisms were in some degree tactical political emphases. Marx emphasized that the various experiments and community reorganization proposals were doomed to failure if they were attempted in the absence of a revolutionary success of the proletariat, an opinion he vindicated in *The Eighteenth Brumaire of Louis Bonaparte*. In contrast, Buber (1949) has documented a number of instances of views of Marx, as well as of Engels, both earlier and later than 1864, that are more sympathetic to these and other utopian experiments. What is important about the views of these experimenters to Buber and Benevolo is their preoccupation with the search for forms of community that would be democratic, nonstatist, socially coherent, and/or socialist in ideals. And if they did not succeed in reorganizing society and abolishing the state, they did provide substantive ideas of a good society, as well as physical forms of community organization, which much influenced early city planning. For Benevolo, the immediate result of the rift between city planning and socialist thought was the encouragement of a purely technical viewpoint in planning and the emergence of a new class of planners and civil servants charged with large-scale projects. And the partial reforms were speedily co-opted by authoritarian regimes. Utopian plans have been in bad repute with the professionals of town planning ever since planning has become well entrenched in government.

If the field of community planning has set aside utopian ideas of the good society, it has paid for its profession with loss of substance and with the reduction of its theme of reason to instrumental rationality. In this century, the intellectual case for this functional rationality has been pressed most effectively by Karl Popper and his followers. Popper launched the debate in 1945 with an attack on political rationalism on the grounds that political rationalism must have a clear view of ultimate ends, the ideal state, as distinguished from means, but that there is no rational way to choose that end state, only utopian aesthetics and perfectionism.[2] Popper attacked this holistic, radical vision as it appeared in Plato's aestheticism and Marx's historicism. He asserted egalitarianism but maintained it must be individual, subjective, piecemeal, and incremental.

The challenge of this position was taken up by a number of critical social thinkers, particularly after the 1964 Heidelberg meeting of the German Sociological Association that dealt with the work of Max Weber. A major concern of this group, from Marxists such as George Lukacs to the Frankfurt School—notably, Adorno, Benjamin, Habermas, Horkheimer, and Marcuse—was the alienation of substantive reason. Their views of the sources of that alienation have varied from Weber's attention to the bureaucratization of the state to Habermas's view of communicative distortion and domination of information in advanced industrial society. But the critical school tends to share the view, also promulgated by writers such as Vogelin and Strauss, that the good society is not a wholly subjective notion but can be developed from the historical dialogue of the informed and unfettered exchange of members of society. In the hands of writers such as Horkheimer and Adorno (1982), this dialogue has taken the form of a savage attack on the domination of mass communication, but the most positive statement of the case and the most influential on planning theorists in the United States is found in the works of Habermas (1970, 1971, 1973, 1975, 1979).

The ideas of Habermas have been most comprehensively applied to U.S. planning practice by Forester (see particularly 1982) but also can be found in the critical analysis of urban planning in Europe (Biarez 1981). There is no need to reproduce these applications for readers, but Forester sums up some of these points with the comment:

> Habermas' attention to social interaction provides a way of showing how an ordinary conversation (or a planner's presentation, analysis, talk, etc.) can work to reproduce relations of power and domination in ways that remain largely invisible to all involved. Set structurally, this is a practical and phenomenological analysis that shows how power is reproduced through concrete human actions (and not just in the market). This is a radicalized version of the agenda-setting arguments, and there's a politics of organizing (demystification, ideology-critique, and mobilization) that follows from both.[3]

For Forester, "if planning theory is to be critical at all, it must have as an absolutely spinal element the analysis of domination and power, and that is to say the analysis of ideology and legitimate authority, too."[4]

The critical analysis of domination and power, of the distortion of communication at the expense of the ideal of reason, and of the democratic expression of social values is an important contribution. But it is necessary to remember that, however critical is the analysis and demystification of power and crooked communication, however effectively the technical manipulation of content is exposed, there remains a faith in society's ability to find its own best reason. Planners have always been optimistic about this ability, whether in the form of utopian vision or in a faith in the principles of a science of society. The latter faith was shared by St. Simon and Marx and given a rather confused, if appealing to planners, statement by Karl Mannheim.[5] Habermas and others of his school appear to trust in a historical reason.[6] Whether this reason, emerging from undominated communication, is itself utopian is a question for another book.

What is important for practice in critical theory is that theory provides a starting point for the analysis of the advanced industrial society in which planning exists. In place of a unitary vision of the good society, critical theory offers a mechanism for finding direction. If that mechanism appears socially utopian to some planners, it has the advantage for others of offering a focus on real agenda.

Toward a Program for Planning Practice

If "subjective consciousness of objective conditions is the first step toward a good society,"[7] what are the objective conditions facing planners today? We are currently in the midst of a reaction against the liberal democratic welfare state. The efforts of the Reagan administration to revoke the social reforms of the 1960s and early 1970s may be seen as a struggle to remove the agenda of the Great Society from the political arena to the marketplace. Far from being antistatist, these moves represent an attempt to purify the capitalist state, to free it from political forces sapping its singleminded effort at accumulation. This stance is manifest in the administration's increasingly belligerent foreign policy, expansion of military expenditures, and protectionism in foreign economic relations; its clearing away of regulation, environmental and social; and its dilution of antitrust and encouragement of mergers. The administration's social policy threatens to colonize minorities, in part by its reductions of welfare and educational support, setting the stage for easier exploitation. At the same time it has moved to make the bureaucracy more compliant, to strengthen secrecy and reduce the flow of information, and to cut off critical social science state support.

This program, despite some initial successes, should be seen as a short-run, and perhaps impermanent, tendency. Whatever the preference for markets over political allocation, modern states cannot evade the necessity for government intervention, given periodic economic crisis. Modern capitalism needs the intervention of the state in many direct and indirect ways. And it needs some types of planning.

If, as Harvey (1978, p. 223) has written, "the planner's task is to contribute to the process of social reproduction and in so doing the planner is equipped with powers vis-à-vis the production, maintenance and management of the built environment which permit him or her to intervene in order to stabilize, to create the conditions for 'balanced growth,' to contain civil strife and factional struggles by repression, cooptation or integration," why not encourage more, not less, planning? To the extent that planners play Harvey's role, they are clearly useful to capital accumulation. In the longer run, they may again be seen to be useful. But planners are not so simply technicians of the state.[8] They are sometimes part of the state apparatus and sometimes independent and distinct from it. They not only formulate state plans and help to set the state agenda but also provide alternative and even counterplans. The planner may be an agent of the state apparatus or a manager of state plans at a remove where he or she can exercise considerable autonomy and interject his or her values. He or she may also be a progressive reformer or an advocate of the underrepresented. This is in part why the planner may be distrusted by the state power, quite aside from the issue of effectiveness. If he or she is concerned with distribution and social effects, as in the liberal model,[9] the planner is likely to be viewed as a drag on the fundamentalist view of accumulation. This liberal stance of planning is just the sort of planning style that would put it in disfavor with the current U.S. regime, whose emphasis is starkly on capitalist efficiency. But the role of the planner in a more liberal welfare state would also be restricted in effect, despite state support of planning.

The progressive role of the planner is ultimately limited by the class nature of society, by the economic need for accumulation and balance in reproduction, and by his or her technician role as a gatekeeper of information. The Marxians have clarified the first two roles; the critical theorists, the third. The postindustrial society has vastly increased the information requirements of state management, has enhanced the power and discretion of the technician, and has strengthened the power for large-scale manipulation, especially through communications. Contemporary society is not able to rid itself of "technostructures," which are bound to reassert themselves when the trappings of a simpler competitive style have faded away.

Fainstein and Fainstein (1982, p. 169) describe the more persistent dilemma of planning practice in the following terms:

> Planners may be part of an emerging class of technical experts whose functions are needed by capitalists, but whose working conditions are becoming

increasingly proletarianized. The "new class" does not derive its income from ownership and is committed to a technical rationality which may help transform capitalism. The question, of course, is whether such a transformation will be progressive.

Their response to this dilemma is an adaptive one, based on the view that revolutionary crisis is remote in the United States. In their view, a progressive program would be based on the following three principles. First, "the better the better, as opposed to 'the worse the better.' To the extent that planning furthers the material situation of the lower classes it is progressive, even if it legitimizes the system in the short run." Second, "the more planning the better. The lower classes are better served by planning in the collective interest of monopoly capital than by the unplanned outcomes of market forces." And finally, "the expansion of the planning and welfare state should be encouraged. State capitalism in liberal regimes represents a marked improvement over market capitalism from the perspective of the proletariat" (pp. 169–170).

For the most part, these rules are not objectionable to Marxians. Their emphasis is, however, a short-run accommodation to a long-run problem. Marx did not oppose reforms but often applauded them (as in the case of the workday limitation, for example). He did, however, oppose the confusion of reforms with fundamental change, as in his critique of the Utopians. He did not oppose the development of capitalism along its lines but thought it a necessary stage in the transition to socialism (as in his curious defense of the British presence in India). Conversely, no one—with the possible exception of some Reaganites—wants to go to a wholly unregulated market system. So this argument is relatively unexceptionable tactically.

Nonetheless, this argument should not blind us to the continuing problem of progressive planning even in a welfare state or to its opportunities. The latter reside in the opportunities for social creativity, those cultural and social insights that comprise the core of our historical development, and as Touraine (1977, p. 262) says, "transcends the functioning of the society while at the same time being embodied in it." The former are familiar difficulties—the bureaucratization, the technical monopoly of knowledge and information, the pressures of power—that must be combatted.

If, as Fainstein and Fainstein (1982) suggest, experts such as planners are being "proletarianized," planners can hardly applaud this reduction of socioeconomic status, but they may turn this fact to short-term advantage. For example, it may allow the planner to identify positively with the groups his or her liberal ideology purports to serve and may clarify the real distribution of power. Whatever the economic fate of planners, their tasks in this moment of adversity should include the following:

1. Rediscover and enrich the content. This task is not limited to physical planning, thanks in part to the liberal reforms of the 1960s, but there is much to be done in sensitive physical planning. Such planning is indivisible from the social and economic content. But physical surroundings are part of the image of the good life, which is indivisible. This is a reasonable objective, even if it implies the revival of utopian thinking.

2. Locate this content in a true political context. The society and the state must be seen for what they are, especially the society, which is primary. While the form of the state is not irrelevant, society will in any case continue to reproduce itself. Its "historicity"[10]—with its imminent possibilities for change—provides the agenda for planners to devise new arrangements, to push for new social forms.

3. Mount a new level of self-criticism. In Forester's (1982) terms, this means finding the false content in our transmissions. Moreover, it implies the opening of dialogue with society on less obscured terms.

4. Develop the instruments of tactical reason. Fainstein and Fainstein (1982) offer but one example. This is an intellectual task, but it should be informed by exchange with powerful and with ordinary people. The liberal rule of carefully measuring effects on distribution is another guide.

5. Put the emphasis on education. Let the planners take the lead in educating the populace to new opportunities. The adversary model, which has been helpful, is inadequate because it presumes a fair judgment. A more frankly political teaching is needed. When have planners ever explained their role? When have they understood their contribution to the maintenance of the system? Let them, as outsiders in the market system, become the tutors of the casualties of the market. This task calls for social imagination. Radical planners can rediscover community, can enter the social system as intelligent advisors, can push for a meaningful agenda.

What might such an agenda contain? My suggestions include the repoliticization of bureaucratic and market decisions and the demystification of technologies; the image, utopian or not, of how community power might be exercised; and new scenarios of the postindustrial society, with its implications for the definition of work, the redefinition of social usefulness, and the variety of payments needed to smooth the transition. They also include the support and guidance to mobilize communities toward the ideal of self-governance in a complex society; explication of the possibilities of the exercise of political power, including the limitations of interest group liberalism;

and contributions to the revival of interest in, and ideas about, the alternative social forms of the good life.

Notes

1. For a critique that is telling on the very grounds of this theory, see, for example, Sen (1970, 1974, 1976, 1977). No one has been more thoroughly skeptical than Sen.

2. Popper's *The Open Society and Its Enemies* was first published in 1945 by Routledge & Kegan Paul. It is more familiar to American students in the 1962 Harper Torchbook version.

3. Personal communication from John Forester, January 25, 1983.

4. Ibid.

5. This point is well traced in Schafers (1973).

6. In his essay "On Theory and Praxis in Our Scientific Civilization," Habermas (1973, p. 281) says, "Only a reason which is fully aware of the interest in the progress of reflection toward adult autonomy, which is indestructibly at work in every rational discussion, will be able to gain transcendent power from the awareness of its own materialistic involvements." Elsewhere, he sees this reason as primary and given by historical experience.

7. This statement could stand as a platform for much critical theory. In this form it is taken from Chang (1983).

8. Touraine (1977, p. 202) notes:

[I]f the distance between power and authority is large, it is more probable that the problems of social domination and those of organizational authority will appear as relatively dissociated, as in the case of public administration whose officials, if they exercise a delegated authority, are somewhat removed from power that is of political origin and refers . . . to a social domination.

9. The liberal model is well stated by Meltzer (1983), who sees it as the norm. He says:

The historical planning objective of creating the "perfect environment" has been replaced by the contemporary conviction that space and its deployment have no validity independent of social and economic differences and considerations. Plans and planning activity are tested not only for their analytical rigor and by efficiency criteria, but for the degree to which they enhance opportunity and reduce social and economic disruption.

10. Touraine's (1977, p. 461) actionist model defines "historicity" as follows:

[The] action exerted by society, on the basis of its own activity, on its cultural and social practices, through the combination of three components: the model of knowledge, which constitutes an image of society and nature; accumulation, which sets aside part of society's available product; and the cultural model, which apprehends and interprets society's capacity for action on itself.

References

American Institute of Planners. 1973. *The Social Responsibility of the Planner.* Washington, D.C.: American Institute of Planners.

Benevolo, L. 1967. *The Origins of Modern Town Planning,* J. Landry, trans. Cambridge, Mass.: MIT Press.

Biarez, S. 1981. Ideological Planning and Contingency Programming: The Case of the Lille-Roubaix-Tourcoing Conurbation, 1967–76. *International Journal of Urban and Regional Research* 5:475–491.

Birnbaum, N. 1977. *Beyond the Crisis.* New York: Oxford University Press.

Buber, M. 1949. *Paths in Utopia,* E.F.C. Hull, trans. Boston: Beacon Press.

Chang, W. 1983. *The Demise of the Rational Model of Planning.* Los Angeles: School of Urban and Regional Planning, University of Southern California.

Fainstein, N.I., and S.S. Fainstein. 1982. New Debates in Urban Planning: The Impact of Marxist Theory Within the United States. In *Critical Readings in Planning Theory,* C. Paris, ed. Oxford: Pergamon Press.

Forester, J. 1982. Understanding Planning Practice: An Empirical, Practical and Normative Account. *Journal of Planning Education and Research* 1:59–71.

Habermas, J. 1970. *Toward a Rational Society: Student Protest, Science, and Politics,* J. Shapiro, trans. Boston: Beacon Press.

———. 1971. *Knowledge and Human Interests,* J.J. Shapiro, trans. Boston: Beacon Press.

———. 1973. *Theory and Practice,* J. Viertel, trans. Boston: Beacon Press.

———. 1975. *Legitimation Crisis,* T. McCarthy, trans. Boston: Beacon Press.

———. 1979. *Communication and the Evolution of Society,* T. McCarthy, trans. Boston: Beacon Press.

Harvey, D. 1978. On Planning the Ideology of Planning. In *Planning Theory in the 1980s,* R.W. Burchell and G. Sternlieb, eds. New Brunswick: Center for Urban Policy Research.

Horkheimer, V.M., and T. Adorno, 1982. *Dialectic of Enlightenment,* J. Cumming, trans. New York: Continuum Press.

Los, M. 1981. Some Reflexions on Epistemology, Design and Planning Theory. In *Urbanization and Urban Planning in Capitalist Society,* M. Dear and A.J. Scott, eds. New York: Methuen.

Lowi, T.J. 1969. *The End of Liberalism: Ideology, Policy, and the Crisis of Public Authority.* New York: W.W. Norton & Company.

Meltzer, J. 1983. Social and Spatial Planning. Unpublished manuscript, School of Social Service Administration, University of Chicago.

Ramos, A. 1981. *The New Science of Organizations.* Toronto: University of Toronto Press.

Rawls, J. 1971. *A Theory of Justice.* Cambridge: Harvard University Press.

Schafers, B. 1973. Voraussetzungen und Principien der Gesellschaftsplanung bei Saint-Simon und Karl Manheim. In *Gesellschaftliche Planung,* B. Schafers, ed. Stuttgart: Ferdinand Enke Verlag.

Sen, A.K. 1970. The Impossibility of a Paretian Liberal. *Journal of Political Economy* 78:152–157.

————. 1974. Rawls versus Bentham: An Axiomatic Examination of the Pure Distribution Problem. *Theory and Decision* 4:301–309.

————. 1976. Welfare, Inequalities and Rawlsian Axiomatics. *Proceedings of the International Conference on Logic, Methods, and Philosophy of Science.* London, Ontario.

————. 1977. Rational Fools: A Critique of the Behavioral Foundations of Economic Theory. *Philosophy and Public Affairs* 6:317–344.

Shuck, P.H. 1976. National Economic Planning: A Slogan Without Substance. *The Public Interest* 45:63–78.

Touraine, A. 1977. *The Self-Production of Society,* D. Coltman, trans. Chicago: University of Chicago Press.

3
Politics in Planners' Practice

Howell S. Baum

Planners have been subjected to increasing study since the 1960s. A central concern in this research is whether planners are political. Several recent developments have stimulated this interest in planners' politics.

Planning was originally institutionalized in local government with the promise of offering a technical, value-free source of assistance for public decision making (Boyer 1983; Brownell 1980; Scott 1969). Nevertheless, planning has always been a political activity in the sense that recommendations affect private interests and interested actors have sought to influence decisions. However, until mid-century the political character of local planning largely went unnoted. Planning's consistent bias toward business interests, if observed, did not seem political because business values were identified with the public interest (Boyer 1983; Scott 1969). Even this bias might not be noticed, however, insofar as planning was a small-scale activity. Master plans often had little effect on local social or economic life (Scott 1969).

This situation changed with the massive expansion of federal programs into the local planning arena, beginning with the Housing Act of 1949. The infusion of federal money made planning conspicuous and increased the stakes involved. As urban renewal forged direct links between planners' activities and program implementation, the political implications of planners' recommendations became clearer. These developments brought about two changes in planners' views of their work.

First, planners were reminded that planning is political in its consequences. Planners' renewed insistence that decision making be rational reflected their growing recognition that various private interests were successfully influencing planning decisions politically. Planners became increasingly sensitive to their limitations in affecting implementation. Often their pro-

An earlier version of this chapter was published in the *Journal of Planning Education and Research* 3:13–22. Copyright © 1983 Association of Collegiate Schools of Planning.

posals either were adopted but did not work as intended or were ignored. Research interests in the university paralleled these new concerns of practitioners. Case studies were assembled to analyze the role of politics in planning (for example, Altshuler 1965; Meyerson and Banfield 1955; Rabinovitz 1969). Implementation has now become a special area of scholarly study (for example, Alexander 1985; Alexander and Beckley 1975; Alterman 1982).

Second, many planners discovered that planning is implicitly political in its intentions. Urban renewal and model cities projects brought planners into increasing contact with members of the public and made traditional claims of disinterest increasingly difficult to maintain in practice. Recommendations affected interests and aroused both support and opposition. Advocate planners took the position that planners could not avoid taking sides in political conflicts and, therefore, should do so explicitly (for example, Davidoff 1965; Heskin 1980; Kaplan 1969; Peattie 1968). More recently the critical theorists have articulated in the planning literature the values embedded in planners' actions (for example, Forester 1980).

Advocacy planning and community action experiences of the 1960s also stimulated a special concern with the interests of the poor. Analyses of community decision making led to a concern about the interests of business in shaping a public agenda that excluded the poor. The planning literature began to include politically Left, often Marxist analyses of planning decisions (for example, Fainstein et al. 1983; Hartman 1974; Tabb and Sawers 1978).

These experiences led many practitioners and researchers to develop new expectations of planners. This new view took for granted the implicitly political character of planners' actions and was concerned that planners should act in politically sensitive ways. They expected planners to think politically about the interests implicated in planning issues. They expected planners to act politically in attempting to influence perceptions of issues and the actions of interested parties.[1] This view of politically sensitive planning rested on the tacit liberal assumption that planning should be participative and that a participatory process would lead to equitable outcomes. More radical observers expected planners to work specifically for the interests of the poor or other deprived populations.

This chapter examines the research on planners' politics. It reviews the meanings of *politics* in the research, analyzes study findings, discusses implications for planning practice, and identifies needed further research.

Politics and Research

Because a political view of planning stands in contrast to traditional norms of planning as a value-free, technical activity, most studies focus on planners' relative emphases on technical analyses and political action. Still, different studies turn on different dichotomies between technical and political planning.

One dichotomy is derived from traditional views of planning as value free and is concerned with whether planners believe that they make value judgments in their work. Planning that involves value judgments is characterized as political, whereas planning with other (for example, engineering) judgments or without judgments is characterized as technical.[2]

A second dichotomy refers to thinking politically. A planner who formulates issues and recommends actions in terms that do not explicitly acknowledge differences in social interests is considered technical. In contrast, a political planner is likely to formulate issues and recommend actions in terms that recognize conflicts of interest and seek to give or mobilize support for particular interests and actors associated with them.

A third dichotomy refers to acting politically. Here researchers are concerned with what planners do with the information they think about or, more generally, how they occupy their time. Thus, a technical planner is likely to engage almost exclusively in a variety of intellectual tasks, collecting and analyzing information, working in relative isolation from most others except a few agency colleagues, and presenting findings or recommendations in a straightforward written form. In contrast, a political planner is likely to engage in not only intellectual work but also a variety of interpersonal or organizational tasks such as interviewing and persuading actors significant in the formulation, adoption, or implementation of future proposals and presenting findings not only in formal written documents but also in informal meetings and public arenas.

One question explored in this chapter is whether planners who are political in one set of terms may be expected to be political in one or both other sets as well. At the same time, the common denominator of most of these studies is the liberal view of politics as participation. The studies are concerned primarily with whether planners are political in the sense of promoting participation of interested actors. Few studies carefully distinguish participation in bureaucratic decision making from participation in public decision making. In addition, few studies are directly concerned with which goals or interests planners may support as at least implicit political actors. Thus, the research examines a diffuse politics that satisfies some but not all of the criteria of the new view of planners.

The studies employ a variety of research methods. A few involve the direct observation of practice.[3] Some ask planners to describe their practice. Other studies ask planners to identify the skills they consider important in practice. A variety of studies survey planners for influential attitudes, beliefs, personality dimensions, or cognitive styles that may influence their practice. This chapter does not analyze the methodologies of these studies. The most important characteristic of the studies is that they are exploratory. For this reason, it is appropriate to relax expectations about the methodological rigor of the research in favor of an interest in what the studies may reveal or suggest about planners.[4] Generalization from the cumulative findings of the studies seems permissible because, despite the variety of research approaches employed, the findings tend to be consistent. The primary limitations of the studies are related not to the rigor of their execution as much as the choice of methodologies. This limitation is discussed later.

Do Planners Regard Themselves as Political?

Studies of planners' self-perceptions take three forms. One group of studies is concerned with planners' cognitive maps of the planning environment. These studies examine ways in which planners may think politically. Do planners see the environment of planning as consisting of information awaiting logical organization or as consisting of people with various interests and different types and amounts of power awaiting political organization? Do planners see the planning process as a relatively rational consideration of information or as a relatively political reconciliation of social and economic interests?

A second group of studies is concerned with planners' role orientation to the planning environment. These studies ask the types of actions in which planners are prepared to engage as part of their professional responsibility. The studies examine a combination of ways in which planners may either think or act politically. Do planners regard themselves as primarily intellectual technicians or as primarily political strategists? What do planners think about the propriety of planners' acting in an explicitly political manner to influence decisions?

The third group of studies is concerned with the types of skills that planners use daily. These studies examine ways in which planners may act politically. Are planners more likely to use and value relatively technical skills involved in collecting and analyzing information or to emphasize relatively political skills involved in communicating with and organizing other people?

Planners' Cognitive Maps

Several researchers examine planners' perceptions of the planning environment to see whether planners formulate issues in explicitly political terms.[5] The researchers all similarly identify two groups of planners. A minority of planners regard the planning process as either properly or inevitably a contest among political interests. In contrast, a majority believe that planning is or should be concerned with only the rational consideration of information. Their descriptions of the planning world emphasize the types of information that planners collect and analyze and tend to exclude political actors who might interfere with planners' rational calculations.

Baum (1980, 1983c) and Needleman and Needleman (1974) interviewed planners in an open-ended manner and attempted to articulate views of the world from common themes in planners' statements. Both studies find a minority, perhaps one-third, of planners who are relatively comfortable with politics, which they understand as a process through which variously interested actors organize power in support of their interests. Recognizing that planning is such a political process, these planners think of themselves as organizers and orchestrators of public participation. They are relatively likely to enter actively into political negotiations or citizen activities as a way of affecting planning decisions, to which they believe they contribute both political strategy and reasoned analysis. When these planners describe the planning environment, they give straightforward recognition to the political contours of decisions. In their world views, planning decisions affect many interests; a number of actors are prepared to influence the planner or elected officials; and the planner conceptualizes planning problems in terms of potential allies or adversaries for a coalition in support of particular positions.

In contrast, a majority of planners think of themselves as intellectual problem solvers. They collect and analyze information about problems and render recommendations that point to optimal solutions. These planners are hostile to politics as a category of activities that involves efforts to subvert the influence of reason. They believe that decisions should be made on the basis of planners' rational analysis, with little or no citizen participation. This group of planners tends to deny, first, the legitimacy and, then implicitly, the reality of political actors in the planning process. When they talk about planning issues, they describe environments in which ideas and information are prominent and in which political actors are unimportant or nonexistent.

These studies suggest that different planners have distinctly different cognitive maps of the environment in which planning issues are formulated and resolved. Planners differ in the terms in which they analyze issues. Planners who appear to think politically are a minority, but a substantial one. These findings raise several questions. Are planners who tend to think politically likely to act politically? If not, what prevents or discourages them from acting politically? Answers to these questions may help to understand an important general question, Are there identifiable differences between planners who think politically and those who do not?

Planners' Role Orientations

Studies of planners' role orientations offer answers for these questions.[6] These studies find a group of planners who advocate a political role, another group who advocate a technical role, and some who argue for a combination of the two, but the most puzzling discovery is a significant group of planners who are ambivalent about taking either of these roles.

Krumholz's (1982; Krumholz, Cogger, and Linner 1975) description of his work and Needleman and Needleman's (1974) description of the community planners whom they interviewed offer a clear picture of planners who enact a political role. These people do not reject technical work, but they supplement it with overt or tacit advocacy for positions they prefer. They make explicit value judgments about the interests affected by issues. They combine rigorous research, dissemination of information about pending decisions, and discussion and negotiation with potential allies and adversaries. These political activists contrast with a majority of planners who eschew positions or tactics that appear to be partisan or that diverge from a technical role.

Howe and Kaufman (1979), interviewing a national sample of American Institute of Planning (AIP) members, offer the first suggestion that there may be another group of planners who are not primarily politicians or technicians. Howe and Kaufman first asked planners to react to statements espousing a political or a technical role. On the basis of responses, they categorized planners in these groups: politicians (18 percent), technicians (27 percent), and an intermediate group of hybrids (51 percent).[7] When these planners were asked whether they regarded various hypothetical overtly political actions of planners as ethical or not, the politicians were consistently most approving, the technicians least approving, and the hybrids in the middle.

The puzzle posed by Howe and Kaufman (1979) is what distinguishes the hybrids from other planners. Are they simply intermediate on a continuum between pure politicians and pure technicians, or are they somehow qualitatively different from other planners? One difficulty in interpreting the discovery of the hybrids is that the survey instruments reports on espoused beliefs and ethical judgments about hypothetical situations rather than planners' actions. It is possible, for example, that subtler ethical distinctions may be found in espousals than are evident in practice. More generally, it is possible that planners do not act as they say they should. Additional research is needed to resolve these questions,[8] but other studies offer evidence that many in this hybrid group may stand between politicians and technicians because they are ambivalent about both roles.

For example, Vasu (1979), also surveying a national sample of AIP members, reveals that a number of planners report simultaneous adherence to apparently conflicting beliefs. Although the aggregate form of the data precludes precise statements, there appears to be a group of planners who at the same time believe that planning involves value judgments and that master plans are not neutral, that planners should not take an active role in influencing planning goals or decisions, and that comprehensive rational planning by government is possible. Vasu interprets the conflict as one between growing role expectations that planners act politically and planners' socialization into traditional norms of planning as value-free, technical work, with professional status attached to their work as technicians. Alternatively, one might interpret the apparent conflict in the context of a "politics of expertise" (Benveniste 1977): Planners may believe that they should act politically but that influence requires them to present themselves as neutral technicians rather than partisan actors in potential conflict with formal decision makers.

Selecting one of these interpretations depends on more information than the data provide. It would be necessary to know whether planners responding to the survey regarded their answers as public or private statements, as comments to a colleague or to an outsider. Apparent conflicts in statements might reflect a perception of the survey as part of a politics of expertise, in which beliefs that planning involves value judgments would be balanced by strategic denials of interest in making or influencing judgments. In this case, there would not be ambivalence, and apparent conflicts of beliefs would reflect deliberate impression management. In addition, or alternatively, planners might feel that their professional status depended on their asserting their neutrality. In this case, the conflict of beliefs might reflect either impression management or genuine ambivalence. Insofar as the conflicting statements are efforts at public relations, then apparent espousals of technical roles may give an inaccurate impression of ambivalence and overstate planners' resistance to a political role. Otherwise—and no data exist to refute this interpretation—it appears that many planners hold conflicting beliefs about political action and are ambivalent about acting politically. Such an ambivalence may be expressed either in a vacillation between political initiatives and retreat to technical roles or in a relatively consistent insistence on a technical role.

Schön (1982, 1983) offers evidence of an ambivalence that involves not simply conflicting beliefs but a conflict between beliefs and feelings. He analyzes the actions of a planner who reviews development applications and makes recommendations to a planning board. The planner believes that he or she is enacting a political role in which he or she mediates between developers and the board, tacitly negotiating proposal modifications with both. However, the planner believes that his or her credibility and influence with both developers and the board rest on their perception of him or her as someone who makes nondiscretionary technical judgments and recommendations. In the end, the planner plays too rigid a technical role and defeats his or her political intentions.

It is possible to interpret this case as an example of the politics of expertise, in which any apparent conflict between technical and political roles reflects only deliberate obfuscation. However, Schön (1982, 1983) emphasizes, the planner uses the technical role excessively as a means of controlling negotiations so that negotiations become overcontrolled and fall through. The planner appears to need, want, and enjoy the control that insistence on unquestionable technical judgments affords. The technical role brings satisfaction that is not just political but also psychological.[9] This planner apparently experiences a conflict between a belief in acting flexibly as a political negotiator and a psychological need to act in a controlling manner. Schön's interpretation suggests that one attraction of a technical role is that it provides a possibility of controlling a situation securely, whereas a political role presents the risk of being more susceptible to question.[10] Thus, anxiety about the challenges of a political role may contribute to ambivalence, causing planners to vacillate between political and technical roles or simply to choose technical roles.

Baum (1980, 1983c), interviewing a sample of Maryland AIP members, provides evidence of ambivalence that involves conflicting beliefs and feelings. In response to questions about political action, many planners make contradictory statements. For example, they say that planners should have more power in public decision making, but they avoid any discussion of specific strategic steps they should take to acquire such power. They suggest that the intellectual quality of their work itself should bring public appreciation, which in turn should bring planners influence, even though they also complain about lack of public appreciation. A number of planners observe that they would benefit from licensing, but they oppose lobbying to enact it. If planners deserve licensing, they say, the quality of their technical work should alone be sufficient to attract the attention and support of laypersons and legislators. These planners recognize that decisions about planning and licensing are political, but they believe that it would be unseemly to attempt to act politically, and they espouse neutral technical roles.

Beneath this ambivalence about political action is ambivalence about the exercise of power in political action. Commitments such as encouraging citizens to participate in planning, organizing collectively to influence public policy, or doing battle with elected officials over planning decisions would force planners to share risks and responsibilities with others, as colleagues, allies, or adversaries. The planners appear to resist committing themselves to political action because they mistrust the exercise of power. They lack confidence that outcomes will be benign, and they hesitate to surrender autonomy to a collectivity regardless of the potential benefits. These planners appear to experience a conflict between the belief that political action is necessary to gain the influence they feel they deserve and feelings of anxiety about the exercise of power. This ambivalence tends to discourage them from political action.[11] They may rationalize this hesitation in terms of intellectual individualism. The role of technical analyst feels secure, and it is represented as properly neutral.

The essence of the ambivalence found in these studies is a combined attraction to and repulsion from a political role. The ambivalence appears to be caused by a conflict between certain activist conclusions from thinking politically and other beliefs or feelings opposing thoughts about politics. The experience of ambivalence is uncomfortable because it involves opposing impulses. One expression of the ambivalence may be constant vacillation between acting politically and taking a technical role. Because such vacillation never succeeds in reducing the discomfort of the ambivalence, another response may be a retreat from ambivalence to a technical role. Another possible response would be to think politically less often, to find fewer reasons for believing that acting politically is appropriate or necessary.

Cole (1975) offers evidence in support of the possibility that planners who are hesitant to act politically tend to exclude political thinking. Studying a group of AIP members and Denver area planners, Cole is interested primarily in the cognitive styles, or ways of thinking, that are common among planners. In particular, he wants to know whether planners tend to think concretely or abstractly. He finds that a little more than half of planners think concretely. Significantly, different views of politics and planners' roles are associated with different cognitive styles. The concrete planners resemble the intellectual planners or technicians in being hostile to politics. They believe that planning decisions should be made rationally and that their strongest contribution should be the force of their analysis. The abstract planners resemble the political planners in accepting politics as either legitimate or unavoidable. They believe that they should encourage citizen participation and that they contribute mediational and organizational skills to decision making.

Cole's (1975) findings are provocative. Planners who choose political roles are more likely to think abstractly than planners who favor technical roles. One explanation for this finding is that an understanding of the political environment of planning decisions requires an ability to think abstractly about a complex network of relationships. In contrast, a concrete view of the world would be more likely to emphasize directly present colleagues and administrators in the planning department as the primary and final participants in the planning process.

This interpretation of Cole's (1975) findings is consistent with Schön's (1982) interpretation in his case. Schön contends that planners and others tend to retreat to controlling positions, such as that afforded by the technical role, because they simply have not learned the more complex framework and skills required for the negotiators of a more open political role. Planners and others choose roles they believe they can most competently enact in the world as they understand it. Thus, planners who select political roles may have a more abstract and more complex framework for interpreting the planning environment than planners who select technical roles.

Cole's (1975) findings that political and technical planners have different cognitive styles are also consistent with speculations about ambivalence about power. It is possible that political and technical planners unconsciously develop abstract or concrete cognitive styles respectively in response to their comfort or ambivalence about political action. For example, planners who are anxious about power may develop a concrete cognitive style that obscures recognition of a complex web of political relationships that might evoke anxiety. Such a development of a concrete cognitive style would tend to hinder thinking politically and to reduce ambivalence about acting politically in favor of a more technical role.

The research, then, suggests some answers to questions raised initially. When planners' inclinations to choose roles are studied, four groups appear. One group of planners follow a primarily political role, in which they seek to influence others to adopt positions or come to agreements. A second group consistently enact a technical role. Howe and Kaufman (1979) find another group, whom they call hybrids. Some in this group undoubtedly combine technical and political roles. However, a number of studies suggest that many hybrids really constitute a distinct group characterized by ambivalence between acting politically and technically. It appears that those planners who think politically also tend to act politically, although the formulation of ambivalence suggests some primarily emotional obstacles to translating political thinking into political action.

Such a view of planners who are ambivalent about acting politically is speculative, yet it is suggested by evidence in several studies with distinct concerns and methodologies. The primary alternative interpretation of some of the evidence is that some apparent ambivalence represents instead more or less conscious efforts to deny political thought or action as part of a politics of expertise. Further research is clearly called for, both to evaluate the interpretations and, if the ambivalence interpretation is valid, to provide a better understanding of the ambivalence. It is reasonable to expect, for example, that only some planners experience significant ambivalence and that, among those who do, the sources, intensity, and consequences of the ambivalence vary. In particular, it would be important to understand when ambivalence may be consistent with acting politically, when it may contribute to a more or less continual vacillation between acting politically and taking a technical role, and when it leads to a simple technical role. It is also important to understand whether ambivalence may prevent planners from thinking politically.

Planners' Skill in Practice

A minority of planners see the world politically and advocate political activism. What happens in practice? Do planners do what they espouse? This question is too complex to answer definitively,[12] but research that asks planners about the skills they employ in practice offers some hints.[13] These studies find planners who value political skills and others who value technical skills, but a puzzling finding is a group of planners who apparently regard political skills as important but do not use them.

Studies of planners' skills tend to distinguish intellectual skills, involving the organization of information, and social skills, involving the organization of people. Consistent with other usage in this discussion, the social skills may be considered political skills. By and large, the intellectual skills may be considered technical (that is, nonpolitical) skills, but a simple equation of intellectual skills and technical skills would be inaccurate insofar as acting politically also requires skills in thinking politically to guide action. The differences in questions asked and the aggregated presentation of findings makes the studies only suggestive.

Some studies find significant support for political skills. Schön et al. (1976) and Foster et al. (1982), surveying alumni of their programs, find that approximately 50 percent of planners most highly value generic skills, which include not only intellectual skills but also political skills such as working with politicians, negotiating, working within power relationships, and consulting with clients.

Other studies, such as Hemmens and colleagues' (Hemmens, Bergman, and Moroney 1978) interviews with social policy planning graduates from several programs, find relatively little support for political skills. For example, even though many social policy planners believe that the political content and context of planning are quite important, relatively few of them nevertheless appear to engage in overtly political activity. Insofar as they do work with other people, relatively little of their activity (for the sample, an average of 19 percent of time spent with others) involves lobbying and selling. These planners believe that they exercise competently most of the skills they frequently use. However, when asked what additional training they would like, many identify high-level mathematical and reasoning skills, even though few social policy planners use such skills. The largest group of these planners believe that social planning is, and should continue to be, a rational problem-solving process. Baum (1980, 1983c) makes similar findings when asking planners to describe their strengths in practice. Approximately two-thirds portray their strengths in terms of the intellectual skills used in a rational problem-solving process, whereas only a third refer to skills in social relations.

Although these divergent findings about political skills may be an artifact of the small number of studies, they do suggest that some planners value political skills but do not use them. The Schön et al. (1976) and Foster et al. (1982) studies indicate that many planners recognize the importance of political issues and actions in planning decisions. However, the Hemmens et al. (1978) and Baum (1980, 1983c) studies, which ask planners to assess their competence, suggest that many planners feel, nevertheless, that exercising intellectual skills is more satisfying or effective for them personally. This interpretation is consistent with the earlier view of ambivalence—that many planners recognize the importance of politics in planning but have difficulty acting politically. An alternative interpretation would suggest that some planners would like to act politically but do not simply because they lack appropriate skills. It is impossible to choose between these interpretations without more information from planners.[14]

Implications for Planners' Practice

These studies were conducted by researchers who share the new expectation that planners' effectiveness requires them to think and act in explicitly political ways. Although the studies combine several different meanings of *politics,* the research appears consistently to identify four relatively discrete groups of planners on the basis of their readiness to think politically or act politically.

A substantial minority of planners think and act politically. Some (it is unclear how many) see the planning environment primarily in terms of social interest, political actors, potential alliances, and opportunities for negotiations. They are prepared to use various explicitly political tactics in influencing decisions. Their repertoire includes organizing and negotiating skills.

Another group, again of uncertain size, combines political thinking and action with technical expertise. It sees the planning environment in terms of both political interests and technical issues. At different times they may emphasize either political strategies or technical analyses as approaches to solving problems. Their repertoire includes both organizational and analytical skills.

A large group of planners consistently act as technicians, avoiding political thinking or action. They see the environment of planning in terms of information and sources of information that may assist them in rational problem solving. They favor a technical, intellectual role and have serious hesitation about even limited political tactics. Their skills are concentrated in analytic problem solving and quantitative skills.

Finally—and perhaps the only surprising finding—a significant group is ambivalent about politics. These planners are more likely to think politically than to act politically, although hesitations about acting in situations involving the exercise of power seem to constrain even their thinking about such situations. They appear both to recognize and to deny the significance of political actors in the planning environment. They acknowledge that political tactics would both benefit them as members of a planning profession and help promote positions they favor on planning issues, but they draw back from a political role. Their repertoire of skills is probably heavily weighted toward the technical.

These findings inform us both about planners and about the practice of planning. First, it is clear that only a minority of planners satisfy the expectation of both thinking and acting politically. In addition, the example of the ambivalents draws attention to the importance of normally unrecognized emotional components of practice. Whether planners become politically sensitive is more than a simple matter of changing ideology. Planning competence evidently entails knowledge of the types of conflicts between beliefs and feelings that may inhibit action, as well as skill in resolving these conflicts. The discovery of the ambivalents raises important questions that these studies cannot answer. Hence, further research should be designed to study, in general, the conditions under which planners are prepared to act politically and, in particular, under which ambivalence about politics or power may hinder political action.

Future Research Needs

One limitation of many studies reviewed here is that they ask planners closed-ended questions, and the responses do not say enough about what planners mean by their brief answers. It is unclear, for example, when responses are meant as public statements and when they express privately held beliefs. It is uncertain what relationship planners see between beliefs they espouse and the actions they carry out and observe. It is difficult to assess when statements may be providing clues to unconscious feelings or sentiments that affect conscious statements, beliefs, intentions, and actions. Understanding the puzzle of planners' ambivalence toward acting politically depends on studying planners with some psychological sensitivity.

The necessary research strategy is to talk with planners, to reflect with them at greater length on what they think and feel while they act. Particularly at the exploratory stage of research it is less important to have an extensive, rigorously selected sample of planners than it is to search in depth with some planners who are willing to reflect on what they do.[15] As much as possible, interviews should be coupled with observations of practice. In this way, researchers may compare planners' descriptions of their work with what the researchers observe, and they may ask the planners about any apparent discrepancies.

Consideration of what field researchers studying planners in practice would observe points to an interesting conceptual limitation in much of the research reviewed here. A field researcher would observe planners as they work in groups, teams, and networks. Yet most studies examine planners as individuals. The studies implicitly assume that the individual planner is the operative unit of planning practice. Although the research is concerned with the political character of the planning environment, the research tends to study planners as if they practiced in social isolation.

This individualistic interpretation of planners' practice is empirically inaccurate. In addition, such an interpretation gives rise to unwarranted conclusions. If current views of planning call for political activism, and if the individual planner is regarded as the operative unit of planning practice, then it is necessary for every planner to become a competent political activist. In this framework, the studies' findings are certainly disappointing. However, this expectation is neither realistic nor necessary.

Much planning work is—and still more should be—carried out by teams of planners sharing responsibilities. If a team is considered the operative unit of planning practice, and if political activism is an appropriate expectation of planners, it need be expected only that some member or members of any team be able to act politically, not that every planner be a political actor. In this framework, the studies' findings are perhaps satisfactory in suggesting that different planners variously emphasize political or technical roles or some combination of the two. Effective planning, incorporating both competent technical analysis and political sensitivities, requires a joining of the political activists with the technicians.

Special research attention should be given to the ways in which planners divide responsibilities in teams and networks. Such a study would help in an understanding of the types of situations about which planners may have intentions and that their intentions may affect. A better conceptualization of the events of practice in teams and networks would contribute to a more sophisticated view of the nature of politics in planning. In particular, the examination of planners' tacit assumptions about other persons may provide the key to some of the sources of ambivalence about acting politically.[16]

This examination of planners' practice would move the study of planners' politics away from what planners espouse and closer to what they do. Then one might ask not simply whether planners are political in the sense of promoting interested participation but which interests and goals planners support.[17] Although four groups of planners emerge from studies of planners' espousals, it is possible that fewer—or more—would appear in observations of practice.[18]

Finally, research on planners' practice links the study of planners' intentions with the study of the consequences of their actions so it is possible to assess the differences in the social world that may be associated with different self-perceptions on the part of planners.[19] Even the most conscientiously technical work may have far-reaching political effects.[20] The possibility for planners to confront the consequences of their intentions would offer them the opportunity to learn to think and to act differently. Many might, even if reluctantly, come to share the conviction that planning competence entails political sensitivity.

This research has major potential implications for planning education. The research is likely to suggest that either acting politically or thinking politically requires personal security with the exercise of power. Moreover, the primary requisite for this security is not ideological clarity but reflective practice in interactions with others. Traditional didactic university education is inadequate for teaching this reflection; experiential education will have to grow in importance.[21] The planning academics and practitioners who most strongly support political activism are not accustomed to speak of planners' emotional lives or psychological issues. The political advocates are more likely to emphasize abstract intellectual analysis than to consider clinical examination of rough-edged practice. And yet the studies point to the inseparability of planners' external actions and their inner conditions. A joining of political and psychological interests in education, research, and practice would be an auspicious partnership indeed.

Notes

1. Needleman and Needleman (1974) identify the expectation of political sensitivity with the new planner and contrast it with the apolitical professional norms of the old planners.
2. It must be emphasized that the research is concerned with planners' views of whether they make value judgments rather than the researchers' views. At the same time, however, the characterization of planners' self-perceptions as either technical or political is that of the researchers.
3. For classification of studies by research methodology, see Baum (1983d).
4. The rigor of the studies varies. While some of this variation indicates differences in the quality of research, much reflects differences in research approaches and methods. For example, studies differ in their degree of conformity to a traditional model of systematic sampling and quantitative analysis of variables. By and large, conformity to or deviance from this model is related to the focus of the studies. The more directly a study is concerned with observing planners' practice, the more likely the study is to sample planners expediently (sampling planners who are accessible) and to find that significant variables are qualitative. Studies based on closed-ended questionnaires, whatever the subject of the questions, permit considerable quantification of variables and analysis.
5. For a summary of the relevant findings in these studies, see Baum (1983a).
6. Ibid.
7. The remaining planners favor neither a technical nor political role.
8. Since their initial study, Howe and Kaufman have collected more information about the meaning of planners' ethical beliefs by interviewing planners at length regarding both their beliefs and situations in their practice. See, for example, Howe (1983).
9. A pure distinction between political and psychological motives is artificial. However, political motives are here meant to be those that support rational political interests, whereas psychological motives are those that serve a variety of conscious and unconscious personal interests and may conflict with political interests.

10. For a discussion of ways in which planners may rely on technical ritualism as a defense against being made scapegoat for problems, see Baum (1981, 1986).

11. For a discussion of ways in which bureaucratic conditions may contribute to ambivalence about power, see Baum (1983b, 1986).

12. Schön (1982, 1983) has explained and shown how it is difficult for either a practitioner or an observer to understand connections between espousals and practice. For a discussion of his research and his conclusions, see also Argyris and Schön (1974, 1978) and Argyris (1982).

13. For a summary of the relevant findings in these studies, see Baum (1983a).

14. For a discussion of reasons why planners may not use political skills, see Baum (1980, 1986).

15. Suggestions about interview topics may be found in Baum (1983d).

16. Argyris and Schön (1974, 1978; Argyris 1982) argue that such assumptions about other persons hinder people from taking actions they espouse.

17. Further, as Forester (1982a) suggests, planners' intentions may be differentiated at three levels: overt decision making, agenda setting, and need shaping.

18. Clearly, how many groups one finds depends on the framework one uses. For example, Argyris and Schön (1974, 1978; Argyris 1982), simply distinguishing an authoritarian Model I and a participatory Model II, would anticipate finding only one type of planner—Model I. For all the reasons mentioned here no simple answer to the question whether planners are political makes general sense. Because politics is multidimensional, no census of planners that simply distinguishes politicians and technicians—even if an intermediate category is included—can provide a clear picture of practitioners' thinking and actions. For instance, Kaufman (1984) points out that different researchers have produced different summary censuses. However, in explaining the differences, he concentrates on methodological differences, as if some methods were better than others for studying what might be assumed to be a well-defined phenomenon, rather than considering the conceptual complexities of the phenomenon.

19. Case studies examine the consequences of planners' actions, but most planning case studies have not looked at linkages between these consequences and specific intentions and self-perceptions.

20. Forester (1980–1981, 1982a, 1982b) has provided useful conceptualizations of the implicit political content of planning practice. His work is particularly helpful in understanding relationships between planners' intentions and the consequences of their actions. His work suggests which intentions may have significant political consequences and what types of social events may be associated with planners' intentions.

21. For recommendations about specific types of experiential education, see Baum (1980, 1983c).

References

Alexander, Ernest. 1985. From Idea to Action: Notes for a Contingent Theory of the Policy-Implementation Process. *Administration and Society* 16:403–426.

Alexander, Ernest, and R.M. Beckley. 1975. *Going It Alone? A Case Study of Planning and Implementation at the Local Level.* Washington, D.C.: U.S. Government Printing Office.

Alterman, Rachelle. 1982. Implementation Analysis in Urban and Regional Planning: Toward a Research Agenda. In *Planning Theory: Prospects for the 1980s,* Patsy Healey, Glen McDougall, and Michael Thomas, eds. Oxford: Pergamon Press.

Altshuler, Alan. 1965. *The City Planning Process.* Ithaca, N.Y.: Cornell University Press.

Argyris, Chris. 1982. *Reasoning, Learning, and Action.* San Francisco: Jossey-Bass.

Argyris, Chris, and Donald A. Schön. 1974. *Theory in Practice: Increasing Organizational Effectiveness.* San Francisco: Jossey-Bass.

———. 1978. *Organizational Learning: A Theory of Action Perspective.* Reading: Mass.: Addison-Wesley.

Baum, Howell S. 1980. Sensitizing Planners to Organization. In *Urban and Regional Planning in an Age of Austerity,* Pierre Clavel, John Forester, and William Goldsmith, eds. New York: Pergamon.

———. 1981. The Planner as Reluctant Scapegoat. Paper presented to the American Society for Public Administration National Conference, Detroit, Michigan.

———. 1983a. Are Planners Political? How Planners (and Researchers) See Planners. Unpublished manuscript. Baltimore: University of Maryland, School of Social Work and Community Planning.

———. 1983b. Autonomy, Shame, and Doubt: Power in the Bureaucratic Lives of Planners. *Administration and Society* 15:147–184.

———. 1983c. *Planners and Public Expectations.* Cambridge, Mass.: Schenkman.

———. 1983d. Politics and Ambivalence in Planners' Practice. *Journal of Planning Education and Research* 3:13–22.

———. 1986. *The Invisible Bureaucracy: Problem-Solving in Bureaucratic Organizations.* New York: Oxford University Press.

Benveniste, Guy. 1977. *The Politics of Expertise,* 2nd ed. San Francisco: Boyd and Fraser.

Boyer, M. Christine. 1983. *Dreaming the Rational City.* Cambridge, Mass.: MIT Press.

Brownell, Blaine A. 1980. Urban Planning, the Planning Profession, and the Motor Vehicle in Early Twentieth Century America. In *Shaping an Urban World,* Gordon Cherry, ed. New York: St. Martin's Press.

Cole, David Bras. 1975. *The Role of Psychological Belief Systems in Urban Planning.* Ph.D. dissertation, University of Colorado.

Davidoff, Paul. 1965. Advocacy and Pluralism in Planning. *Journal of the American Institute of Planners* 31:331–338.

Fainstein, Susan S.; Norman I. Fainstein; Richard Child Hill; Dennis Judd; and Michael Peter Smith. 1983. *Restructuring the City.* New York: Longman.

Forester, John. 1980. Critical Theory and Planning Practice. *Journal of the American Planning Association* 46:275–286.

———. 1980–1981. What Do Planning Analysts Do? Planning and Policy Analysis as Organizing. *Policy Studies Journal* 9:595–604.

———. 1982a. Planning in the Face of Power. *Journal of the American Planning Association* 48:67–80.

———. 1982b. Understanding Planning Practice: An Empirical, Practical and Normative Account. *Journal of Planning Education and Research* 1:59–71.

Foster, Howard H., Jr.; Amy Abramson; and Mary Parella. 1982. Planners' Skills and

Planning Schools: A Comparative Study of Alumni. Paper presented at the Annual Meeting of the Association of Collegiate Schools of Planning, Chicago, Illinois.

Hartman, Chester. 1974. *Yerba Buena: Land Grab and Community Resistance in San Francisco.* San Francisco: Glide Publications.

Hemmens, George C.; Edward M. Bergman; and Robert M. Moroney. 1978. The Practitioner's View of Social Planning. *Journal of the American Institute of Planners* 44:181–192.

Heskin, Allan David. 1980. Crisis and Responses: A Historical Perspective on Advocacy Planning. *Journal of the American Planning Association* 46:50–63.

Howe, Elizabeth. 1980. Role Choices of Urban Planners. *Journal of the American Planning Association* 46:398–409.

———. 1983. Planners' Views of the Public Interest. Paper presented at the Annual Meeting of the Association of Collegiate Schools of Planning, San Francisco, California.

Howe, Elizabeth, and Jerome Kaufman. 1979. The Ethics of Contemporary American Planners. *Journal of the American Planning Association* 45:243–255.

Kaplan, Marshall. 1969. Advocacy and the Urban Poor. *Journal of the American Institute of Planners* 35:96–101.

Kaufman, Jerome. 1984. Review of Howell S. Baum, *Planners and Public Expectations. Planning* 50:42–43.

Krumholz, Norman. 1982. A Retrospective View of Equity Planning: Cleveland 1969–1979. *Journal of the American Planning Association* 48:163–174.

Krumholz, Norman; Janice Cogger; and John Linner. 1975. The Cleveland Policy Planning Report. *Journal of the American Institute of Planners* 41:298–304.

Meyerson, Martin, and Edward C. Banfield. 1955. *Politics, Planning, and the Public Interest.* Glencoe, N.Y.: Free Press.

Needleman, Martin L., and Carolyn Emerson Needleman. 1974. *Guerrillas in the Bureaucracy.* New York: Wiley.

Peattie, Lisa. 1968. Reflections on Advocacy Planning. *Journal of the American Institute of Planners* 34:80–88.

Rabinovitz, Francine F. 1969. *City Politics and Planning.* Chicago: Aldine Publishing Company.

Schön, Donald. 1982. Some of What a Planner Knows: A Case Study of Knowing-in-Practice. *Journal of the American Planning Association* 48:351–364.

———. 1983. *The Reflective Practitioner.* New York: Basic.

Schön, Donald; Nancy Sheldon Cremer; Paul Osterman; and Charles Perry. 1976. Planners in Transition: Report on a Survey of Alumni of M.I.T.'s Department of Urban Studies, 1960–1971. *Journal of the American Institute of Planners* 42: 193–202.

Scott, Mel. 1969. *American City Planning Since 1980.* Berkeley: University of California Press.

Tabb, William K., and Larry Sawers, eds. 1978. *Marxism and the Metropolis.* New York: Oxford University Press.

Vasu, Michael Lee. 1979. *Politics and Planning: A National Study of American Planners.* Chapel Hill: University of North Carolina Press.

4
Usable Planning Theory: An Agenda for Research and Education

Judith Innes de Neufville

Despite recent signs of life, planning theory remains in the doldrums, where it has been for years. Few new ideas have been generated from within the field, while old ones are unsupported by consensus. Documentation is growing that planning theory provides little guidance to the practitioner, contributes to frustration, and even hinders practice. It is a matter of considerable urgency to develop theories of planning that will both mesh with the realities of practice and be useful and inspiring to the practitioner. The theories must be richer, more evocative, and more intellectually productive than those now in currency if the field is to mature. The question is, How can these goals be achieved?

The Doldrums of Planning Theory

Evidence of the inadequacy of planning theory comes from many directions. Klosterman (1981) reports a survey of planning theory courses showing few contributions by planners in recent years, with the most popular being mainly review articles. He finds little commonality among course bibliographies, few items appearing in more than a quarter of them, and seemingly no common structure to courses. No text, or even collection of writings, has gained general acceptance.

Not only is there no agreement on what body of ideas constitutes planning theory, but also much of the literature raises insoluble dilemmas and conundrums. How can the planner choose between roles as a value-neutral analyst and committed, effective political actor? If there is no single public interest, how can planners know what interest or value to serve? How can they do long-term, comprehensive, and systematic planning in an environment in which action is undertaken incrementally and power is shared? Should a plan be a vision of the future, a contract, or a first step in a process?

An earlier version of this chapter was published in the *Journal of Planning Education and Research* 3:36–45. Copyright © 1983 Association of Collegiate Schools of Planning.

Such questions have no answers. They are the stuff of armchair debate, the product of logical-deductive argumentation in which the implications of extreme viewpoints are drawn in relief and the contradictions exposed.

Because much of planning theory stops short at this exercise, it offers little aid to the understanding of how planning actually works. This type of argumentation offers promise of neither creating new models of planning nor of building usable theory for practice. In planners' education, the dilemmas are posed, but little guidance is offered in thinking about how to solve them. Each planner must invent a rationale and strategy for practice. This gap of theory and practice is well recognized in planning curricula, which include studio courses, field placements, and experiential learning. But the void between the world of practice and most of what is formally taught will remain until planning theory provides a framework for understanding and evaluating the experience.

Cognitive Dissonance in the Profession

Empirical studies increasingly document that the dilemmas of planning theory are reflected in planners' thought and attitudes. For example, Vasu (1979), after surveying a large sample of planners, concludes that they suffer from cognitive dissonance. They are caught on the one hand by an acute awareness that their environment is dominated by politics and that rational, comprehensive planning may well be futile, and on the other by a conviction that they should attempt it anyway. Conflict among planners' roles and lack of congruence between their goals and their achievements are important sources of job dissatisfaction (Mayo 1982). Planners are confused about what is ethical behavior (Marcuse 1976). Howe and Kaufman (1979), in a study of planners' attitudes, identify three groups—technicians, political planners, and hybrids. The third group, which represents nearly 50 percent of the sample, do not choose between technical excellence and value commitment but try to achieve both. Planning theory, however, gives little image of the content or logic of this latter stance, despite its prevalence. Instead it suggests that the role is logically and psychologically untenable. Baum (1980, 1983) argues that planners are often ineffective and frustrated because they expect to be analysts and plan makers, but instead they must operate as bureaucrats and negotiators, although they are unprepared for these roles. In another study, de Neufville (1981a) finds that planners subscribe to the rhetoric that information and analysis are important components of planning, although few actually use data in any significant way in practice.

Defining Planning: A Cooperative Enterprise

What is meant by *planning*? It is my contention that defining planning is in part a task for research to discover rather than simply the a priori basis for argumentation. Planning is an "open concept," in Kaplan's terminology (1964), not fully articulated and with fuzzy boundaries yet in use and generally understood. We can tacitly recognize a certain core of activities as planning, although we might disagree on some at the boundaries. It is important to avoid premature closure because the meaning of open concepts varies according to context, purpose, and the understanding of the overall situation. For example, to a child a book is a bound set of pages with words and pictures; to a librarian such books may be considered periodicals; to a university tenure committee a bound volume made up of reprinted articles does not count as a book, while a stack of loose manuscript pages may be quite acceptable. The term *planning* has an even greater range of variations than this example suggests because its purpose and contexts are even more varied.

We can use research simultaneously to analyze and define planning in the same way that, as children, we learn the meanings of words. A phenomenon is identified and labeled for us; we observe it and experience it in various contexts and forms; we generalize from our observations; we consider explanations from others; we modify the original definitions and develop principles that allow us to recognize even peculiar variations of a phenomenon. The principles may be tacit, but as long as they are more or less shared, we can communicate and analyze. The exercise of elaborating understanding has both objective and subjective components, as we go back and forth between experiencing and analyzing.

Academics and researchers normally are the ones who try to make the link between experience and interpretation (Berger and Luckmann, 1966), but those who do planning must also provide their own perspective in the definition process; they must evaluate the researchers' conceptions and test them in practice. The study of practice is essential, along with the engagement in practice. The definitions of planning should ultimately be ones with which those who study planning and those who engage in it can be comfortable. A kind of negotiation over ideas is needed, but this will require deliberate efforts. Planning theorists should not only aim at understanding the practitioner's position but also must present and publish their ideas in forums in which practitioners may encounter them. Practitioners must reflect on their experience, read widely on other experience, and publish their ideas which go beyond descriptive and self-congratulatory accounts to more analytical assessments that involve comparison of experience to ideas about planning. Each group needs to try seriously to understand the enterprise of the other. Discourse can take place at conferences, in classrooms, and in many other settings.

Practitioners with whom to begin a definition process may be sought in the formal planning profession, represented in part by members of the American Planning Association (APA) and served by planning schools. But many other practitioners belong in this first cut: national planners operating in planned economies, people working in state planning agencies, social planners, policy analysts, program planners, budgetary analysts, and policy advisors. Their continued inclusion in planning theory research depends on the objectives of the research and the degree of commonality among the groups.

Another starting point is to make a first cut at an a priori definition of planning. I propose the following for use in the rest of the discussion: Planning is a set of activities intended to improve the quality of decisions for a community and help prepare for its future. Planning theory tackles the problem of defining, assessing, and prescribing roles and activities for those who try to guide those in power. Planning is comprehensive in attempting to deal with many factors; it makes some systematic use of information; and it involves creation of images of the future and strategies to reach them. These are all preliminary definitions, open to evaluation and even rejection as part of the further specification process.

Planning as a Field in Crisis

One way to understand the situation of planning is to see it as a field in crisis, in a way which parallels Kuhn's (1970) discussions of progress and revolution in science. Revolutions in thought, or paradigm changes, occur when anomalies—observations in practice that are not accounted for by theory—are severe enough to cause significant malaise among both theorists and those doing empirical work. The evidence is that theories of planning are increasingly at odds with the experience of research and practice. If we follow out the implications of the analogy, it is time for a revolution in planning thought. It is time to develop a new way of seeing the problems and the task of planning—to make a gestalt shift to a paradigm that will provide a more satisfactory mesh with reality, a more usable set of goals for practice, and a more fruitful direction for theoretical inquiry.

The notion of paradigm is elusive but useful in the context of this discussion. It refers to a cluster of ideas and methods—theories, models, techniques, and practices—that is shared among a group of practitioners. It is a common mindset about the nature and purposes of a research discipline or, in this case, about practice. In science, as in planning, this paradigm can often be best understood by reference to an exemplar, or the prime model of effective research and practice emulated by those in the field. This exemplar becomes the basis for education and thus institutionalizes a particular way of approaching the field. In macroeconomics, for example, the prime exemplar is found in the work of John Maynard Keynes. In a profession, an exemplar may be a model of practice well enough elaborated and widely enough accepted and used to shape education and provide a basis for defining and doing research on practice. To understand the degree to which planning can claim a dominant paradigm, it is useful to examine possible exemplars.

The Master Plan

The best developed candidate for an exemplar of U.S. planning is the Master Plan approach, complete with planning commission; long-range, comprehensive, and visionary plan; planning tasks such as goal setting, information gathering, alternative generation, and solution design; a nonpolitical role for planners as staff to planning commissions; and clients (the commissions or the city council) that could be viewed as representing the public interest. The system was intended to insulate planners from bureaucracy and from the tasks of getting political support for plans, managing or even designing implementation activities. The approach represents an effort to avoid many dilemmas, such as the issue of whose values to promote. It provides a comparatively workable set of institutional and political arrangements and, under the Standard City Planning Enabling Act, has become the framework for much local planning across the United States. Kent's *Urban General Plan* (1964) became the prime exposition of the model, and later texts gave it prominence.

The Master Plan approach never has achieved the status of planning's exemplar, however. Some part of the profession saw it at the outset as too oriented to physical planning. Certainly it has been directed primarily to U.S. city planners, although it could have been adapted to other types of planning. After some experience, many planners and planning theorists have concluded it does not work as intended. It has been hard to develop a plan that would be influential and long term, as well as pragmatic and implementable, without turning the planning process into something quite different from the image originally projected—namely, something that was part and parcel of daily practice. The whole approach could simply mask a political process, allowing planners to serve class- and power-based interests while acting as disinterested servants of the public interest (Weiss 1985).

Whatever the reasons for the failure of the Master Plan approach to gain full support from planners—it is not the purpose of this chapter to reiterate the many arguments on this subject—the model has become the straw man for much of planning theory. Attempts have been made to modify the model, for example, by talking about the middle-range bridge (Meyerson 1956), to justify it through public finance theory (Moore 1978b; Lee 1981), and to outline alternative planning roles like advocate, facilitator, or analyst. Countless diatribes have been launched against the logic, practicality, and rationality of the Master Plan. None of the critiques, however, has produced an alternative equally well developed for practical application.

Policy Analysis as Planning Paradigm

Another strong recent contender for a U.S. planning exemplar has been best articulated and practiced by those trained in public policy (which has parallel difficulties to planning in agreeing on a paradigm and exemplar). In this approach, the planner is analyst and advisor to a chief executive or agency head, applying economic and systems analysis to produce recommendations. Meltsner (1976) documents the practices of policy analysts, and many textbooks with methods have appeared. Some planning schools have begun to identify with this model, as they loosen traditional ties to architecture and link themselves with public policy or public administration.

However, no clear trend has moved planning practice and education into a policy analysis mode. Despite the limitations of the Master Plan approach, the latter expresses several ideas important to many planners, which are not embodied in other approaches. These are, most notably, comprehensiveness in the sense of developing a plan for the whole rather than working on only a part of the problem; a concern with outcomes rather than simply a focus on method and process; and a design perspective that is synthesizing, creative, and visionary rather than primarily analytic and reactive to immediate political agendas or to narrowly specified problem formulations (see MacRae and Alterman 1983 for a comparison of planning and policy analysis).

An Agenda for Planning Theory

The predicament of planning—the crisis, the malaise, the disjunction between what we teach and claim planners do and what they actually do, the sharp divergences of opinion within the field—is, I believe, largely the responsibility of planning faculty. The job of those who teach planning is to explain the profession to itself, to make explicit the nature of practice, and to develop theories about how and why certain modes of practice tend to produce one or another type of result. The theories should provide a framework to understand action and to create a new exemplar for practice.

To accomplish these goals, I propose a research agenda that has three parts. The first is to address the dilemmas that planning theory has bequeathed to planning. The second is to address other questions that are central to planning but are poorly understood. The third is to explore and apply research and analytic approaches borrowed from fields that have hitherto had only a modest influence on planning thought.

Dilemmas to Address

A major purpose of reframing planning theory must be to resolve or at least to reduce the centrality of the crippling dilemmas that have dominated thought about planning. The most important of these include the following.

Planner as Technician. On the one hand, planners must be objective and value neutral if they are to be credible or legitimate in their technical roles.

On the other, they choose problem definitions, methods, and indicators; they shape questions and point to answers, each of which embodies values. How can these tasks be reconciled?

Planning as the Application of Knowledge. While planners and others pay lip service to the importance of information for public decisions, such decisions often seem to make little use of formal knowledge. Is the concern with information merely window dressing? If so, from what source can planners assure their legitimacy? If not, how can information be made useful?

The Values Problem. Is there a public interest and, if so, how is it recognized? If there is no such interest, which values should planners represent? And what should a planner do with his or her values—acknowledge, ignore, or work for them?

Stance toward the Political Process. Does the political process reflect the will of the people or the interests of the few? Even if it does reflect the popular will, is there any assurance that the results of the process will be desirable on other counts?

Comprehensiveness versus Incrementalism. Can planners reconcile the desirability of comprehensive, long-term plans with the practical reality that decisions are made in piecemeal, incremental fashion, that information is inadequate, and that even partial and short-term plans are often not implemented?

Synthesis versus Analysis. Should the planner expect to analyze and solve problems or to create new ideas? While the temptation is to say yes to both, the tasks are not clearly reconcilable. Analysis involves taking things apart; it is reactive to problems. Design is creative and putting together (Teitz 1974).

Professional Dilemmas. Who is the client—the immediate boss, the one who pays, the agency, the segment of the public being served, or the public as a whole? What is a planner's special expertise? How should the planner interact with clients—on the model of the lawyer, doctor, social worker, or in some unique way? Where within government should planners serve—as advisors to executives: staff to legislative bodies, citizen-based commissions, or line agencies; or in some other capacity?

Context Issues. Is it possible to assume an autonomous role for planning, or is it simply subject to the larger forces of a society? Is there a general model for practice, or should it be conducted differently in different organizational environments or degrees of technological and political uncertainty?

Uniqueness. How can planners use knowledge of general laws to deal with the one-of-a-kind nature of practice situations? What, if any, systematic approaches can they use when each task or problem is unique?

Implementation. Is planning a matter of designing outcomes, or does it include designing and following through on implementation strategies? Can the planner be accepted as impartial advisor, while simultaneously being involved in action?

Research Topics

Some of the foregoing questions may be reframed in useful ways if attention is given to some neglected but critical elements of planning. Important topics for future research and theorizing include the following.

Problem Definition. Analysts have begun to study how problems are defined, exploring, for example, the routinized ways problems are identified by managers (Pounds 1969) or the role of quantitative measures in framing policy problems (de Neufville 1981c). They have identified the values associated with particular ways of defining problems and the implications for policy, as Moore (1978a) has done in the case of drug addiction, or to link stakeholders and their assumptions to different problem definitions, as Mason and Mitroff (1981) have for airport planning. The challenge is to outline the problem identification process, to link it to other planning tasks, and to develop criteria to define problems in technically adequate or ethically acceptable ways.

Language, Symbols, and Indicators. Public debates focus on so-called signifiers—language, numbers, and shorthand labels for policies that are layered with meanings and mythologies (Mandelbaum 1982a, b; de Neufville 1983). Rallying cries such as "a decent home for all Americans" and "close tax loopholes" link into deeply held emotions (Edelman 1977) and values, but a common meaning never fully exists (de Neufville 1985). Planning theory should give attention to how to uncover meanings, to the process by which meanings are ascribed, and to the implications of the fact that complex and ambiguous stories underlie explicit debates. Planners must not only work with the elusive tools of language but also be symbol makers.

Communication. This broad term covers many planning tasks that are poorly integrated into planning thought. Language is the foundation of communication, but there is a need to focus on specific tasks such as advising (Krieger 1981), attention shaping (Forester 1980), negotiating and mediating (Susskind and Ozawa 1984), and developing further the implications of the transactive and social learning models of planning (Michael 1973; Friedmann 1973).

Forms of Knowledge and Ways of Providing It. Since the traditional model of information provision and use appears inadequate, theorists need to search for a more effective model by identifying what works in practice and why. For example, contrary to the traditional model, formal research often has more role in framing issues than in solving problems; more in setting targets and standards than in comparing alternatives; more in the education of decision makers than in policy choice; more in program design, management, and monitoring than in evaluation; and more in stopping unwanted programs than in creating new policy concepts (Rein and White 1977; de Neufville 1981a; Weiss 1977). The institutional process of creating information, moreover, is as important as its content in assuring it will be meaningful, legitimate, and used (de Neufville 1975, 1978–1979). The link of power to the process of informing decisions requires study (Forester 1982), as do decision processes that use one or another form of information.

Values. Social values are elusive because they emerge in relation to specific situations. Planning theorists need to understand the content of public belief systems and ideologies, the processes and influences that transform them into public preferences, and the ways in which they are negotiated and modified. Works by Bellah et al. (1985) on individualism and commitment in the United States and by Barton (1985) on citizen views of property rights and community in local land use conflicts represent efforts to understand public values.

Scenes and Settings. Attention must be paid to the settings in which planning is done, to how these can and should influence the way the planner thinks and acts. Theory should address how strategies for practice are dependent on different political, technological, and organizational contexts. It should address ways in which planners can deal with uncertainty and uniqueness. Schön (1983) and Bolan (1980) have pioneered in studies of the latter kind.

Ethics. Planning theorists should incorporate philosophical ideas of justice and equity in their work. They should address the practical question of how planners' ethics can support or undermine their credibility, influence relations with clients, and affect practice in agency and political environments. Planning theory should generate debate over issues the profession needs to decide, such as for whose welfare it should work and what values it represents. Planning theory should take the lead in confronting the field with arguments for consistent and appropriate ethical systems for the profession.

Theoretical and Analytical Perspectives

Much of the available research on practice is atheoretical, but progress in planning theory will depend on strong conceptual frameworks that illuminate rather than simply describe. Several perspectives offer promising structures of planning theory research.

History. One strategy is to study what planners have done or thought over time and how or why planning has come into being in one form or another and had one or another set of consequences. History allows a holistic view of both practice and context, action and outcome. It permits tracing the influences of ideas and identifying the sources of change as they are exposed to practice and as predominant understandings of society evolve. But historical study will not be useful unless it takes a clear point of view and endeavors to be explanatory rather than merely descriptive. Too much planning history falls in the latter category.

Political Economy. Planning needs to be seen in relation to the state and the economy, and its unintended as well as intended functions need to be explored. Political economists offer a framework for understanding these relationships, and their ideas belong in the mainstream of planning theory. Their contributions include the concepts that planning may function to facilitate capital accumulation and maintain social control; that planners, even if unintentionally, serve as agents of the state and of powerful forces that work through the state; and that planning, in the name of rationality, may depoliticize the actions of the state and limit the arena of legitimate political conflict (Fainstein and Fainstein 1982). Political economists often regard planning as a result rather than a cause, with the ability to effect only marginal change. One contributor to this genre is Cohen (1977), who defines the form and logic of French indicative planning in terms of the state, educational system, bureaucracy, and economy. Another is Boyer (1981, 1983), who traces the history of U.S. city planning and views planning and regulation as responses to the needs of capital for widened investment or for limits on speculation.

Political Theory. Planning theorists and practitioners are vulnerable in their limited ability to link ideas about practice with an understanding of power and political process. The value of looking at planning through the political science lense is amply demonstrated by Altshuler (1965). Two decades later, a sequel to this work is needed.

Organizational Behavior. Planners operate within organizations that exist within a complete set of interrelationships of governmental and private groups. Planning theory usually fails to incorporate understanding of this environment. Theory and research need to address how practice varies according to the organizational environment, how professional and organizational roles come into conflict or merge, and how to design strategies for making organizations responsive to demands for change. Contributions thus far include the work of Christensen (1985), Bryson and Delbecq (1979), and Boschken (1982), who draw on organizational theory to predict and prescribe planning strategy for types of problems in various situations. Studies of implementation are also useful because they combine political and organizational perspectives (see, for example, Bardach 1977; Mazmanian and Sabatier 1981).

Anthropology. Planning theorists can draw on the analytic and research style of anthropology to identify cultural systems that ascribe meaning to events and create norms for behavior and choice. Anthropological methods can uncover expectations that are so taken for granted that participants no longer are conscious of them. The most notable planning study of this type is Perin's (1977), documenting the meanings ascribed to residential land uses by local officials and ordinary citizens who influence the zoning process. Her work is a model for research in the way that it identifies, interprets, and analyzes a structure of values that influences planning.

Epistemology

A field such as planning, which is so centered around informing and communicating as well as attempting to know and create the future, must have a firm basis in philosophical thought about the nature of knowledge. It requires an epistemology appropriate to the tasks of planning that provides a consistent, intuitively satisfying, and workable way to link knowledge to action.

The Limits of Positivism. The epistemology that has most influenced planning theory in recent decades is positivism. Positivism is represented by the ideal of scientific method, which views the researcher as a disinterested observer of facts that have an independent existence. The search for knowledge involves the hypothesizing of general laws and proceeds via logical deduction and empirical tests using concepts that can be measured. Values or other subjective phenomena are not considered in this view.

Positivism has led to analytic advances and empirical findings in many fields, but in planning theory it has contributed to dilemmas. For example, the positivist separation of knower and doer as a model for planning suggests that planners must be either value-neutral technicians or activists but not both. The standard model is that a decision maker sets goals while a planner provides information on the basis of which decision makers act. Knowledge and action are virtually unlinked except insofar as the rational decision maker is moved to act because information reveals truth. In practice, however, when knowledge has an impact the process is more complex (de Neufville 1981a, b; Scott and Shore 1979).

The positivist view has encouraged a focus on quantifiable issues and discouraged the study of meanings, intentions, and values. The search for laws encourages the use of limited hypotheses rather than efforts to understand whole systems in their full complexity and unique contexts. Theorizing is done a priori, and empirical studies must rely on definitions and concepts posed at the outset of research rather than discovered in the process. An effect on planning theory can be found in its search for simple principles and in the quantitative and hypothesis-testing nature of much research on practice. Such research has value but cannot generate new categories and images for planning theory. The effect on practice has been to drain legitimacy from many of the intuitive and holistic ways of knowing on which planning practitioners depend.

Phenomenology. Phenomenology is an alternative to positivism that is gaining acceptability in social science research. It provides a path through some of the paradoxes of planning theory (Patton 1980). The phenomenological view takes many forms (Bernstein 1976) but has several recurring themes. The basic idea is that the knower tries to understand a phenomenon in its own unique terms. Subjective and unmeasurable issues such as meanings and intentions are not only accepted but also central to this understanding. Facts are viewed as socially constructed within a community, and their truth depends on shared understanding. One can learn about subjective phenomena by bracketing one's feelings and values and putting oneself in the place of those being studied (Berger and Luckmann 1966). Since there is commonality or intersubjectivity across people, one can interpret the reasons for actions by knowing enough of the circumstances and meanings of events to people. One learns through the technique of *verstehen,* or interpretation—making sense of complex circumstances and relating them to experiential and abstract knowledge. The results of open-ended, exploratory, and qualitative research may include typologies, stories, case studies, ideal-typical descriptions of behavior, and explanations of events and attitudes that are rich in the detail that makes a situation unique. Differing interpretations of situations among actors and researchers are resolved through a negotiated process.

Phenomenology provides alternatives to some planning dilemmas. For example, the planner can be both a disinterested technician and a user of subjective understandings. Indeed, part of a planner's technical expertise lies in the ability to identify and formulate the socially shared meanings of facts. There is less of a gap between the knowledge of the expert and that of the citizen with whom the planner works. The research permits an approach to planning problems that is comprehensive and that deals with the special aspects of the particular problem instead of with partial general laws that are difficult to apply in specific cases. Thus, phenomenology offers a view of knowledge that meshes more closely with practice than the positivist view. Moreover, it provides an opportunity to search for new images and conceptions of planning.

Recent contributions to planning theory illuminate through their methods the phenomenological approach to research and, through their findings, to practice. For example, Schön (1983) watched and listened to practitioners solving client problems in an effort to understand their thought processes and analytic strategies. He argues that reflective practitioners use positivist knowledge of principles or theories in a limited way but depend heavily on generalizations derived from experience and also remain alert to the possibility that a particular problem may require a unique solution. Practitioner and client work interactively in a kind of negotiation process until both are satisfied with the problem formulation and solution. In another example, Bolan (1980) tries to understand the theories of planning in the minds of practitioners and explores the relationship between these and the more formal, or institutional, professional theory. His analysis emphasizes language, the meanings participants bring to the action, and the uniqueness of each planning episode. My research on social indicators in public policy concludes that to be politically significant and socially meaningful, indicators have to be developed through lengthy negotiated processes and reflect a convergence of public and expert understandings (de Neufville 1975).

Critical Theory. The critical theorists may offer the potentially richest and most useful ideas for planning theory. The work of these theorists remains relatively inaccessible and has not been developed into operational and widely usable concepts (McCarthy 1978). This set of ideas may deal with even more dilemmas than the phenomenological approach. Habermas (1973) provides an all-encompassing perspective linking action, knowledge, ethics, and politics, all the ingredients of the dilemma. Moreover, his view accepts the necessity of employing many ways of knowing and learning—the positivist, empirically based method; the phenomenological, holistic, and interpretive method; and the method of critique. Each of these has pertinence in planning.

The notion of critique demands that the knower question all assumptions and be aware of how formal knowledge reinforces the status quo. The relativity of facts and methods to values and understandings becomes the foundation for further thought rather than a dilemma. The knowing process is dialectical and does not require the observer to be disinterested. The knower takes a position and learning proceeds through discourse and disagreement within a group where power has been equalized. This perspective provides a potential intellectual framework for understanding and prescribing for problematic but central planning roles such as negotiation and the generation of citizen involvement.

Critical theory posits no truth independent of those who think and argue about it. A set of claims to truth allows us to decide what to take as valid. These claims include the comprehensibility of what is said, the logical truth of a proposition, the legitimacy and expertise of the person making the truth claim, and the veracity of the speaker. These concepts have already provided a useful analytic framework to some planning theorists for conceptualizing and evaluating what planners do (Forester 1980, 1982; Krieger 1981).

The dialectical approach accepts the shifting and self-contradictory nature of truth—the notion that every truth implies its opposite. Faith in the dialectic would make it easier for planners to live with the uneasy contradictions, which are inevitable in their work, and to deal with changing environments and goals. One implication is that theorists and planners should generate debate among differing points of view. Examples include two recent works on planning theory and land use policy that incorporate a range of disciplinary and political perspectives and attempt to provide a framework for the comparison (Healey, McDougall, and Thomas 1982; de Neufville 1981b). The dialectical approach also implies that research on planning must include a historical perspective and deal with competing forces and frameworks for explanation. This approach is illustrated in the work of Markusen (1985), who traces the history of U.S. regional planning and development and explains phenomena simultaneously from microeconomic, geographic, political, and political economy perspectives.

Critical theory offers the strongest linkage between knowledge and action of the three epistemologies, not only because its concepts mirror important realities of practice but also because in this view the knower must act in order to know. While the disinterested observer is necessary to some forms of knowledge, it is only through praxis that many ideas can take shape. Some critical theorists argue that discourse is a crucial tool for change. Moreover, Habermas (1973) suggests that part of the knower's task is to oppose the status quo. The argument that existing knowledge protects those in power translates to the notion that the knower should advocate for the powerless.

Habermas's view has advantages as an approach to planning theory. It suggests that planners should take a more active role than many do, but it also spares them the difficult choice between political involvement and detached analysis. It offers them a value position from which to operate, which is not incompatible, at least in theory, with their technical role. One message for planning theorists is that practice is part of research. Another message is that the growth of planning theory depends not only on debate among those with differing views but also on the inclusion of practitioners in the process.

Much needs to be done to elaborate and apply critical theory to planning, and many points will be challenged and argued. How can discourse lead to change? How can practice be transformed into knowledge? Is it possible to advocate for the powerless while in the employ of the powerful? Critical theory will generate its own dilemmas. But it is a promising source to enrich and revitalize planning thought.

Strategies for Research and Education

Research

To revitalize planning theory and make it usable for practice, planning theorists must get their hands dirty with data and do firsthand study of planning and of the meaning systems in which it takes place. Howe (1980), Howe and Kaufman (1979), and Vasu (1979) provide valuable models in their surveys of planners' attitudes. However, the survey has limitations as a research tool. If the right question is not asked at the outset, the survey gives no answer. Moreover, a survey is limited to finding out what people say they do and say they believe and cannot uncover what they hide or do not recognize. Finally, while responses can be correlated with measurable variables like age, sex, or education, a survey will not discover if the causal system is more complex.

The challenge is to go beyond positivist, quantitative studies to more holistic research. The new research would involve many types of knowledge and variables, including actions and ideas of participants, characteristics of planned environments, and outcomes of planning strategies. It would rely on a range of methods, including surveys, open-ended interviewing, direct observation, historical study, language and content analysis, and in-depth case studies.

An important result of such research will be complex stories, so-called thick descriptions, rather than laws linking variables or offering conclusions generalizable to well-specified categories or situations (Geertz 1973). Such stories enlighten by their insights, by deepening understandings, as well as by raising theoretical questions for further empirical study. Learning from them is in part at a tacit level like learning from experience. Schön (1983) provides the clearest example of this type of research in planning.

Planning research should go beyond descriptions, typologies, and measurements to theory building and theory testing. It should seek to explain what works and how and under what conditions. It should deal not just with attitudes but with belief systems, not just with individuals but with organizations, not just with actions but with norms and institutionalized practices, and not just with plans but with outcomes. Quantitative research should become richer and qualitative research better structured, with cases carefully selected to allow valid comparisons and generalizable conclusions.

Education

Planning education must more effectively link theory and practice. It is not enough to hire practitioners to teach, to insist on student internships, or to rely on studio and workshop courses to convey experiential learning. Instead, educators should find ways to integrate theoretical and experiential learning throughout the curriculum. Not only should such practice education be informed by theories of planning, but also theory courses should be taught in ways that make them directly meaningful to students. In teaching, as in research, planning academics should move away from a predominantly positivist conception of learning to one that incorporates ideas from phenomenology and critical theory. The idea that knowing is an interactive and social process suggests that the classroom be used to provide structure and meaning to students' experience. The notion that learning occurs through a dialectical process and a challenging of assumptions is also readily transferable to the classroom.

Many educational strategies provide the opportunity to challenge ideas and make sense of experience. For example, students can go to their internships with questions designed to help them observe, evaluate, and interpret. When they return, an opportunity to assess the experience in a structured way with faculty, peers, and practitioners is essential. Small classes can be brought into planning offices for organized discussion with staff. Exercises can be used where students observe and evaluate planning activities and documents. Alumni and other local planners can be interviewed by students and discussions of findings shared and challenged in class. Group problem solving, simulations, role playing, and debates can be integrated into lecture and seminar courses. Practitioners and faculty can teach together, each consciously bringing his or her perspective to the task, debating directly or building cooperatively on what each knows. Studios and workshops can be explicitly framed according to the instructor's theory of the planning process, and students can be invited to critique and alter it as they learn. Doctoral programs should not be exempt from these structures. It is important that those who will build the next stage of theory and teach the next generation of planners understand the nature of practice.

These ideas suggest a qualitatively different approach to teaching. They imply relinquishing some control in the classroom to the students, who after all must learn on their own (Finkel and Monk 1983). Teaching in this fashion can be difficult for those accustomed to an authority role. But if the goal is for students to become thinking practitioners who can use or even build their own theories, then the effort is essential. The reward for faculty is that teaching can be more stimulating and can help to bring practice and theory closer together.

Conclusion

Planning theory cannot seek simple answers but should develop accounts dealing with the full complexity of planning and its many contexts. It should be about meanings and embrace rather than deny ambiguity. It should be grounded in empirical study and in the knowledge that those who do planning take for granted. It should account for structural and historical forces and delineate planners who are immersed in interaction—communicators, and simultaneously actors, researchers, and facilitators. It should define ethical practice, establish typologies of the settings in which planning takes place, and expand knowledge of strategies effective in each. A new exemplar, or series of them, should emerge. The result should be richer insights on which to build usable and evolving theories of planning.

References

Altshuler, Alan A. 1965. *The City Planning Process.* Ithaca, N.Y.: Cornell University Press.

Bardach, Eugene. 1977. *The Implementation Game.* Cambridge, Mass.: MIT Press.

Barton, Stephen. 1985. Property Rights and Democracy: The Beliefs of San Francisco Neighborhood Leaders and the American Liberal Tradition. Ph.D. dissertation, Department of City and Regional Planning, University of California, Berkeley.

Baum, Howell S. 1980. Analysts and Planners Must Think Organizationally. *Policy Analysis* 6:479–494.

Baum, Howell S. 1983. *Planners and Public Expectations.* Cambridge, Mass.: Schenkman Publishing Co.

Bellah, Robert; Richard Madsen; William M. Sullivan; Ann Swidler; and Steven M. Tilton. 1985. *Habits of the Heart: Individualism and Commitment in American Life.* Berkeley: University of California Press.

Berger, Peter L., and Thomas Luckmann. 1966. *The Social Construction of Reality.* New York: Anchor Books.

Bernstein, Richard. 1976. *The Restructuring of Social and Political Theory.* New York: Harcourt, Brace, Jovanovich.

Bolan, Richard S. 1980. The Practitioner as Theorist: The Phenomenology of the Professional Episode. *Journal of the American Planning Association* 46:261–274.

Boschken, Herman. 1982. *Land Use Conflicts: Organizational Design and Research Management.* Urbana: University of Illinois Press.

Boyer, M. Christine. 1981. National Land Use Policy: Instrument and Product of the Economic Cycle. In *The Land Use Policy Debate in the United States,* Judith I. de Neufville, ed. New York: Plenum Press.

Boyer, M. Christine. 1983. *Dreaming the Rational City: Myths of American Planning, 1893–1945.* Cambridge, Mass.: MIT Press.
Bryson, John M., and Andre L. Delbecq. 1979. A Contingent Approach to Strategy and Tactics in Project Planning. *Journal of the American Planning Association* 45:167–179.
Christensen, Karen. 1985. Coping with Uncertainty in Planning. *Journal of the American Planning Association* 51:63–73.
Cohen, Stephen. 1977. *Modern Capitalist Planning: The French Model.* Berkeley: University of California Press.
de Neufville, Judith I. 1975. *Social Indicators and Public Policy: Interactive Processes and Application.* New York: Elsevier.
de Neufville, Judith I. 1978–1979. Validating Policy Indicators. *Policy Sciences* 10: 171–188.
de Neufville, Judith I. 1981a. *Federal Requirements and Local Planning Capacity: The Case of CDBG.* Berkeley: Institute of Urban and Regional Development, University of California.
de Neufville, Judith I., ed. 1981b. *The Land Use Policy Debate in the United States.* New York: Plenum Press.
de Neufville, Judith I. 1981c. Social Indicators. In *Handbook of Applied Sociology: Frontiers of Contemporary Research,* M. Olsen and M. Micklin, eds. New York: Praeger Publishers.
de Neufville, Judith I. 1983. Symbol and Myth in Land Policy. In *Values, Ethics, and the Practice of Policy Analysis,* W. Dunn, ed. Lexington, Mass.: D.C. Heath, Lexington Books.
de Neufville, Judith I. 1985. Policy Problems and the Public: Uncovering the Myths Beneath the Surface. Paper presented at the Annual Conference of the American Society of Public Administration, Indianapolis.
Edelman, Murray. 1977. *Political Language: Words That Succeed and Policies That Fail.* New York: Academic Press.
Fainstein, Norman I., and Susan S. Fainstein. 1982. New Debates in Urban Planning: The Impact of Marxist Theory Within the United States. In *Critical Readings in Planning Theory,* Chris Paris, ed. Oxford: Pergamon Press.
Finkel, Donald L., and G. Stephen Monk. 1983. Teachers and Learning Groups: Dissolution of the Atlas Complex. In *Learning in Groups: New Directions for Teaching and Learning,* C. Bouton and R.Y. Garth, eds. San Francisco: Jossey-Bass.
Forester, John. 1980. Critical Theory and Planning Practice. *Journal of the American Planning Association* 46:275–286.
Forester, John. 1982. Planning in the Face of Power. *Journal of the American Planning Association* 48:67–80.
Friedmann, John. 1973. *Retracking America: A Theory of Transactive Planning.* New York: Anchor Press.
Geertz, Clifford, 1973. *The Interpretation of Cultures.* New York: Basic Books.
Habermas, Jurgen. 1973. *Theory and Practice,* J. Viertel, trans. Boston: Beacon Press.
Healey, Patsy; Glen McDougall; and Michael J. Thomas, eds. 1982. *Planning Theory: Prospects for the 1980s.* Oxford: Pergamon Press.
Howe, Elizabeth. 1980. Role Choices of Urban Planners. *Journal of the American Planning Association* 46:398–409.

Howe, Elizabeth, and Jerome Kaufman. 1979. The Ethics of Contemporary American Planners. *Journal of the American Planning Association* 45:243–255.

Kaplan, Abraham. 1964. *The Conduct of Inquiry: Methodology for Behavioral Science*. San Francisco: Chandler Publishing Company.

Kent, T.J., Jr. 1964. *The Urban General Plan*. San Francisco: Chandler Publishing Company.

Klosterman, Richard E. 1981. Contemporary Planning Theory Education: Results of a Course Survey. *Journal of Planning Education and Research* 1:1–11.

Krieger, Martin. 1981. *Advice and Planning*. Philadelphia: Temple University Press.

Kuhn, Thomas. 1970. *The Structure of Scientific Revolutions*. Chicago: University of Chicago Press.

Lee, Douglass B., Jr. 1981. Land Use Planning as a Response to Market Failure. In *The Land Use Policy Debate in the United States*, Judith I. de Neufville, ed. New York: Plenum Press.

MacRae, Duncan, Jr., and Rachelle Alterman. 1983. Planning and Policy Analysis: Converging or Diverging Trends? *Journal of the American Planning Association* 49:200–215.

Mandelbaum, Seymour J. 1982a. Too Clever By Far: Communications and Community Development. *Communications* 7:103–114.

Mandelbaum, Seymour J. 1982b. What Is Philadelphia? Philadelphia: School of Public and Urban Policy, University of Pennsylvania.

Marcuse, Peter. 1976. Professional Ethics and Beyond: Values in Planning. *Journal of the American Institute of Planners* 42:264–274.

Markusen, Ann R. 1985. *Profit Cycles, Oligopoly, and Regional Development*. Cambridge, Mass.: MIT Press.

Mason, Richard O., and Ian I. Mitroff. 1981. *Challenging Strategic Planning Assumptions: Theory, Cases and Techniques*. New York: John Wiley & Sons.

Mayo, James M. 1982. Sources of Job Dissatisfaction: Ideals Versus Realities in Planning. *Journal of the American Planning Association* 48:481–495.

Mazmanian, Daniel A., and Paul A. Sabatier, eds. 1981. *Effective Policy Implementation*. Lexington, Mass.: D.C. Heath, Lexington Books.

McCarthy, Thomas. 1978. *The Critical Theory of Jurgen Habermas*. Cambridge, Mass.: MIT Press.

Meltsner, Arnold J. 1976. *Policy Analysts in the Bureaucracy*. Berkeley: University of California Press.

Meyerson, Martin. 1956. Building the Middle-Range Bridge for Comprehensive Planning. *Journal of the American Institute of Planners* 22:58–64.

Michael, Donald. 1973. *On Learning to Plan and Planning to Learn*. San Francisco: Jossey-Bass.

Moore, Mark. 1978a. Anatomy of the Heroin Problem. *Policy Analysis* 2:639–662.

Moore, Terry. 1978b. Why Allow Planners to Do What They Do? A Justification from Economic Theory. *Journal of the American Institute of Planners* 44:387–398.

Patton, Michael Quinn. 1980. *Qualitative Evaluation Methods*. Beverly Hills: Sage Publications.

Perin, Constance. 1977. *Everything in Its Place: Social Order and Land Use in America*. Princeton, N.J.: Princeton University Press.

Pounds, William F. 1969. The Process of Problem Finding. *Industrial Management Review* 11:1–19.

Rein, Martin, and Sheldon J. White. 1977. Policy Research: Belief and Doubt. *Policy Analysis* 3:239–271.

Schön, Donald, 1983. *The Reflective Practitioner: How Professionals Think in Action.* New York: Basic Books.

Scott, Robert A., and Arnold R. Shore. 1979. *Why Sociology Does Not Apply: A Study of the Use of Sociology in Public Policy.* New York: Elsevier Press.

Susskind, Lawrence, and Connie Ozawa. 1984. Mediated Negotiation in the Public Sector: The Planner as Mediator. *Journal of Planning Education and Research* 4:5–15.

Teitz, Michael B. 1974. Toward a Responsive Planning Methodology. In *Learning from Turbulence: Planning in America,* David Godschalk, ed. Washington, D.C.: American Institute of Planners.

Vasu, Michael Lee. 1979. *Politics and Planning.* Chapel Hill: University of North Carolina Press.

Weiss, Carol. 1977. Research for Policy's Sake: The Enlightenment Function of Social Research. *Policy Analysis* 3:521–545.

Weiss, Marc. 1985. Scientific Boosterism: The Real Estate Industry and the Origins of Local Government Land Use Regulation in the U.S. Ph.D. dissertation, Department of City and Regional Planning, University of California, Berkeley.

Part II
Strategies and Skills in Practice

5

Strategic Planning in the Public Sector: Approaches and Directions

John M. Bryson
R. Edward Freeman
William D. Roering

overnment leaders in the United States face difficult challenges in the years ahead.[1] Their environments have changed dramatically in the past decade—as a result of economic crises, tax problems, demographic shifts, value changes, federal budget cuts, and the devolution of responsibilities to local areas. These developments have led to a now familiar dilemma. On the one hand, traditional sources of revenue for most governments often are unstable, unpredictable, or declining. On the other hand, demands for government services have not slackened.

These changing circumstances challenge government leaders to become more effective strategists. They need to exercise as much discretion as they can in areas under their control, to develop strategies to cope with changing circumstances, to develop a coherent and defensible basis for decision making, and to be more concerned than ever with the successful implementation of their strategies.

Strategic planning can assist governments with these tasks. As two early proponents of the use of strategic planning by governments note, "strategic planning is a disciplined effort to produce fundamental decisions shaping the nature and direction of governmental activities within constitutional bounds" (Olsen and Eadie 1982, p. 4). When strategic planning of this kind takes place, the result can be a broad-scale yet effective collection of information, exploration of alternatives, and emphasis on the future implications of present decisions. Such planning can facilitate communication and participation, accommodate divergent interests and values, strengthen analytical and orderly decision making, and improve chances of successful implementation. Done well, strategic planning can help revitalize and redirect government and public service.

Strategic planning focuses specifically on a government corporation or agency and on what it can do to improve its performance. This focus distinguishes strategic planning from comprehensive planning, which typically focuses on a territory and specific functions (for example, land use, public facilities, transportation) rather than on an organization and usually leaves the means of implementing the plan relatively unspecified. This focus also distinguishes strategic planning from program or project planning. The former is concerned with a basic government or agency mission and the appropriate strategies to pursue that mission, while the latter is concerned with planning for and implementing new programs, projects, or services.

Strategic planning, as one approach that governments might take to deal with their changed circumstances, can be viewed as old wine in new bottles. Successful government leaders have always thought and acted strategically (Leuchtenberg 1983; Lewis 1980; Luttwak 1977). Many government and public agency officials have not, however, and the price of ignoring this important tool can be devastating in a time of change.

It should be emphasized that such strategic planning provides a valuable counterbalance to the tendency for the public sector to be organized into specific policy networks and programs that cut vertically across general purpose governments at the federal, state, and local levels. In essence, much of the public sector is organized not horizontally by unit of government across programs but vertically by programs across levels of government (Milward and Wamsley 1982; Wildavsky 1979a, 1979b; Milward 1984). Strategic planning provides governments with an opportunity to make connections and changes across programs — and therefore to make more of a whole out of the disparate parts of public policies and programs.

This chapter reviews alternative approaches to strategic planning in the public sector. It presents examples of the application of strategic planning models in the public sector and suggests directions and prospects for the future of both strategic planning theory and practice.

Approaches to Strategic Planning

Strategic planning has a long history of use in this private sector,[2] which has been amply documented by others (Ansoff 1977; Lorange 1980b; Schendel and Hofer 1979). We shall briefly set forth the major schools or models of strategic planning in terms of their applications to the strategic problems of public sector organizations. The approaches include the Harvard policy, portfolio, industrial economics, stakeholder, and decision process models.

The Harvard Policy Model

Originating in the business policy course taught at the Harvard Business School since the 1920s, the Harvard policy model is fundamental to recent work in strategic management (see Christensen et al. 1983). According to Andrews (1980), strategy is a pattern of purposes and policies defining the company and its business. Ansoff (1965) argues that corporate strategy is the common thread or the underlying logic that holds a business together. Thus, it is possible to understand this foundational logic of a business by analyzing the resources of the company and the values of senior management, together with the threats and opportunities in the environment and the social obligations of the firm. The way a firm combines these elements will yield its pattern of purposes and policies.

Research in this tradition is quite voluminous, but several studies are particularly important. The first is Chandler's (1962) classic study of DuPont, Sears, General Motors, and Standard Oil in which he argues that strategy and organizational structure are inherently connected. Chandler's thesis, that structure follows strategy, has become the focus of much current academic research (Hofer 1975). Second is Rumelt's (1974) study of the relationships among corporations in various stages of their growth and economic performance. He finds that firms that were unrelated diversifiers performed less effectively than firms that were related diversifiers. Although several follow-up studies have failed to confirm the accuracy of Rumelt's thesis, he has connected the work at Harvard with economic theory and developed the idea that appropriate strategy leads to improved economic performance.

There are obvious parallels and applications for public sector organizations. We will elaborate on these later but note here that any organization must understand its underlying logic (even if that logic is dictated by responsiveness to interest groups) and that knowledge of underlying purposes and policies can lead to improved performance.

Portfolio Models

An important contribution to strategic planning is the concept of a portfolio of businesses. Just as investors may have portfolios of stocks that allow them to manage risk, so too could corporate managers think of the businesses within a corporation as a portfolio within which investments could improve potential and maximize cash flow. The intellectual history of portfolio theory in corporate strategy is complex. We shall illustrate one particular portfolio model developed by the Boston Consulting Group, the BCG matrix.

Bruce Henderson, founder of the Boston Consulting Group, argues that all business costs follow a well-known pattern—namely, they drop by one-third for every time that volume or turnover doubles (Henderson 1979; Wind and Mahajan 1981). Hence, he postulates a relationship between costs and volume, known as the *experience curve*. This relationship leads naturally to some generic strategic advice: Do whatever is legally possible to gain market share, for if a firm gains market share, costs will fall and profit potential will increase. Henderson argues that a business can be categorized into one of four types, depending on how fast its industry and the business's market share are growing. These include (1) high-growth/high-share businesses, or stars; (2) high-growth/low-share businesses, or question marks; (3) low-growth/high-share businesses, or cash cows; and (4) low-growth/low-share businesses, or dogs. Generic business strategies can be adopted to maximize cash flow for the entire set of businesses. A firm certainly must have a balanced portfolio because if there are too many cash cows it will have too much cash, and if there are too many question marks then it will not have enough cash, and so on.

This theory has led to an increasingly sophisticated understanding of firms with multiple businesses. Hambrick, MacMillan, and Day (1982), for example, argue that dogs long thought to be albatrosses around corporate managers' necks are in fact cash generators. More research is needed on portfolio theory.

This model may have less obvious applications to public sector organizations than the Harvard policy model, but the parallels are just as powerful (MacMillan 1983). Many public sector organizations are in multiple businesses that are only marginally related. Resource commitments, often from a single source, must be made to these unrelated businesses. Thus, public sector managers, in effect, often make portfolio decisions, although usually without the help of analytical portfolio models that frame decisions in a strategic fashion. This should be a fruitful area for further research.

Industrial Economics Models

In the spirit of both the Harvard policy model and portfolio theories, Michael Porter and his students have theorized that the forces that shape competitive strategy in an industry can be analyzed and used to determine the success or failure of a particular pattern of action. Porter (1980), building on the work of economists such as Richard Caves and Michael Spence, hypothesizes that five key forces shape an industry: (1) relative power of customers, (2) relative power of suppliers, (3) threat of substitute products, (4) threat of new entrants, and (5) amount of rivalrous activity among the players in the industry. Several studies present these forces in detail, and Harrigan (1981) has added a sixth factor by arguing that exit barriers can influence success or failure in some industries. The major proposition is that the greater the forces in the industry, the lower the returns. Thus, in an industry such as metal containers, there is the constant threat of backward integration by customers and forward integration by suppliers of metal; extreme price pressure due to the oligopolistic structure of both industries; new materials, such as plastics and compounds, on the horizon; and tremendous competition within the industry. Consequently, the metal can industry has had low returns.

We can list some public sector analogies within each force. Client or customer power is often exercised in the public arena, and suppliers of services are equally important. There are fewer new entrants, but recently the private sector has begun to compete with public organizations. An effective public sector organization must understand the forces at work in its industry even though *industry* is a difficult term to define. Industrial analysis models may help solve the problem of economic development for many state and local governments. Since governments must understand the forces at work in the industries they want to develop, this model represents an excellent starting point.

Stakeholder Models

Freeman (1984), building on the work of Ansoff (1965), Evan (1966), and Ackoff (1974), argues that corporate strategy can be understood as the corporation's mode of relating to or building bridges with its stakeholders, which are defined as any group or individual who is affected by or can affect the future of the corporation. Typical stakeholders are customers, employees, suppliers, owners, governments, banks, and critics. Freeman argues that a corporate strategy will be effective only if it satisfies the needs of multiple groups. Traditional models of strategy have focused solely on economic actors, but Freeman argues that in the turbulent environment of today, other political and social actors must also be considered. Another way to understand the stakeholder model is to argue that relative power of other stakeholders is another force that shapes industry strategy, and thus, Porter's industrial economics model becomes a special case of a more general theory.

The stakeholder model, through its integration of economic, political, and social concerns, is highly applicable to the public sector. Multiple interest groups have stakes in public organizations, and effective managers must formulate and implement explicit strategies for dealing with these groups. Controversies such as the development of the Supersonic Transport Program, the Oil Shale Project, the reform of the Social Security system and other efforts can be understood in stakeholder terms. Such analyses fit the familiar pattern of pluralist research and advice to practicing politicians and managers (Coplin and O'Leary 1976; Dahl 1984) and have precedent in the planning literature (Bolan 1969; Kaufman 1979).

Decision Process Models

Corporate strategy is a process in which managers make important decisions across functions and levels in the firm. Lorange (1980a) argues that any strategic management process must address four fundamental questions: (1) Where are we going (mission)? (2) How do we get there (strategic programs)? (3) What is our blueprint for action (budgets)? and (4) How do we know if we are on track (control)? These four questions are relevant for making decisions about industry positioning or developing stakeholder strategy. Freeman (1984) integrates several of these questions; Lorange (1979) summarizes considerable research on decision process models of strategy; and Freeman and Lorange (1985) formulate a model for synthesizing much of the research.

The decision process approach is relevant to public sector organizations, for regardless of the particular nature of the organization, it makes sense to talk about its mission and its plans for accomplishing it across functions and levels. Furthermore, the emphasis on control means that a public sector organization can understand how well its mission is being met and how well it is doing strategically, in addition to attending to the yearly incremental budget decisions that dominate public agency life (Wildavsky 1979a).

These five approaches guide most strategic planning research and represent the major intellectual differences in the field. They provide a basis for understanding strategic planning in the public sector. Two of the approaches—the portfolio and industrial economics models—are content approaches. Their use leads to specific strategic advice, and the social and political process for developing the advice is ignored. The others are process approaches. They do not provide any single answer but instead offer a process for developing answers.

Examples of Public Sector Strategic Planning

This section presents three examples of public sector strategic planning. Two are process applications of strategic planning models, and one is a content application utilizing a portfolio approach. The first example is the Ramsey County, Minnesota, Nursing Service, which is typical of strategic planning by a single agency and illustrates an application based on the Harvard and stakeholder approaches. Second is the *Philadelphia Investment Portfolio,* which is based in the portfolio model tradition. This example is not typical of public sector strategic planning because it focuses on a set of organizations or stakeholders in a geographic area rather than a specific organization. It also is not typical because portfolio methods are rare in the public sector. The final example is the government of Hennepin County, Minnesota, which fits the decision process tradition, in which key strategic issues across functions and levels are identified and decisions are made by top management. Hennepin County is one of the few cases known to the authors of an entire government engaged in strategic planning. The examples together represent the range of public sector strategic planning efforts, and each exemplifies the tradition of which it is part. Only the industrial economics tradition, the one least frequent in public sector strategic planning, is not represented here.

Ramsey County Nursing Service

Ramsey County, Minnesota, includes the state capital of St. Paul and has the second largest population among Minnesota counties. The county executive director decided to explore the utility of strategic planning for the county by asking three of the major units within the county government to undertake their own strategic planning exercise. One of these units was the Ramsey County Nursing Service (RCNS).

The RCNS is required by statute to provide communicable disease control services, and it also provides a variety of public health services at its clinics throughout the county. In 1984 the RCNS had more than eighty staff members and a budget of approximately $3.5 million.

The RCNS has been engaged in its first formal strategic planning effort. The process was developed by the senior author, who serves as a consultant to the nursing service. It is intellectually rooted in the Harvard and stakeholder model traditions and is presented in figure 5–1.

The process began with the identification of the agency's mandates, mission, and values. Mandates were included since they are an important feature of the environment of most public sector organizations. Mission and values were added because they have such a strong impact on the identification and resolution of strategic issues (Peters and Waterman 1982; Gilbert and Freeman 1985). The process draws attention to similarities and differences among stakeholders in their missions and values.

Next came the identification of strengths, weaknesses, opportunities, and threats—the typical Harvard analysis. Analysis of these elements, along with mandates, mission, and values, allowed participants to identify strategic issues, including fundamental policy choices affecting the organization's mandate, mission, values, or product or service level and mix; clients or users; cost; financing; or management. It is vital that such issues be identified expeditiously and effectively.

The RCNS identified four key strategic issues and is developing strategies to deal with them. The strategic issues in order are:

1. What business should we be in? The issue is one of mandate, mission, and values.

2. How do we ensure an adequate funding base to fulfill our mission?

3. How do we organize and manage the agency in order to fulfill our mission effectively?

4. How do we influence public policy at the state and local levels to assure appropriate gatekeeping to, and quality of, public health services for the community?

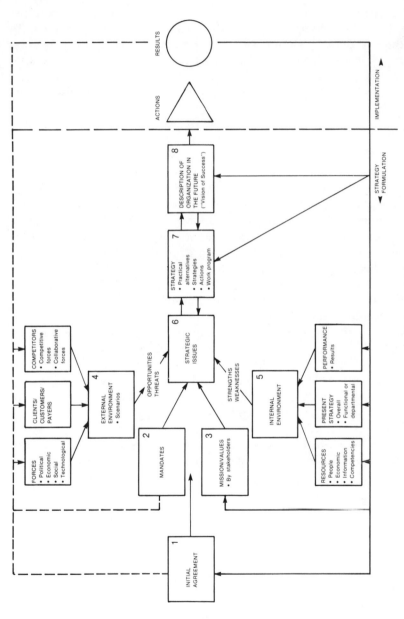

Source: Based on materials of the Management Support Services Unit, Amherst M. Wilder Foundation, St. Paul MN; the Institute for Cultural Affairs, Minneapolis, MN; and the Office of Planning and Development, Hennepin County, MN.

Figure 5–1. Strategic Planning Process

The first issue, as noted, concerns the mandate, mission, and values of the RCNS. When the process began, the RCNS staff were reasonably sure they knew what their mission was. After completing their analysis of strengths, weaknesses, opportunities, and threats, however, they were no longer quite as sure. In the authors' experience such a revelation is fairly typical. If the RCNS concludes its mission has changed and articulates exactly what that changed mission is, one might expect to identify additional or changed strategic issues. In particular, one might expect to see less abstract strategic issues — a development that probably would facilitate the identification of effective strategic options.

Strategy development begins with the identification of practical alternatives and then may move to a consideration of the barriers to their achievement rather than to developing strategies to realize the alternatives. A focus on barriers at this point is one way of assuring that any strategies developed deal with implementation difficulties directly rather than haphazardly. For this reason actual strategies in some cases may be strategies for overcoming the barriers rather than for directly realizing the alternatives — although the nurses in such cases will check to assure that the strategies can also help realize desired alternatives.

After strategy development comes an atypical step: describing the organization in the future. This description is the organization's outline of what the organization would look like if it successfully implemented its strategies and achieved its full potential. The importance of such descriptions has long been recognized by excellently managed companies (Ouchi 1981; Peters and Waterman 1982) and organizational psychologists (Locke et al. 1981). These descriptions help people learn what success looks like and how they should behave to achieve it. Such descriptions typically include the organization's mission, basic strategies, performance criteria, certain decision rules, and ethical standards expected of organizational employees.

The ultimate effectiveness of the RCNS strategic planning process remains to be seen. However, the RCNS example does provide an example of strategic planning by a single government agency representing a variation on the Harvard and stakeholder models, probably the most common approaches to strategic planning in the public sector.

Philadelphia Investment Portfolio

The *Philadelphia Investment Portfolio* was the final product of the Philadelphia: Past, Present, and Future project of the Center for Philadelphia Studies of the School of Urban and Public Policy at the University of Pennsylvania. The portfolio was published along with an introductory prospectus. Both documents grew out of the collaborative task force and committee efforts of approximately 750 interested individuals, drawn from public, private, and nonprofit organizations (Center for Philadelphia Studies 1982a, 1982b). The portfolio consists of 56 investment options organized around four developmental themes or strategies for Greater Philadelphia. The four strategies were derived after examination of a variety of scenarios that matched local assets and organizational capabilities with future needs, threats, and opportunities. The four strategies outlined in the prospectus, along with some of the investment options, are as follows.

City as Innovator. This strategy is based on promoting the city as a place for innovation by individuals and enterprises. Examples of investment options include a high technology business development zone in West Philadelphia, formation of local private venture capital funds, a Philadelphia Youth Conservation Corps, and a Literacy Commission of Philadelphia.

City as Conservator. This approach calls on the city to conserve and maintain its physical and social infrastructure. Investment options for pursuit of this strategy include a citywide effort to cut residential energy consumption, housing and economic development capital funds to improve the quality of life in communities, an integrated hazardous waste program, and a Center for Neighborhood Self-Reliance.

City as Mediator and Broker. As a mediator, the city manages conflict, builds appropriate coalitions, and negotiates settlements across a broad range of issues. Examples of options that fit this strategy include in-plant and industrywide labor-management cooperative efforts aimed at improving the competitive position and quality of work life in the Delaware Valley, replacement of teachers' contracts with school-based performance contracts, a venture capital information referral system, and a technical support network for community-based enterprise development.

City as Enhancer. Finally, the city is called on to improve the quality of life for residents, workers, and visitors. Proposals that promote this strategy would include, for example, regional commercial-industrial tax base sharing, a public education program on property tax reform, a regional tourist development program, and a downtown convention center for Philadelphia.

The creators of the portfolio view Greater Philadelphia as an organizing structure of interests and stakeholders in which the activities of disparate parties can be loosely coordinated through a focus on specific investment options (linked to the four strategies) that are attractive to specific organizations or coalitions of organizations. An organization or coalition would pursue a specific investment option that fits its needs or desires, but the city as a whole also would benefit. The more options that were pursued by organizations and coalitions, the greater the benefit to the city as a whole.

The creators of the portfolio envisioned a three-stage process of investment. First, portfolio options are either presented to specific organizations or serve as the agenda for multi-organizational conferences. Second, option are discussed and modified through a process of negotiated goal setting. Finally, statutory organizations, such as the Greater Philadelphia First Corporation (GPFC), would monitor developments with the help of a portfolio assessment matrix and manage the portfolio as a strategic development tool. GPFC is a consortium of the region's major economic development agencies, civic institutions, and the Greater Philadelphia Chamber of Commerce, along with an executive staff. It was formed just prior to the conclusion of the Philadelphia: Past, Present, and Future project.

The matrix is a modified version of the Position-Attractiveness Screen developed by General Electric, Shell Oil, and McKinsey and Company and is presented in figure 5–2. Analysts would use the matrix to assess projects and programs according to the degree to which they take advantage of ongoing trends (that is, their position) and the degree to which they facilitate achievement of the strategic objectives of the prospectus (that is, their attractiveness).

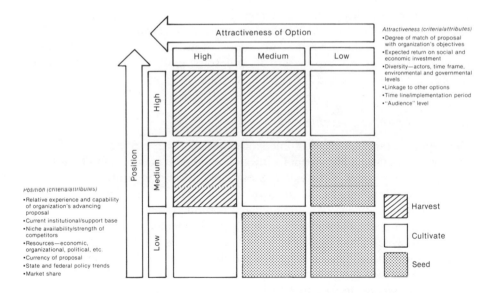

Figure 5–2. *Philadelphia Investment Portfolio* Proposed Portfolio Assessment Matrix

The position of an option would be based on a variety of criteria or attributes, including the experience and ability of the organization advancing it, the support and resource base for the proposal, its market and marketability, and the economic or political forces that enhance or constrain successful implementation. The attractiveness of an option would be based on its social or economic return, its fit with the sponsoring organization's goals, and its linkage to other proposals.

Based on the positioning of a proposal in the matrix, three kinds of decisions are proposed:

1. Seed the proposal. The proposal should be treated like seed—that is, stored for future use—if it is neither positioned well nor particularly attractive.
2. Cultivate the proposal. The proposal should be developed further to improve its position or attractiveness.
3. Harvest the proposal. The proposal should be implemented now.

The portfolio is an interesting adaptation to the public sector of a tool that is widely used in the private sector. Because the focus is on the mix of organizational entities in an area rather than directly on a government within a locale, the approach is not typical of public sector strategic planning efforts. However, it does provide a way of loosely coordinating the actions of a wide variety of independent actors and therefore can be related to stakeholder approaches as well as to more traditional portfolio methods. It remains to be seen how effective the portfolio and process of investment will be, although implementation efforts are underway and some early successes have been recorded.

Hennepin County Government

Hennepin County, home of Minneapolis, has the largest population of any county in Minnesota. Hennepin County's government is the second largest in budget and employees in the state, second only to state government. In 1983 county government began a strategic planning process. This move illustrates one of the few instances of strategic planning undertaken by an entire major unit of government, as opposed to a single government agency, and indicates one way in which planning can be linked across levels and functions within a unit of government. The example fits the decision process tradition of strategic planning, although there also are elements of the Harvard model.

In 1982 Hennepin County's Office of Planning and Development began to explore the applicability of the strategic planning concept to the county. The process selected by the county executive and his cabinet is outlined in figure 5–3.

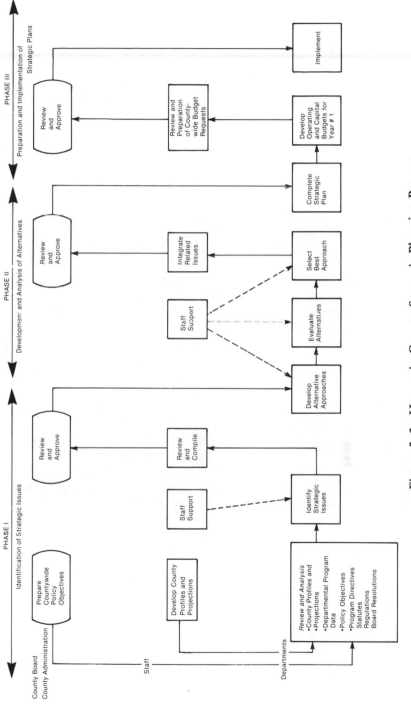

Figure 5–3. Hennepin County Strategic Planning Process

The process began with preparation of countywide policy objectives and demographic and economic profiles and projections, which were distributed as two components of a strategic planning manual. Individual departments then identified strategic issues through a process that included steps to review the strategic planning manual, review the department's mission, identify key external and internal forces, develop a three- to five-year scenario, develop strategic issues statements, and submit strategic issues. The departmental level process thus was similar to the Harvard policy model approach to the identification of strategic issues.

These strategic issues were then synthesized by the county executive and his cabinet — with the assistance of the Office of Planning and Development — into a set of forty issues organized into fifteen areas of strategic concern. These issues typically cut across departments. In the area of financing, for example, the key issues were: What can the county do to ensure that the tax base will increase sufficiently to sustain growth in service demands without substantially raising mill rates and taxes paid by property owners? What action(s) can the county take to maximize non–property tax revenues to ensure that residents' basic needs for governmental services do not outstrip the financial capabilities of the county's taxpayers? In the area of environmental quality, the key issues were: What actions should Hennepin County take to ensure the effective management of hazardous wastes? What should the county's role and responsibilities be in the areas of surface and ground-water management? What waste management method or methods should the county use to dispose of the remaining solid wastes? The first phase in the process ended with the compilation of the forty issues in a report prepared for the county board and the public (Hennepin County 1984).

The second phase began with the formation of interdepartmental task forces to address each of the strategic issues. Although no fixed reporting date has been set for the task forces, each is to proceed in a timely fashion and involve appropriate members of the public in its deliberations. As issues are analyzed and recommendations prepared, they will be presented to the county executive or county board for action. In the third phase, specific alternatives for implementation will be selected, reviewed, and approved.

It is too early to assess the effectiveness of the Hennepin County process. However, the process does appear to provide a good example of government-wide strategic planning. The process is relatively formal, perhaps too formal. It centralizes considerable power in the county executive, with relatively little public and board involvement. But the case merits attention as one of the first major efforts of its kind. Hennepin County officials and citizens are learning a great deal as they proceed through the process for the first time, and students of strategic planning elsewhere can learn from their experience.

Future Directions

This chapter has presented alternative approaches and selected examples of strategic planning in the public sector. This section concludes with some future directions for strategic planning research and practice if strategic thinking is to become central in public management. These directions are suggested by several issues.

First, governments need more experience and knowledge of strategic planning. The three examples presented illustrate the major traditions in strategic planning, except for the industrial economics approach. But more empirical studies of the effectiveness of various strategic planning approaches need to be undertaken. Strategic planning as a subject of research—and as a public sector activity—is simply too new to say anything conclusive about the effectiveness or applicability of alternative models to the public sector.

Second, most models of strategy are noncontingent in that they do not clearly specify the boundary conditions of the model or how each should be applied in specific circumstances. For example, the Harvard model is a generic approach that a naive user might presume is applicable in all situations. However, most planning theorists now recognize that a contingent approach to planning is necessary in which the appropriate structure and process for planning is contingent on the situation (Bryson and Delbecq 1979; Alexander 1984). If strategic planning models are to become more useful to public sector organizations, they must be formulated in a contingent manner.

Third, most process models of strategic planning do not tell the user how to identify strategic issues. This is a serious shortcoming since the identification of strategic issues is the heart of most process models. In Bryson's adaptation of the Harvard and stakeholder models, for example—the one used by the RCNS—five arrows lead to the strategic issues box, but exactly how specific strategic issues emerge from that conjunction of arrows in specific situations is unclear. For strategic planning process models to be more useful to public organizations, more detailed guidance must be offered on how to formulate strategic issues constructively.

Fourth, questions remain about how to formulate specific strategies for dealing with strategic issues once the issues are identified. Some of the strategy models discussed earlier—for example, the portfolio and industrial economics models—prescribe specific strategies for firms depending on where the model positions them. But these content models have been applied rarely in the public sector. As noted, most public sector strategic planning efforts have involved the application of process models—specifically, the Harvard and stakeholder models. These models outline a process for formulating a strategy, but they do not say what specific strategies should be pursued in a given circumstance. A useful addition to the literature would be development of a typology of public sector strategies and an elaboration of the conditions under which to pursue one strategy rather than another.

Fifth, most models of strategic planning are not formally or explicitly political, and yet the public sector typically is explicitly and legitimately a politicized environment (Ring and Perry 1985). The literature on public sector strategic planning is not very instructive when it comes to dealing with the political aspects of strategic planning, other than to recognize that politics plays a part. The strategic planning model that comes closest to being explicitly political is the stakeholder approach, and it would seem wise for public sector strategic planners to incorporate stakeholder analyses and involvements into their efforts. Additional work is needed on the politics of strategic planning.

Sixth, questions remain on how to deal with the plural, ambiguous, and often conflicting goals and objectives in the public sector. Most strategic planning models do not emphasize such situations other than to prescribe the formulation of explicit goals and objectives. Such an approach, however, might in practice prove disastrous in the public sector, depending on how or if it were done at all. The stakeholder approach offers one method of dealing with this difficulty in its specification of the different goals, objectives, and interests of various stakeholder groups. Such specification should prove useful to strategic planners, even if the results are not made public.

A related question is whether or not mission statements ought to be prepared for public agencies in all cases. The answer would appear to be no. Some situations are so conflict ridden that no agreement on mission could be reached. The best that might be expected is agreement on the means, or next actions or steps, that might be taken by the agency. Public sector participants do not necessarily have to agree on mission or goals to agree on next steps (Cleveland 1973). However, one possibility is the preparation of a mission statement that incorporates different missions for different constituencies or stakeholders. Such an approach is often used in the private sector, for example, in which different missions might be outlined for customers, employees, stockholders, and communities in which the firm operates. As long as the mission statements remain general enough, it may be possible to live with the potential conflict implied by different missions for different stakeholders.

Seventh, most models of strategic planning are not clear on how to link tools and processes. Many of the tools are actually antithetical to process. The portfolio and industrial economics approaches, for example, are analytic tools that prescribe an answer. Process is irrelevant and might, in fact, block the way of determining the correct solution to the organization's strategic problems. Among the few exceptions in the literature is Nutt (1984), who describes a strategic planning process, prescribes the use of specific tools in different phases of the process, and outlines generic strategies based on the conjunction of processes and tools.

Eighth, the appropriate unit of analysis or application is unclear for many of the models. In the case of portfolio analyses, for example, what should a city government emphasize if it is the organization engaged in strategic planning? Should portfolio analyses focus on the region, the city as a place, the city government as an organization, or specific lines of business that the city might pursue? In the case of the Harvard approach, should the model be followed by the city government as a whole, by each department separately, or both? There is little general literature, and even less of an empirical nature, on how best to apply either tools or processes.

Ninth, much of the literature on private sector strategic planning assumes a competitive model in which firms compete with one another for volume, market share, and revenue. While private sector strategy formulation may involve major collaborative efforts with competitors—as, for example, through trade association activity, joint ventures, or price fixing—government strategy formulation may involve even more collaborative activity. The literature is not particularly helpful on how to engage in collaborative efforts at strategy formulation among different public organizations (Porter 1985).

Finally, what is the appropriate role for the strategic planner? This is an old debate in the planning literature. Should the planner be an expert on experts (Bolan 1971)? Should the planner be a technician, a politician, or a hybrid (Howe and Kaufman 1979; Howe 1980)? Or should the planner not be a planner, at least formally, but instead be a line manager (Bryson, Van de Ven, and Roering 1984)? We believe that what is most important about strategic planning is the development of strategic thinking, and therefore, it may not matter who does it. However, it does seem that the most useful strategic planning influences decision making in desirable directions and that strategic planning done by line managers is most likely to be implemented. Exactly how people formally designated as planners fit into that formulation is unclear and is an important subject for further investigation.

If the literature on strategic planning can address these issues in such a way that valuable empirically based advice to strategic planners emerges, then strategic planning is likely to improve. To the extent that strategic thinking becomes a conventional part of planning practice, the profession is likely to improve its usefulness to decision makers and its standing among the other public professions.

Notes

1. We thank Barbara C. Crosby, Phil Eckhert, Barbara O'Grady, Michael Rubin, Louise Straus, and Jean Allen for their valuable help with the preparation of

this chapter, but we take responsibility for any errors in the text. While concerned with strategic planning in the public sector in general, we focus primarily on strategic planning by and for governments.

2. There is controversy in the literature over the similarities and differences among the terms *strategy, strategic planning,* and *strategic management,* but we use these terms interchangeably here.

References

Ackoff, R. 1974. *Redesigning the Future.* New York: John Wiley & Sons.

Ackoff, R. 1981. *Creating the Corporate Future.* New York: John Wiley & Sons.

Alexander, E.R. 1984. After Rationality, What? A Review of Responses to Paradigm Breakdown. *Journal of the American Planning Association* 50:62–69.

Andrews, K. 1980. *The Concept of Corporate Strategy.* Homewood, Ill.: R.D. Irwin.

Ansoff, I. 1965. *Corporate Strategy.* New York: McGraw-Hill.

Ansoff, I. 1975. Managing Strategic Surprise by Response to Weak Signals. *California Management Review* 18:21–33.

Ansoff, I. 1977. The State of Practice in Planning Systems. *Sloan Management Review* 18:1–24.

Ansoff, I. 1979a. The Changing Shape of the Strategic Problem. In *A New View of Business Policy and Planning,* D. Schendel and C. Hofer, eds. Boston: Little, Brown.

Ansoff, I. 1979b. *Strategic Management.* New York: John Wiley & Sons.

Ansoff, I.; R. Declerk; and R. Hayes, eds. 1976. *From Strategic Planning to Strategic Management.* New York: John Wiley & Sons.

Boal, K.B., and J.M. Bryson. 1984. *Representation, Testing and Policy Implications of Planning Processes.* Minneapolis: Strategic Management Research Center, University of Minnesota.

Bolan, R.S. 1969. Community Decision Behavior: The Culture of Planning. *Journal of the American Institute of Planners* 35:301–310.

Bolan, R.S. 1971. Generalist With a Specialty—Still Valid? Educating the Planner: An Expert on Experts. *Planning 1971: Selected Papers from the ASPO National Conference.* Chicago: American Society of Planning Officials.

Bryson, J.M. 1981. A Perspective on Planning and Crises in the Public Sector. *Strategic Management Journal* 2:181–196.

Bryson, J.M. 1983. Representing and Testing Procedural Planning Methods. In *Evaluating Urban Planning Efforts,* I. Masser, ed. Aldershot, England: Gower Publishing Company.

Bryson, J.M., and A.L. Delbecq. 1979. A Contingent Approach to Strategy and Tactics in Project Planning. *Journal of the American Planning Association* 45: 167–179.

Bryson, J.M.; A.H. Van de Ven; and W.D. Roering. 1984. Strategic Planning and the Revitalization of the Public Service. Paper presented at the Twentieth Annual Conference of the Association of Collegiate Schools of Planning, New York City.

Center for Philadelphia Studies. 1982a. *Philadelphia Investment Portfolio.* Philadelphia: University of Pennsylvania.

Center for Philadelphia Studies. 1982b. *A Philadelphia Prospectus.* Philadelphia: University of Pennsylvania.

Chandler, A. 1962. *Strategy and Structure.* Cambridge, Mass.: MIT Press.

Chandler, A. 1977. *The Visible Hand.* Cambridge: Harvard University Press.

Channon, D. 1980. Business Government Planning Agreements—Ideology Versus Practicality. *Strategic Management Journal* 1:85–97.

Charan, R. 1982. How to Strengthen Your Strategic Review Process. *The Journal of Business Strategy* 2:50–60.

Charan, R., and E. Freeman. 1980. Planning for the Business Environment of the 1980s. *The Journal of Business Strategy* 1:9–19.

Child, J. 1972. Organizational Structure, Environment and Performance: The Role of Strategic Choice. *Sociology* 6:1–22.

Christensen, R.; K. Andrews; J. Bower; R. Hammermesh; and M. Porter. 1983. *Business Policy: Text and Cases.* Homewood, Ill.: R.D. Irwin.

Cleveland, H. 1973. *The Future Executive.* New York: Harper & Row.

Coplin, W.D.; and M.K. O'Leary. 1976. *Everyman's Prince: A Guide to Understanding Your Political Problems.* Boston: PWS Publishers.

Dahl, R.A. 1984. *Modern Political Analysis.* Englewood Cliffs, N.J.: Prentice-Hall.

Emshoff, J. 1980. *Managerial Breakthroughs.* New York: Amacom.

Emshoff, J., and A Finnel. 1979. Designing Corporate Strategy. *Sloan Management Review* 21:41–52.

Evan, W. 1966. The Organizational Set: Toward a Theory of Inter-Organizational Design. In *Approaches to Organizational Design,* J. Thompson, ed. Pittsburgh: University of Pittsburgh Press.

Freeman, R.E. 1983. Managing the Strategic Challenge in Telecommunications. *Columbia Journal of World Business* 18:8–18.

Freeman, R.E. 1984. *Strategic Management: A Stakeholder Approach.* Boston: Pitman Publishing.

Freeman, R.E., and P. Lorange. 1985. Theory Building in Strategic Management. In *Latest Advances in Strategic Management,* R. Lamb and P. Srivastava, eds. Greenwich, Conn.: JAI Press.

Gilbert, D.R., and R.E. Freeman. 1985. *Strategic Management and Corporate Responsibility: A Game Theoretic Approach.* Minneapolis: Strategic Management Research Center, University of Minnesota.

Hambrick, D.; I. Macmillan; and D. Day. 1982. Strategic Attributes and Performance in the BCG Matrix—A PIMS-based Analysis of Industrial Product Businesses. *Academy of Management Journal* 25:510–531.

Harrigan, K. 1981. Barriers to Entry and Competitive Strategies. *Strategic Management Journal* 2:395–412.

Henderson, B. 1979. *Henderson on Corporate Strategy.* Cambridge, Mass.: Abt Books.

Hennepin County. 1984. *Strategic Planning, Phase I, Executive Report.* Minneapolis: Office of Planning and Development, Hennepin County Government.

Hofer, C. 1975. Towards a Contingency Theory of Business Strategy. *Academy of Management Journal* 18:748–810.

Hofer, C., and D. Schendel. 1978. *Strategy Formulation: Analytical Concepts.* St. Paul, Minn.: West Publishing Company.

Horwitch, M. 1982. *Clipped Wings: The Story of the American SST.* Cambridge, Mass.: MIT Press.

Howe, E. 1980. Role Choices of Urban Planners. *Journal of the American Planning Association* 46:398–409.

Howe, E., and J. Kaufman. 1979. The Ethics of Contemporary American Planners. *Journal of the American Planning Association* 45:243–255.

Kaufman, J.L. 1979. The Planner as Interventionist in Public Policy Issues. In *Planning Theory in the 1980's,* R. Burchell and G. Sternlieb, eds. New Brunswick: Center for Urban Policy Research.

King, W. 1981. The Importance of Strategic Issues. *The Journal of Business Strategy* 1:74–76.

Lenz, R. 1980. Environmental, Strategy, Organization Structure and Performance. *Strategic Management Journal* 1:209–226.

Leuchtenburg, W.D. 1963. *Franklin D. Roosevelt and the New Deal.* New York: Harper & Row.

Lewis, E. 1980. *Public Entrepreneurship: Toward a Theory of Bureaucratic Political Power.* Bloomington: Indiana University Press.

Locke, E.A.; K.N. Shaw; L.M. Saari; and G.P. Latham. 1981. Goal Setting and Task Performance: 1969–1980. *Psychological Bulletin* 90:125–152.

Lorange, P. 1979. Formal Planning Systems: Their Role in Strategy Formulation and Implementation. In *A New View of Business Policy and Planning,* D. Schendel and C. Hofer, eds. Boston: Little, Brown.

Lorange, P. 1980a. *Corporate Planning: An Executive Viewpoint.* Englewood Cliffs, N.J.: Prentice-Hall.

Lorange, P. 1980b. Evolution des methods de planification. *Revue economique et sociale* 38:134–166.

Lorange, P. 1984. Strategic Control. In *Competitive Strategic Management,* R. Lamb, ed. Englewood Cliffs, N.J.: Prentice-Hall

Luttwak, E. 1977. *The Grand Strategy of the Roman Empire.* Baltimore: The Johns Hopkins University Press.

MacMillan, I. 1978. *Strategy Formulation: Political Concepts.* St. Paul, Minn.: West Publishing Co.

MacMillan, I. 1983. Competitive Strategies for Not-For-Profit Agencies. *Advantages in Strategic Management* 1:61–82.

Mason, R., and I. Mitroff. 1982. *Challenging Strategic Planning Assumptions.* New York: John Wiley & Sons.

Mazmanian, D.A., and P.A. Sabatier. 1983. *Implementation and Public Policy.* Glenview, Ill.: Scott, Foresman.

Milward, H.B. 1984. Current Institutional Arrangements That Create or Require Shared Power. Paper prepared for the 1984 Humphrey Conference on Shared Power, Minneapolis.

Milward, H.B., and G.L. Wamsley. 1982. Policy Networks—Key Concept at a Critical Juncture. Blacksburg: Center for Public Administration and Policy, Virginia Polytechnic Institute and State University.

Montgomery, C. 1982. The Measurement of Firm Diversification: Some New Empirical Evidence. *Academy of Management Journal* 24:299–307.

Nutt, P.C. 1984. A Strategic Planning Network for Non-Profit Organizations. *Strategic Management Journal* 5:57–75.

Olsen, J.B., and D.C. Eadie. 1982. *The Game Plan: Governance With Foresight.* Washington, D.C.: Council of State Planning Agencies.

Ouchi, W. 1981. *Theory Z: How American Business Can Meet the Japanese Challenge.* Reading, Mass.: Addison-Wesley.

Peters, T.J., and R.H. Waterman, Jr. 1982. *In Search of Excellence: Lessons From America's Best-Run Companies.* New York: Harper & Row.

Porter, M. 1980. *Competitive Strategy.* New York: Free Press.

Porter, M. 1985. *Competitive Advantage.* New York: Free Press.

Ring, P.S., and J.L. Perry. 1985. Strategic Management in Public and Private Organizations: Implications of Distinctive Contexts and Constraints. *Academy of Management Review* 10:276–286.

Rumelt, R. 1974. *Strategy, Structure and Economic Performance.* Cambridge: Harvard Business School, Division of Research.

Schendel, D., and C. Hofer, eds. 1979. *A New View of Business Policy and Planning.* Boston: Little, Brown.

Sorkin, D.L: N.B. Ferris; and J. Hudak. n.d. *Strategies for Cities and Counties: A Strategic Planning Guide.* Washington, D.C.: Public Technology.

Taylor, B. 1984. Strategic Planning—Which Style Do You Need? *Long Range Planning* 17:51–62.

Wildavsky, A. 1979a. *The Politics of the Budgetary Process.* Boston: Little, Brown.

Wildavsky, A. 1979b. *Speaking Truth to Power.* Boston: Little, Brown.

Wind, Y, and V. Mahajan. 1981. Designing Product and Business Portfolios. *Harvard Business Review* 59:155–165.

6
Making Planners More Effective Strategists

Jerome L. Kaufman

At a time when confidence in public planning agencies is declining, agencies may be judged increasingly by the scope of their influence in public decisions. To increase impact in decisions that involve equity and other traditional planning values, planners need to think and act strategically. Skillful planning strategists can help chart paths for their agencies in analyzing and influencing the decision process.

Strategy can be defined in dictionary terms as "the science or art of military command as applied to the overall planning and conduct of large scale combat operations." Although often cast in military terms, strategy is also well recognized in political and business spheres.[1] The war room, where military strategists plot ways to win battles against the enemy, is a popular image. So, too, is the smoke-filled room, where political strategists exchange ideas on how to win elections. Within the corporate world, strategic planning is increasingly accepted, with strategists becoming influential in charting paths for corporations to follow in gaining and maintaining a more competitive edge in the marketplace (Steiner 1979).

Despite the widespread notion of planning agencies as neutral fact-finding advisory bodies, many act with deliberate normative intent to help adopt and implement policies that otherwise might be viewed skeptically or resisted in the community. Strategy can play an important role in public planning, yet the strategist is hardly mentioned in the literature on planner roles (Alexander 1979; Burke 1979; Catanese 1984; Rabinovitz 1969; Rondinelli 1975; Susskind 1974). These authors acknowledge a multiplicity of roles. They view the planner as not only advisor, analyst, designer, or educator but also advocate, entrepreneur, evaluator, facilitator, manager, mediator, negotiator, organizer, or publicist. However, specific recognition of the planner's role as strategist is missing from this literature.

But planners do function as strategists, as illustrated in the small body of writings by practicing planners on their experiences. Jacobs (1978), former planning director of San Francisco, analyzes several cases that reflect a flair for strategic thinking. These include an unsuccessful effort to prevent construction of the giant Transamerica building and an effective campaign to influence adoption of a controversial citywide urban design plan. Krumholz, former planning director of Cleveland, and co-workers (1975) analyze the strategies and tactics used to include equity considerations in the regional transportation plan, prevent a large mixed-use development complex from construction downtown, and build support for a previously contested housing allowance policy. Other accounts of strategic thinking by planning practitioners include Bertsch and Shafer (1971) on the Miami Valley Regional Planning Commission's fair share housing plan, and Schoop and Hirten (1971) on efforts to establish a permanent Bay Conservation Development Commission in California. Despite their strategic intervention, none of these practitioners refers to him- or herself as a strategist. Lewis (1983, p. 12) substantiates ways that planners act as strategists in her account of planning agency directors in big cities:

> [I]n the agencies with million dollar budgets and dozens or even hundreds of employees, directors must, above all, be good at plotting strategy to make sure their policies fly. They leave the hands-on work—tasks such as budgeting, administration, and technical reports—to their staff. In many respects, the planning office is like the military, except that the battles aren't so bloody. The lieutenants do the field work while the generals mull over tactics in the war room.

She points to an important but rarely acknowledged activity of many planning agencies. Planners, more often than conventional wisdom holds or than they are willing to admit publicly for fear of jeopardizing their image as neutral and objective advisors, do plot strategies at times to improve chances that policies might fly.[2] But she is too restrictive in identifying only planning agency directors in big cities as engaging in strategic thinking. Strategy is not the province of the generals alone. Lieutenants, corporals, and privates in all kinds of planning offices also plot strategies at times.

Consider, for example, the following hypothetical scenario:

> It was Friday afternoon. The county planning director's door was slightly ajar. His deputy came in and sat down opposite him. "There's a move afoot to remove the right-of-way reserved for the future expansion of the Blue Mountain Highway from the official map," said the deputy director.
>
> He went on, "The neighborhood organization in that area is beginning to pressure some county board members to take action to prevent that highway from ever being widened. The residents feel that if it was widened, the neighborhood would quickly succumb to the developers."
>
> The planning director turned his swivel chair toward the window. "That can't be," he said. "All our studies show that highway will have to be widened in the next few years the way development is occurring in its vicinity. It would be costly and irresponsible to remove the right-of-way reservation."

He paused and reflected for a moment. Then with assurance he said, "We've got to do something to keep the official map designation as is. Call the city traffic engineer and county planning transportation director and see if you can arrange a meeting next week. We need to have strategy session soon to decide what to do."

This example depicts a situation that many practicing planners experience, albeit about different issues of varying complexity. An awareness by planners of a competing proposal originating from elsewhere within the community may or may not trigger a response. But the temptation to protect favored policies is an understandable element of practice. And when the temptation leads to action, strategic thinking often affects the actions taken.

How effective are planners when they think or act strategically? My view is that planners have shortcomings as strategists, not because they are averse to acting as strategists but because they approach the task of strategic analysis—which underlies the formulation and choice of strategies and tactics—far too casually and haphazardly.[3] Consequently, some selected strategies may be inappropriate or misdirected.

This chapter focuses on the kinds of information that planners should collect and analyze to become more adept as strategists. It includes information drawn from strategic analysis schemes developed in diverse fields, including political science, social work, community organization, educational policy, and industrial engineering, as well as planning. It reviews the state of the art of strategic analysis in planning today and presents one strategic analysis scheme that illustrates the practical value of devising strategies that have a better chance of producing desired outcomes.

State-of-the-Art Strategic Analysis

When planners function as strategists, they usually operate at two levels: at the general community or functional system level and at the level of specific issues in which they intervene. Because most planners are long-term participants in their communities, they usually have a good sense of how decisions are made. The planning strategist may pose questions at the general community or functional system level. Who are the most influential individuals and groups in the community or functional system, and what are their beliefs and values? What issues are associated with which groups? How are important decisions usually made—by consensus, interest group bargaining, or strong centralized leadership? Which groups tend to support planning policies, and which tend to oppose?

Contextual information like this is useful to the planning strategist who is considering specific issues and actions. It clarifies elements in the broader environment that may facilitate or deter contemplated actions. It provides a reservoir of information for planners each time they undertake analyses to devise strategies at the issue-specific level.[4] Lewis (1983) describes a planning director who regularly keeps a card file on influential community members to anticipate where they might stand on any given issue. This planner also maintains computer files on community groups and a matrix showing how city council members voted on various issues.

Although contextual information about the community or functional system is helpful to the planning strategist, my focus here is strategic analysis at the issue-specific level, on what happens when planners intervene on a particular issue. They usually begin with a working objective or objectives they want to achieve—initiate a policy, modify a policy, or prevent a policy from being enacted. As initiator, the agency may try to promote policies that represent those recently developed, policies kept off the public agenda for awhile, or those that represent a change from the status quo. They may find apathy or engender resistance in response.

Decisions in a community or functional system reflect a continuous process and dynamic system. A number of ideas, policies, and proposals emanate from outside the planning agency—for example, from the chief executive's office, legislators, business community, neighborhood organizations, other governmental agencies, service providers, and service beneficiaries. Planners may think that some of these outside proposals would undermine a preferred policy if enacted. If so, the agency may either stay out of the issue, try to modify the proposal to make it more consistent with its own policy views, or try to prevent the outside policy from enactment.

The next stage of the process may involve deliberating about how to achieve a set objective. In theory, here is where most strategic analysis may be done and change strategies chosen.[5] The final stage may involve deploying tactics that complement strategy and achieve desired outcomes.

Some level of analysis may be undertaken at each stage of the process. What is the quality of such analyses? My image is that planners spend more time on analyses leading to the choice of objectives—that is, what the planning agency wants to accomplish—than on analyses at other stages of the process. The forum for devising strategies may be no more than a staff brainstorming session, lasting at most an hour or two for any significant issue. Analysis in such sessions is often cursory and unstructured, a haphazard blend of professional instincts and political hunches. Planners rarely perform systematic analysis to generate helpful clues for assessing strategic possibilities. Thus, the most appropriate strategy may not emerge from these sessions.

This image is based in part on conversations over several years with veteran planning practitioners who described the kinds of strategic analyses they undertake. These conversations suggest that such planners give relatively low priority to strategic analysis, but my methodology was informal and my sample unsystematic.[6]

This image also is based on more systematic interviews with planning directors of selected medium-sized Wisconsin cities, ranging in size from 50,000 to 170,000 people. Each agency had a planning commission with seven to nine members, as well as a small professional staff. Each director was asked to identify from five to seven recent decisions that in his or her judgment had a significant effect on their city's growth and development. Each was asked to describe, for any three decisions, the analysis used in choosing strategies and the methods employed to influence the outcomes.

The study showed that agency directors were casual and unsystematic about their analyses to formulate strategies and select tactics. Political intuition and hunches were instrumental. They identified the most visible potential supporters and potential opponents of the agency's position in most cases, but their analyses were usually superficial. They rarely analyzed the specific skills and resources of these groups, their stake in the issue, or their reasons for supporting or opposing the agency's position. They seldom analyzed the characteristics of the issue. For example, what were the costs and benefits to specific groups if the favored policy or issue were adopted? Was the issue easy or difficult to understand? Would the proposed change be viewed as permanent or temporary? What were the perceived costs of the proposed policy? They rarely asked or answered such questions. Instead they usually spent less than an hour in analyzing the situation and designing strategies and tactics for action. Moreover, even this cursory analysis was often not used in their selection of strategies and tactics to influence decisions. The findings reflect the questionable quality of strategic analysis undertaken by planners.

Strategic Analysis Schemes

How can planners become more adept as strategic analysts? One answer can be found in the body of eclectic writings that includes strategic analysis schemes. Some of these schemes have been devised by planners, but most have been developed by people in other fields. One common thread in these approaches is their focus on obtaining information on target groups—the individuals, organizations, and institutions involved in specific policy issues.[7] While some schemes seek general contextual information about the environment of the issue or the characteristics of the proposal, most minimally focus on target groups.

The schemes differ in several respects. Some are relatively simple, requiring analysis of only a few target group characteristics (Coplin and O'Leary 1976; Havelock 1973; Speeter 1978; Warren 1965). Others are more complex, involving a lengthier list of target group characteristics for analysis (Bardach 1972; Bolan 1969; Gustafson 1979; Kaufman 1978; Mazmanian and Sabatier 1981; Meltsner 1972; Morris and Binstock 1966; Rothman,

Erlich, and Teresa 1976). Most schemes assess target group characteristics in qualitative terms. Others convert qualitative information into numeric terms (Coplin and O'Leary 1976; Gustafson 1979). Most schemes apply analysis to the policy adoption stage. Others apply analysis to implementation after the proposal is adopted (Gustafson 1979; Mazmanian and Sabatier 1981). Most schemes are not strategy specific, and contingent strategies are possible whatever the findings. Others clearly link the findings of the analysis to particular strategies (Speeter 1978; Warren 1965).

Despite their differences, these schemes all can be used both prospectively and prescriptively. Used prospectively, they can provide the planner with information on the difficulty of achieving an objective. If analysis shows overwhelming and broad-based resistance, then the sensible course of action may be to jettison the objective and avoid the issue in accordance with an amended old saying, "Fools should *not* rush in where angels fear to tread." Efforts in pursuit of a hopeless course may produce frustration, waste scarce resources, and eventually fail.

If analysis shows strong but narrowly based resistance to a particular desired objective, the planner might try to modify the objective so it better fits the base of possible support. In this case, as well as in only moderate resistance, the information collected can be used prescriptively. It can provide the planner with clues to consider in selecting strategies to achieve either the original objective or a modified one. Regardless of the objective sought, however, efforts can aim at trying to move target groups toward either greater support of the objective, reduced opposition to it, or a neutral, noninvolved position.

Analyzing the Target Group

What information about target groups can help in formulating strategy? Although different in their purpose and terminology, strategic analysis schemes appear to share certain categories of information, including the basic position each target group holds toward the objective sought by the planning agency, the specific concerns each target group has about the working objective, the likelihood that each target group will get involved in the issue, the resources each target group possesses that affect its capacity to influence the decision outcome on the working objective, and the pattern of relationship among the target groups involved in the issue. The following sections describe each type of information.

Basic Position

Strategic analysis schemes seek information on the position each target group holds toward the objective sought. Is a group for, against, or neutral toward the objective? For example, Coplin and O'Leary (1976) use a numeric system to score a target group's degree of support or opposition. Bolan (1971) divides supporters and opponents by their interest or sentiment. A supportive interest group is one that perceives it will gain directly from adopting the proposed change, whereas an oppositional interest group perceives it will directly lose from such adoption. In contrast, a sentiment group sees the gain (if supportive) or loss (if in opposition) more indirectly, in symbolic or ideological terms or in terms of an adjustment in status if the proposed change is adopted.

Specific Concerns

Some strategic analysis schemes direct the analyst beyond support or opposition to probe more deeply into the target group's specific concerns about the objective. Even supportive groups may have concerns about some aspects of the proposal, including concerns about features of the proposal or about possible negative effects on the target group if the proposal is adopted or implemented. By focusing on the concerns of target groups, the analyst can chart a clearer course for designing strategies to increase support and overcome opposition to an objective.

Different issues have different levels of concern. Two groups may oppose a plan to save a marshland from development. But one may base its opposition on the belief that more affordable housing is needed, whereas the other may oppose on grounds that private property rights are threatened and that the community has a restrictive no-growth policy. Or groups may oppose a new shopping center proposal for different reasons. For example, one may be concerned about neighborhood impacts, another about the poor design of the center, and another about the high public improvement costs to service the center. Whatever the concerns, the analyst will find it helpful to identify those most bothersome to target groups involved in the issue.

It is possible to identify types of concerns about objectives. For example, Gustafson (1979) identifies four features of any proposal that may trouble groups: complexity, radicalness, nonadaptability, and uncertainty about its working as intended if enacted.[8] Morris and Binstock (1966) emphasize the possibility that the dominant faction of a group may perceive a proposal as being opposed to its interests. Thus, knowledge of the interests of groups is needed.

Bolan (1969) identifies several attributes of proposals that may affect their acceptability. Target groups may have concerns about a specific working objective because they perceive it to be too ideologically controversial, too difficult to change once adopted, too uncertain in its consequences, too hard to understand, or too complex to administer. Mazmanian and Sabatier (1981) focus on how tractable the proposal is. They claim that certain concerns such as costs to target groups, extent of political support, diversity of the behavior proscribed, and number of groups affected by the policy, affect tractability.

Zaltman, Florio, and Sikorski (1977) analyze several concerns rooted in the proposed change that may lead to resistance. The proposal may be perceived as too difficult to communicate; too radical, risky, complex, or costly to operate; too difficult to reverse once enacted; or too incompatible with the existing environment. Whatever the concerns of target groups, strategists should know about them in specific terms so they can anticipate or lessen perceived negative aspects.[9]

Likelihood of Involvement

Two approaches in strategic analysis schemes can aid the strategist in assessing the likelihood that a target group will actually work for or against the objective. One approach addresses the target group's intensity of feeling or concern about the issue. *Salience, stake,* and *motivation* are terms used to gauge intensity of feeling (Bardach 1972; Bolan 1969, 1971; Coplin and O'Leary 1976; Gustafson 1979; Meltsner 1972).

The other approach deals with opportunity. Although an issue may have salience for a group, the group may have little opportunity for involvement because of scarce resources, demands, or other factors. Bolan (1971) defines opportunity in terms of time, money, or situational factors that enable an actor to participate. Others view opportunity as the capacity of a target group to deliver its resources. Bardach (1972, p. 222) suggests that groups who are "likely to be relatively free to commit political currency and production resources to the struggle" should be inventoried.

There are several strategic implications of a target group's salience or opportunity. If a supportive group's salience is low, the strategist might try to lessen concern about an objective or provide an incentive for the group to become more active. If a group with low salience opposes the working objective, then the strategist might try to keep that salience low so it will give little opposition to the objective. The strategist should not overestimate the role supportive groups with little opportunity can play in affecting the outcome of the issue because such groups may be unable to deliver their support. The best approach may be to consult them at critical times when their support is deemed essential. The strategist also should be wary of high-salience, high-opportunity target groups that are in the opposition. It may require careful and creative thinking to neutralize their opposition.

Resources

Even if a target group has high salience and high opportunity, its ability to influence outcomes may be limited if it lacks resources. Most strategic analysis schemes thus identify target group resources. For example, Coplin and O'Leary (1976) emphasize power (defined broadly as the ability to accomplish or prevent an outcome from occurring) as the most critical resource. Bolan (1971) suggests analysis of group resources in terms of four capacities—performance, support, management, and integration. Bardach (1972) focuses on weightiness and effective resources to differentiate among strong and weak actors.

Resources more commonly found in strategic analysis schemes include power, legitimacy, knowledge, and performance skills. Power resources represent means to influence or compel. In the extreme, a group with power resources might have the capacity to impose sanctions or to veto proposals. Bardach (1972) broadens the notion to high functional indispensability, or the leverage a group can exert in the form of a threat as an indicator of power. Bolan (1971) views power in terms of group ability to control and coordinate. Havelock (1973) identifies leaders who control wealth as having power. Morris and Binstock (1966) find power in those who can coerce and offer inducements as well as receive and control the flow of information by virtue of their special positions.

Another resource is legitimacy. Groups with political or social standing (Morris and Binstock 1966), high standing with influentials (Bardach 1972), an image of clear representation (Havelock 1973), and high positions within the system (Meltsner 1972) may be viewed as legitimate. Target groups that lack legitimacy may find it more difficult to develop alliances and participate effectively in decisions.

Another resource is knowledge. Bolan (1969) identifies groups with general knowledge of the issue under consideration and those with special knowledge of contextual matters that bear on the issue such as laws, regulations, and procedures. Havelock (1973) refers to cognitive knowledge—that is, the degree of understanding and sophistication an actor has in the issue area. Meltsner (1972) considers information as an important resource if it is valued or wanted by other actors. Planners who understand which groups are most and least knowledgeable about an issue may deal with them more effectively.

Yet another resource involves performance skills. These affect the ability to deploy other resources and include communication skills (Bardach 1972; Bolan 1971), organizing skills (Bolan 1971), interpersonal skills like negotiation and mediation, and strategic skills. Speeter (1978, p. 88) emphasizes that "strategizing becomes the nuts and bolts work of the community organizer. Like the daily encounters of any long-range journey, it requires extensive knowledge of a situation (who or what you're dealing with), and flexible use of strategies and tactics." Meltsner (1972, p. 862) emphasizes the importance of timing as "when to use norms of reciprocity, when to remind others of the rules of the game, when to propose issues."

Relationships

Some strategic schemes seek information on relationships and interactions among target groups. For example, Bolan (1971) refers to the power or dependence relationship between the planner and his or her client groups, such as the planning commission, mayor, or governor. He argues that the extent of the planner's power or dependence in relation to client groups will affect policy influence and the technical, interpersonal, or other skills needed.

Havelock (1973) analyzes relationships among innovators, resisters, and leaders involved in issues, particularly the influence of innovators and resisters on leaders. Gustafson (1979) suggests study of alliances among affected parties. Kaufman (1978) emphasizes the importance of knowing which individuals or groups have the respect of target groups. Bardach (1972) gives low priority to groups that are inaccessible and lack formal or informal communication channels. Coplin and O'Leary (1976) devise a friendship-neutrality-hostility chart as a way of better understanding how actors perceive others involved in an issue.

Knowledge of relationships among target groups can serve several strategic functions. It can help the strategist know more about how to reach groups and others who may be better able to reach them. It can help the strategist identify potential allies and how easy or difficult it may be to gain access to them. It also can reveal potential allies who might be willing to act on behalf of the planning agency and reduce resistance from groups who oppose the agency's position on an issue.

Strategic Analysis in Practice

The preceding section focuses on target group information that planning strategists might obtain to influence the outcome of decisions. The aim was to suggest a wide range of information for possible collection, leaving aside constraints in time and money and differences in importance of issues. But all issues do not warrant the optimum approach. This section illustrates the practical value of strategic analysis by applying one scheme to a hypothetical case.

In a clever and entertaining book, Coplin and O'Leary (1976) present an approach they claim can lead to success in politics. They advise the individual to *probe* surroundings to identify the most important actors, *interact* with these actors to find out their inclinations and influence on important issues, *calculate* how to get them to behave in the desired way, and *execute* the plans.[10] They coin the acronym *prince* from the first letters of the steps—an allusion to Machiavelli's classic work—and arrive at what they call the Prince Political Accounting system.

How can the system apply to a planning situation? Our hypothetical case involves a planning agency that tries to get a favored but dormant policy adopted by community decision makers.[11] The planning strategist would begin at the probe stage and identify the important actors or target groups involved in the issue. In this stage, the strategist would cast widely to catch many actors or groups, including those with little interest in the issue at the outset but who might become more important later on. The media might be an example of such a late bloomer.

The strategist would then score each actor or group on the position, salience, and power factors, then multiply these numbers to reach a total score for each.[12] He or she then would sum the total scores for all actors or groups to derive a total score for the entire issue. This figure becomes a way to gauge how difficult or easy it may be for the planning agency to achieve its objective before it considers any change strategies.

Table 6-1 illustrates how the scheme would work, up to this stage, for our hypothetical case. The findings reveal a total score of − 10 for the issue. This score suggests moderate resistance to the agency. From a prospective standpoint, the agency might achieve its objective through appropriate strategic action. However, if the total score were − 25 instead of − 10, the agency might choose to avoid the issue since resistance would be formidable.

Table 6-1 also offers prescriptive information on several clues for possible strategic tactical actions needed to change the − 10 figure to a less negative or more positive number. Coplin and O'Leary (1976) view this as the time for the planning strategist to calculate how to get the actors or groups to behave in a more desired way. They also would include additional information on the pattern of relationships among actors in terms of their friendship, neutrality, and hostility toward each other, as indicated in table 6-2.

Table 6-1
Position, Salience, and Power of Target Groups on Planning Issue

Target Group	Position	Salience	Power	Totals
A	− 3	2	1	− 6
B	+ 1	1	2	+ 2
C	− 2	2	2	− 8
D	− 2	1	2	− 4
E	− 2	2	1	− 4
F	+ 2	2	1	+ 4
G	+ 2	2	1	+ 4
H	+ 1	1	− 2	+ 2
Total				− 10

Table 6–2
Relationships among Target Groups on Planning Issue

Target Group	A	B	C	D	E	F	G	H
A	X	+	+	−	−	−	=	=
B	+	X	−	+	=	=	+	+
C	−	+	X	=	+	−	+	=
D	+	−	+	X	−	=	−	−
E	=	+	−	−	X	−	−	=
F	−	−	−	=	−	X	=	−
G	=	+	+	−	+	+	X	−
H	=	+	=	=	=	−	−	X

Key: + friendly toward
= neutral toward
− hostile toward

Following are possible strategic and tactical actions from a review of these two tables.

Target groups B and H have similar profiles (see table 6–1). Both mildly favor (+ 1) the policy position, have some power (2), but have low salience (1) about the issue. Since each has power that might be used to support the policy, the strategist might ask if their salience can be raised so that they are more likely to exercise their power. The strategist can further discern that actor G is even more favorable toward the policy (+ 2) than B and H. If G would act as an ally for the planning agency on B and H, salience in the issue might be raised. Table 6–2 provides helpful information to determine whether or not this is a good tactic to try. It shows that although B and G are friendly to each other, H and G are not. So in this instance, the strategist might consider trying to induce G to exert its influence on B, by virtue of their friendship, but avoid trying to use G as an ally on H because these two groups are hostile to each other.

Target groups C and E both oppose the policy (− 2 on position). But they differ on power because C (2) has more than E (1). The strategist might address some of their concerns by trying to lessen their opposition. Furthermore, since the supportive G is friendly with C (see table 6–2), G might be asked to help reduce C's concerns, thereby lessening C's opposition. This tactic should not be attempted for E, since as table 6–2 indicates, G and E do not get along. The astute strategist would note that C is the more important group to address because it has more power to wield against the planning agency's policy than E and because it could do more damage if its opposition remained strong.

Target group A is strongly opposed to the policy (− 3 on position). But

Table 6–3
Position, Salience, and Power of Target Groups before and after
Strategic Action

Target Group	Position		Salience		Power		Total	
	Before	After	Before	After	Before	After	Before	After
A	−3	−3	2	2	1	1	−6	−6
B	+1	+1	1	2	2	2	+2	+4
C	−2	−1	2	2	2	2	−8	−4
D	−2	−2	1	1	2	2	−4	−4
E	−2	−2	2	2	1	1	−4	−4
F	+2	+2	2	2	1	1	+4	+4
G	+2	+2	2	2	1	1	+4	+4
H	+1	+1	1	1	2	2	+2	+2
Total							−10	−4

the effort is questionable because of the difficulty of changing its views and because A (1) has relatively little power to exert on this issue. From the strategist's standpoint, the potential damage is minimal.

Target Group F is a reasonably strong supporter (+2 on position). On first glance, it may appear good to get F involved in the issue. But since F has poor relations with most other groups (table 6–2), encouraging it to become more active in support of the policy would probably be a mistake.

Further analysis of the findings in tables 6–1 and 6–2 suggests other possible actions, but these four points can stand for purposes of simplification. If each action works as intended, then the total issue score of −10 would drop to −4 (see table 6–3) and the chances of achieving the objective would improve.

Although the Coplin and O'Leary (1976) scheme is relatively easy to use for both prospective and prescriptive purposes, it does have shortcomings. For example, the variables are insufficiently defined and fail to articulate why one actor or group strongly opposes (−3) the position while another moderately favors (+2) it. The strategist would have a more accurate basis for placing an actor or group on the continuum if the variables were better defined. Such information also would provide better material to tailor messages and communicate with an actor or group in strengthening support or reducing opposition. Also, the model fails to recognize the important opportunity variable that serves to gauge whether or not an actor or group's salience will be activated. Finally, the model defines power too loosely. Coplin and O'Leary draw no distinction among the several kinds of resources an actor or group may possess to exert influence. What kinds of resources does an actor or group have to affect the outcome of any particular issue? For example, does it have veto power, review authority, social standing, political legitimacy, communication skills, strategic skills, or special knowledge about the issue?

The Coplin and O'Leary (1976) model could be expanded and improved for strategic analysis. Any actor or group's position on an issue could be set by better understanding what it does and does not like about an objective. An actor or group's score on salience could depend on assessing its opportunity for involvement as well as its perceived stake in the issue. And resources could substitute for power, with any target group's resources ranked from 0 to 3. Power could then become one of four resource variables in addition to legitimacy, knowledge, and performance skills. The strategist could then assess each resource for each target group to derive an overall score. He or she then could multiply the figures for position, salience modified by opportunity, and resources to reach a total score for each target group and then sum all group scores to derive a total score for the entire issue. This model has impressive strategic possibilities for planning.

Conclusion

Two approaches typify much of the discussion about planner roles. One calls for fundamental changes in role behavior. These changes are difficult to achieve given the environments in which most U.S. planners operate. The proposed transactive (Friedman 1973), radical (Grabow and Heskin 1977), communicative (Forrester 1980), and overt advocate (Krumholz, Cogger, and Linner 1975) roles are questionable for most public agency planners to pursue, even though one may sympathize with the underlying values that modify such proposals. The prevalent social, political, and institutional system in which U.S. planning operates poses too many obstacles for these roles to work in practice, however much some may prefer that practicing planners follow these alternative directions.

The other approach to planner role behavior seems to fit better the real world in which planning takes place. The roles of planner as technical analyst, policy advisor, facilitator, mediator, and manager seem more in harmony with the institutional environment in which planning functions. The basic premise underlying these planner role conceptions is that good performance will lead to more effective practice. There is evidence that planners can influence public decisions by functioning in these roles, but even when impact is evident, questions remain: Are the results socially beneficial? Do they further the public interest? Can effective planning serve the wrong purposes?

My interest here lies in the second, more feasible approach to planner roles. My contention is that planners can be effective in acting as analysts, advisors, facilitators, mediators, and managers and that they do function as strategists more often than conventional wisdom holds. My concern is not that planners avoid acting as strategists but that they apply strategic analysis less rigorously than they should.

This chapter shows that a body of knowledge is available for adaptation by planners to improve their capacities as strategists. When planners perform more adeptly as strategists, they can expect more powerful impact on policy decisions. My focus here is on strategic analysis that follows the selection of objectives and precedes the selection of strategies and tactics. The contention is that more careful and systematic strategic analysis can improve chances of success. Reliance on intuition can work in some instances for a few planners, but intuition is insufficient for most planners. And quick-and-dirty analysis in selection of strategies is all too casual and haphazard to expect much success. Planners should take strategic analysis more seriously. The potential payoffs in more imaginative and effective practice are well worth the effort.

Notes

1. The term *tactic* is closely related to the term *strategy*. Tactics, in dictionary terms, are "adroit devices to accomplish an end."

2. Lewis (1983) attributes the following statements to big city planning directors who reflect a strategic approach to thinking:

> It's not only longevity that's important. It's the willingness to keep pressing forward with your objectives. Then the other players in the game have to adjust their strategies. Pretty soon, you can negotiate. . . . [p. 16] Sometimes I worked with other city agencies to isolate a maverick. . . . [p. 16] Most significant . . . is that other departments thought of us as having a very good rapport with top decision makers, including the mayor. Whether or not they were correct is less important than the fact that that was their perception. [p. 17]

3. Only a few graduate schools of planning attempt to train planners to be effective strategists. The casual way in which most planners approach the task of formulating strategy may result in part from this gap in their formal planning education.

4. Several authors focus on the general contextual knowledge that planners should have. For example, Rabinovitz (1969) focuses on the political system within the community. She suggests that planners should adapt their role to the nature of the local political system, including cohesive, executive-centered, competitive, and fragmented systems. Bolan (1969) advocates analysis of the formal and informal decision environment to gauge the chances of any proposal's acceptance. Bolan (1971) also advocates analysis of the planner's relationship with his or her client. He describes a power-dependence continuum, placing the planner in relation to his or her client as a means to guide subsequent behavior. Other analysts emphasize the need to obtain information about the interests of dominant factions in the community (Morris and Binstock 1966) or about the beliefs and motivations of actors involved in policy issues (Meltsner 1972).

5. Zaltman, Florio, and Sikorski (1977) group change strategies into three broad categories: (1) rational strategies involve transmitting high-fidelity messages that justify change; (2) manipulative strategies involve a deliberate arranging of messages and aspects of the environment to produce change, and (3) power strategies are based on the offering or application of basic rewards and punishments.

6. As one well-known planning director candidly admitted to me, "We are strategizing, but we're strategizing without doing the analysis of the people who will be arrayed against us."

7. Coplin and O'Leary (1976) refer to what I call target groups as political actors. They use this term because they see political problems as widespread and ubiquitous in everyday life; that is, "a political problem is one in which you must get some other people to act or stop acting in a certain way in order to achieve a goal important to you" (p. 3). Thus, most issues—for example, getting a better job, making a successful sales pitch, finding a new living mate—become political issues involving political actors, in their view.

8. Gustafson (1979) focuses on twenty-nine factors that affect the chance of implementation success. The proposed change is but one of six general categories to be analyzed. The others are the planning process, implementation process, change agent, target group, and context. Gustafson uses a numeric scale to assess each factor.

9. The strategist can also identify specific aspects of a desired proposal that target groups may like, even though these groups may be neutral or mildly opposed to the proposal. With such information, the strategist might try to augment features perceived positively by such groups to try to lessen their opposition or move them from a neutral to a more supportive position.

10. Coplin and O'Leary (1976) probe and interact stages in similar ways to my use of strategic analysis. Their calculate stage is analogous to my choosing strategies and tactics, and their execute stage is analogous to my carrying out the strategies and tactics.

11. The Coplin–O'Leary (1976) approach also could apply to other kinds of working objectives, such as modifying an outside-initiated proposal or preventing enactment of an outside-initiated proposal.

12. Coplin and O'Leary (1976) use a numeric scale for each factor. The score for position can range from +3 (favorable) to −3 (unfavorable) and for salience and power, from 0 (low) to 3 (high).

References

Alexander, E. 1979. Planning Roles and Context. In *Introduction to Urban Planning,* A. Catanese and J. Snyder, eds. New York: McGraw-Hill.

Bardach, E. 1972. *The Skill Factor in Politics.* Berkeley: University of California Press.

Bertsch, D., and A. Shafer. 1971. A Regional Housing Plan: The Miami Valley Regional Planning Commission Experience. *AIP Planners Notebook* 1:1–8.

Bolan, R. 1969. Community Decision Making: The Culture of Planning. *Journal of the American Institute of Planners* 35:301–310.

————. 1971. The Social Relations of the Planner. *Journal of the American Institute of Planners* 37:386–396.

Burke, E. 1979. *A Participatory Approach to Urban Planning.* New York: Human Services Press.

Catanese, A. 1984. *The Politics of Planning and Development.* Beverly Hills: Sage Publications.

Coplin, W., and M. O'Leary. 1976. *Everyman's Prince: A Guide to Understanding Your Political Problem.* North Scituate, Mass.: Duxbury Press.

Forrester, J. 1980. Critical Theory and Planning Practice. In *Urban and Regional Planning in an Age of Austerity,* P. Clavel, J. Forrester, and W. Goldsmith, eds. New York: Pergamon Press.

Friedman, J. 1973. *Retracking America: A Theory of Transactive Planning.* New York: Anchor Press.

Grabow, S., and A. Heskin. 1977. Foundations for a Radical Concept of Planning. *Journal of the American Institute of Planners* 43:115–124.

Gustafson, D. 1979. *An Approach to Predicting the Implementation Potential of Recommended Actions in Health Planning.* Madison, Wis.: Institute for Health Planning.

Havelock, R. 1973. *The Change Agent's Guide to Innovation in Education.* Englewood Cliffs, N.J.: Educational Technology Publications.

Havelock, R., and A. Huberman. 1977. *Solving Educational Problems: The Theory and Reality of Innovation in Developing Countries.* New York: UNESCO.

Jacobs, A. 1978. *Making City Planning Work.* Chicago: ASPO Press.

Kaufman, J. 1978. The Planner as Interventionist in Public Policy Issues. In *Planning Theory in the 1980's,* R. Burchell and G. Sternlieb, eds. New Brunswick: Center for Urban Policy Research.

Krumholz, N.; J. Cogger; and J. Linner. 1975. The Cleveland Policy Planning Report. *Journal of the American Institute of Planners* 41:298–304.

Lewis, S. 1983. How to Survive as a Big City Planning Director. *Planning* 49:12–17.

Mazmanian, D., and P. Sabatier, eds. 1981. *Effective Policy Implementation.* Lexington, Mass.: D.C. Heath and Company, Lexington Books.

Meltsner, A. 1972. Political Feasibility and Policy Analysis. *Public Administration Review* 32:859–867.

Morris, R., and R. Binstock. 1966. *Feasible Planning for Social Planning.* New York: Columbia University Press.

Rabinovitz, F. 1969. *City Planning and Politics.* New York: Atherton Press.

Rondinelli, D. 1975. *Urban and Regional Development Planning, Policy, and Administration.* Ithaca, N.Y.: Cornell University Press.

Rothman, J.; J. Erlich; and J. Teresa. 1976. *Promoting Innovation and Change in Organizations and Communities: A Planning Manual.* New York: John Wiley & Sons.

Schoop, J. and J. Hirten. 1971. The San Francisco Bay Plan: Combining Policy with Police Power. *Journal of the American Institute of Planners* 37:2–10.

Speeter, G. 1978. *Power: A Repossession Manual.* Amherst: Citizen Involvement Training Project, University of Massachusetts.

Steiner, G. 1979. *Strategic Planning: What Every Manager Must Know.* New York: Free Press.

Susskind, L. 1974. The Logic of Planning Practice: A New Focus for the Teaching of Planning Theory. Paper presented at the Annual Conference of the Association of Collegiate Schools of Planning, Denver.

Warren, R. 1965. *Studying Your Community.* New York: Free Press.

Zaltman, G.; D. Florio; and L. Sikorski. 1977. *Dynamic Educational Change: Models, Strategies, Tactics and Management.* New York: Free Press.

Zaltman, G., and R. Duncan. 1977. *Strategies for Planned Change.* New York: John Wiley & Sons.

7
Policy Analysis with Implementation in Mind

Carl V. Patton

Much attention has been given during recent years to methods of policy analysis and evaluation under the assumption that analysis of alternative policies and programs before adoption provides a better chance of producing the desired results. For example, efforts have gone into refining cost-benefit analysis, incorporating citizen input into the design of policies and programs, and conducting real world experiments to pretest programs. However, few of these efforts have had more than a minimum impact on the quality of programs implemented. In this chapter I argue that many policies have not had their intended impact because the policy analyses were not conducted with implementation in mind and that implementation feasibility analysis should be incorporated into the policy analysis process.

Implementation has been given a variety of definitions (see, for example, Bardach 1980; Hargrove 1975; Pressman and Wildavsky 1973), but Williams (1980, p. 1) defines it succinctly as "the stage between a decision and operations. . . . It is the hard, next step after the decision, involving efforts to put in place—to make operational—what has been decided." Williams calls this type of implementation "implementation proper," and he points out that the issue is "how to get changes in organizational behavior—that is, what people in the organization do—to reflect what the decision envisions" (p. 3). He notes that there is also a more general aspect of implementation, the "capacity problem," the continuing effort of an organization to increase its ability to carry out future decisions (Williams 1975a). Although both types of implementation issues may be present when an organization attempts to implement a policy, we are concerned here primarily with implementation as doing what has been decided on.

The chapter begins with a discussion of the reasons policies fail. It then distinguishes between technical feasibility and political viability, identifies where implementation concerns can be addressed during the policy analysis process, and draws these issues together in a set of tips for effective implementation. The message is that implementation should be considered throughout the policy process, that implementation methods should be explicitly recognized at several steps in the policy analysis process, and that policy professionals can and should have an impact on successful policy implementation.

We Cannot Assume Policies Will Be Carried Out

Policies and programs fail primarily for two reasons. The program either is not or cannot be implemented as designed or is implemented as designed but does not have the desired effect. The first instance has been termed *program failure;* the second instance has been termed *theory failure* (Weiss 1972). Policy or program evaluation has tended to look primarily at theory failure, under the assumption that the policy was implemented as designed and that failure was due to a flaw in the design or underlying theory. However, we should examine the possibility that the policy or program failed because it could not be implemented as designed or was not implemented because of inadequate instructions, staff resistance, or error.

Administrators know that policies will not be automatically carried out as designed. Kaufman (1973) carefully documents the many places in the administrative hierarchy where orders can go astray. Edwards and Sharkansky (1978) discuss the numerous actions that top officials must take to help guarantee that policies are properly implemented, and others discuss the agonizing complexity in implementation that results from the multitude of actors involved in the many different bureaucratic and governmental layers of the process (Elmore 1975; Gramlich and Koshel 1975; Nakamura and Smallwood 1980). Zeleny (1982) discusses the fact that implemented policies may be quite different than their design, attributing the differences to the tendency to view decision making and implementation as separate processes. In the same vein, Nakamura and Smallwood make an important distinction between policymakers and policy implementers. They hold that policymakers usually do not implement policy but rely on implementers and intermediaries to carry out their policies. These authors conceptualize three policy environments, in which policy is formed, implemented, and evaluated. They place great importance on the directions and instructions that policymakers in the first environment pass on to the implementers in the second environment. This is consistent with the argument by Edwards and Sharkansky (1978, p. 295) that "the first requirement for effective implementation is that those responsible for carrying out a decision must know what they are supposed to do."

Gramlich and Koshel (1975) argue that it is difficult to implement policies because of uncertainty over whether instructions will be followed. In a study of the Office of Economic Opportunity educational performance contracting experiment, they describe "difficulties ranging from launching the experiment to problems operating the programs to problems in analyzing test scores" (p. 512).

These analysts emphasize the need to examine the many steps between policy conceptualization and policy implementation as sources of policy failure. Once there is understanding of the many points at which policy may break down, it is possible to take steps to prevent this from happening. Although it may seem obvious that policies are not self-implementing, that their implementation should be monitored and aided, the nation's policy history is littered with abandoned, broken, and failed policies. There is a long list of famous policies that failed to be implemented properly because the feasibility of implementation was not assessed beforehand, including the Clean Air Act (Jacoby and Steinbruner 1973), New Towns in Town Program (Derthick 1972), job creation under Economic Development Administration Programs (Pressman and Wildavsky 1973), Title I of the Elementary and Secondary Education Act (Stockman 1975), and CETA (Van Horn 1978). Failure to implement plans as designed is not limited to the United States but exists worldwide (Haywood 1979; United Nations 1975).

It is a huge, but not impossible, assignment to guarantee that policies are implemented as designed. Edwards and Sharkansky (1978) believe that top officials can take a number of steps to help guarantee that policies are implemented properly, including assuring that the policy is unambiguously stated, that instructions for execution are consistent and clearly communicated, that adequate numbers of trained and informed staff are available and have the authority and incentive to execute the policy, and that staff actions are reviewed.

These steps require the participation of many actors, and analysts note that the individuals involved in the process of implementation must have some commitment to the policy if it is to be implemented properly. Zeleny (1982) describes a process of building support for implementation by formulating alternatives, reassessing goals and objectives, fine tuning evaluations, making partial decisions, and involving the people who will implement the final decision in the decision-unfolding process. This process aims at gaining a consensus on a decision so that less selling has to be done when the decision is implemented. The reasoning is that there is little advantage in making fast, efficient, optional decisions that require enormous efforts to be sold and that could become obsolete, suboptimal, or wrong before they are implemented.

Zeleny's (1982) position parallels the argument that people obey laws only if they believe in them, and Bardach (1980) argues similarly that the policy analyst can take steps to design policies that have a chance to survive the implementation process. Bardach views the implementation process as a set of games in which many actors maneuver around one another to get what they want. He believes that policies can be designed to survive the game by ensuring that the basic social, economic, and political theory behind them is reasonable and sophisticated; by selecting a basic administrative strategy that relies on actual or simulated markets rather than bureaucratic processes; by identifying program elements and the organizations, groups, and individuals who might be able to provide them; by identifying supporters and opponents; by identifying facilitative and fixing mechanisms; and by determining how to phase in a new program so it draws more supporters than opponents.

Bardach (1980) and others argue that implementation analysis should be handled as art rather than as science. For example, Levin (1981) concludes from case studies that the conditions contributing to effective implementation are idiosyncratic rather than generalizable, although he finds that strong leadership, a favorable context, and private interest groups make useful contributions to effective implementation. His analysis suggests that the possibility of generating effective implementation is low because the conditions that permit it cannot often be replicated; leadership talent is scarce, effective leadership is costly, potential client groups are insufficiently organized, and policy actors and the general public are not easily convinced that a crisis exists. Levin suggests a move toward policies that are more self-administering and self-executing rather than trying to replicate these conditions. These tentative findings suggest that much more needs to be learned about factors affecting a successful policy and about interrelationships among policy analysis, political analysis, and policy evaluation.

Good Implementation Cannot Overcome Bad Policy

In the process of examining possible policy alternatives, much attention is usually given to the selection of the technically or economically feasible alternative. However, limiting the selection process in this way can result in the identification of policies that are technical successes but political failures (Greenberg, Lipson, and Rostker 1976). If an alternative is not politically viable—if it does not have the backing of politicians, government officials, and others who can effect its implementation—then there is doubt about it being the proper alternative.

Selecting the right alternative thus involves political analysis, not as an afterthought but as an integral part of the policy analysis process. In one sense, political analysis refers to the acceptability of the alternatives to participants in the political system. How will politicians, decision makers, and voters respond to the preferred alternative? However, this question cannot be answered in isolation since clients and analysts are part of the political process and can affect the outcome of policy decisions. Therefore, political analysis also involves a need to help clients discover preferences and to consider actions that might make the preferred alternative politically acceptable to other participants in the decision process. Other analysts, decision makers, politicians, voters, and elected officials may need persuasion to support a particular option.

This situation raises the question of whether alternatives should be initially selected on the basis of political viability. At the outset several alternatives may be infeasible because they demand excessive resources, violate moral or ethical values, run counter to basic laws, or violate civil liberties. Most often a wide range of alternatives should be considered and their technical feasibility and political viability estimated. It would be as much a mistake to rule out possible alternatives at the beginning of analysis as it would be to select an alternative that is doomed from the outset. No matter how hard we try, good implementation cannot overcome bad policy (Bardach 1980).

If policies are to be successfully implemented, then, they must be both technically feasible and politically viable. If an alternative that is not technically feasible is taken to the implementation stage, then even the most skillfully directed implementation will not generate the desired results—unless there is an in-process evaluation that feeds back information about how the policy is working and needed changes are made. Although good implementation cannot correct a bad policy, the effectiveness of implementation will bear on whether a technically feasible policy will be a success.

Problems must be defined, criteria for selecting alternatives must be specified, and alternatives must be selected in light of political forces and the values held by clients, the community, and relevant groups and organizations. In these early stages of the policy analysis process, the relative influence of individuals and groups may affect the way a problem is defined, the options that are identified, and the selection criteria employed. Political factors should also be considered in the comparison of alternatives. Analysts have provided checklists, outlines, and other suggestions for political analysis (Meltsner 1972; Patton and Sawicki 1986), but the analyst will develop a good feel for political issues as the policy problem is defined, as relevant evaluation criteria are identified, and as politically acceptable alternatives are sought.

We Must Think of Implementation throughout the Policy Continuum

Williams (1975b, p. 531) warns us not to view implementation as only the "brief interlude between a bright idea and opening the door for service" but to think about it as part of the overall policy process. In fact, he argues that implementation should be a major concern before a complete decision is made but that questions about difficulties of implementing various alternatives almost never arise. At what points should we consider implementation? Elaborate descriptions of several multistep policy development processes are available. Although the steps in the policy processes are typically interlinked and feed back on one another, the processes usually contain several discreet steps, including ex ante policy analysis, implementation analysis, policy maintenance, policy monitoring, and ex post program evaluation.

Several discussions among steps in the policy process are useful when we consider policy analysis with implementation in mind. These distinctions are made not because they are clearly separable steps but because they help illustrate the numerous points at which implementation problems must be kept in mind. The continuum ranges from policy analysis to policy termination.

Ex Ante Policy Analysis

Ex ante policy analysis involves the identification and clarification of policy problems, the specification of criteria used in examining the pros and cons of possible alternatives, the identification of a range of potential alternatives, the quantitative and qualitative evaluation of these alternatives to estimate the extent to which the alternatives will meet the evaluation criteria, and the comparison of the relative benefits and costs of the alternatives. Ex ante policy analysis may also include a recommendation for a preferred alternative and the identification of the steps necessary to implement the policy.

Implementation Analysis

Implementation analysis in this conceptualization is a step in the policy analysis process that involves an examination of the reasonableness of the policy and the steps necessary to implement it. This examination includes identifying the person responsible for implementation and whether staff can do what has been designed and how they should do it. Williams (1975b, p. 532) defines implementation analysis as "scrutiny of (1) the preliminary policy specifications, to determine their clarity, precision, and reasonableness; and (2) staff, organizational, and managerial capabilities, to determine the degree to which the proposed policy alternative can be specified and implemented in its bureaucratic/political setting." This process involves an analysis of technical and political problems that may be encountered during implementation, administrative strengths and weaknesses, and changes necessary to permit implementation. Williams points out that implementation analysis must be conducted before a decision is made and should be available simultaneously with policy recommendations if it is to be useful.

Policy Implementation

Policy implementation is the set of activities necessary to put the policy into effect. Such activities would include translation of the policy into a clear, unambiguous statement; preparation of program directions for participating units; recruitment and training of staff; and printing of instructions and program eligibility statements. Depending on the type of policy or program, this step also might include hundreds of technical, administrative, and political activities to put even a modest policy into effect. It also should include a review to determine whether the final design is equivalent to the one envisioned at the end of the policy analysis step, whether implementation instructions are clear, and whether policy maintenance, monitoring, and evaluation plans are in order.

Policy Maintenance

Policy maintenance includes the set of activities undertaken to ensure that the policy or program is implemented as designed. Such efforts involve watching for any changes made in the policy as it passes out of the decision maker's hands into operating or implementing agencies or bureaus and the prevention or correction of such changes. It also involves the analysis of possible changes to the policy after it has been instituted because the persons responsible for program operation misunderstood or were unable to follow instructions, made modifications to initiate the program, or made changes during the program operations to keep it running or to make it run more smoothly. The purpose of policy maintenance is not to prevent necessary changes but to prevent haphazard changes, to record purposeful changes so that they can be recognized and considered during the evaluation of the program, and to provide necessary feedback to ensure proper policy maintenance.

Policy Monitoring

Policy monitoring is the process of recording and analyzing changes in key variables that are being monitored as a result of policy or program implementation. Policy monitoring attempts to identify whether any changes took place as a result of policy implementation. Although policy monitoring sounds relatively simple and direct, it requires that key variables be identified, that ways to measure changes in those variables quickly be identified, and that this process remain free of biases from program supporters or detractors.

Ex Post Policy Evaluation

Ex post policy evaluation in the most general sense involves the analysis of whether policy objectives were achieved or the extent to which they were achieved. This requires relating the information derived during policy monitoring to program goals, objectives, and criteria and making a decision about whether the policy should be continued, modified, or terminated because of a lack of effect or because of unintended negative consequences. Policy evaluation is a complex area and is not discussed extensively here. Current issues include whether product or process or both ought to be evaluated, whether the original or modified goals should be evaluated, and whether evaluation does feed back into the decision process (see, for example, Palumbo, Fawcett, and Wright 1981).

Policy Termination

Policy or program termination may be called for as a result of program evaluation. Programs are often difficult to terminate, however, because of general resistance to termination, technical limitations to obtaining sufficient evidence to justify termination, or a variety of strategies used by agencies to survive. Until recently, very few evaluations resulted in the termination of government programs (Nakamura and Smallwood 1980). Key criteria for program termination include financial constraints, program inefficiency, and political ideology, with political ideology playing an increasingly strong role (de Leon 1983).

Tips for Effective Implementation

The literature, case examples, and experience suggest several requirements for effective implementation. Implementation must be considered at all steps in the policy process; policies must be both technically feasible and politically viable; policies must be clearly defined; the steps to implement them must be specifically spelled out along with the responsibilities of various actors; and the policy analyst can play a role in increasing the chances for policy implementation.

Mazmanian and Sabatier (1981) reviewed the literature on implementation and concluded that a set of minimum crucial conditions is necessary to implement successfully a policy decision that is a substantial departure from the status quo. Their conditions include:

Enabling legislation or other legal directives that mandate clear and consistent policy directives,

Sound theory that links policy objectives to target group behavior,

An implementation process structured to maximize the probability that implementing officials and target groups will comply with directives,

Agency commitment to goals and confidence in staff managerial and political skills,

Active support by constituency groups and key legislators, and

No new policies or changing socioeconomic conditions to undermine the policy.

Sabatier and Mazmanian (1979) explain that although these conditions may not always be achieved, several steps might be taken to increase the probability of success, including incorporating the development of a valid technical theory into a learning process when such a theory is not available, initiating legislation to clarify ambiguous policy directives, providing for outside intervention when implementing agencies are not supportive, mobilizing support from existing organizations when the policy has no active interest group, and convincing a legislator to support and closely monitor the implementation process when one is not already so disposed.

Systematic approaches to analyzing implementation feasibility are under development. However, Hatry et al. (1976) provide a checklist of factors to consider in assessing the implementation feasibility of alternatives, including the number of agencies involved; threats to officials, jobs, and groups; changes in behavior of government employees; availability of funds; presence of legal issues; and level of public support. Nakamura and Smallwood (1980) provide another checklist that includes questions about the political climate (key actors and their beliefs and resources), the resource base (leverage or inducements to actors), mobilization potential (sources of opposition, support, and compromise), and assessment indicators (criteria for measuring success).

What are some suggestions and tips for successful policy implementation? The risks in providing such a list are that it will be incomplete and that there is no assurance that the tips will result in succesful implementation. There appears to be substantial agreement among analysts, however, that these tips are among the most important.

Identify Real Problems

Analysts have discussed the need for clearly stating the policy option and the objective being sought. Bullock (1981) considers this the most important implementation variable. It is crucial to identify the problem that the policy is designed to address to reduce ambiguity in the implementation analysis process. Skillful implementation cannot overcome bad policy, and policy resulting from improper problem definition will be good only by accident.

Devise Real Alternatives that Can Be Implemented

Can the policy be implemented? Does the implementing agency have trained staff, capable administrators, committed field staff, and the technical capacity to do what is asked? A number of programs have been placed into operation without a clear understanding of how they could be implemented or whether what would be established in the field would correspond to the design. The follow-through planned variation experiment and the performance-contracting experiment are two examples in the area of education (Williams 1975a).

Implementation typically relies on local officials and local conditions over which program designers have little control, and the programs often tax the technical and administrative capabilities of program personnel. The follow-through planned variation education experiment involved nearly 175 local school districts, about 75,000 children, and more than 20 treatments (Elmore 1975). Our experience with a large-scale centralized information and referral system illustrated clearly that policies and programs may be designed that have little chance of success, no matter how hard staffers try, because they are too complex and demanding, involving many actors at many levels of government (Brooks, Patton, and Taber 1973).

The need to specify details of policy alternatives presents a dilemma. A good, convincing policy analysis need not include a great amount of detail. The first goal of the analyst is to get the client's or director's attention with a good idea. Great detail can obscure good ideas, so there is a tendency for analysts to leave detail for later. This can be a good working strategy, but it can also backfire when a policy is adopted for which the details of how it can be implemented cannot be worked out. Real alternatives that respond to specific objectives must be identified early in the analysis, however. Some idea of the technical, financial, and fiscal requirements, as well as expected outcomes, must be specified early in implementation analysis, even though these specifications may be modified during the analysis. The absence of concreteness in either objectives or the delivery system is a warning of trouble (Williams 1975b).

Seek Clear, Simple Solutions

A number of authors have argued that what is needed in policy analysis is not new, powerful techniques but more attention to the available data and the ability to put together conflicting information from various sources in a way that makes sense and can be done quickly. Williams (1975b) has made the point that in both policy and implementation analysis the critical requirement is for reasonable people to ask sensible questions.

It is unrealistic to expect to implement successfully a program that depends on major changes such as a redistribution of power or a restructuring of the social system, as was the case in numerous educational experiments including Head Start and Follow Through (Elmore 1975). Success is more likely to obtain when small changes are sought and when those changes are sought in a target group that is a small percentage of the total population (Mazmanian and Sabatier 1981). We should target not only small problems but also should look for the simplest solution to any problem. Solutions should be simple in the sense that behavior modification is minimized not in the sense that they are simpleminded. Sound theory must link the proposed policy to the behavioral change that is sought.

Students of policy implementation failures have found that good policy implementation also requires simple, unambiguous instructions. Although there is no conclusive evidence that policies will be implemented correctly only if program operation details are spelled out clearly, studies suggest that there is little hope for successful implementation without these details. Weikert and Barnet (1975) argue that it is difficult to train professionals to implement a model, even in their areas of expertise, without specific instructions and details.

Incorporate Political Factors into Analysis

Effective implementation requires that political factors be incorporated into all phases of the policy process. It is not sufficient for the implementing agency to examine only existing political problems and devise alternatives that recognize these problems. It should also establish plans to deal with political problems that arise during implementation, including winning the support of politicians and officials who can help keep the policy on track, prevent modification to legislation, or pressure participating agencies to maintain their effort.

Observers have argued that implementation is, above all, a bureaucratic and political problem and that results improve if political and bureaucratic factors operate in favor of rather than against policies (Williams 1975b). Behn (1981) asserts that the complete policy analyst not only will recommend the best policy alternative but also devise the best political strategy for implementing that option. Berman (1978) similarly argues that social programs should be modified to respond to the nuances of local political systems to have a chance of implementation. Nakamura and Smallwood (1980) point out that the strength of a policymaking coalition determines whether policies get implemented, but the minor political issues, such as jurisdictional disputes among lower-level bureaucrats, often stand in the way of implementation.

Meltsner (1972) suggests that political problems should be analyzed in terms of the actors involved, their beliefs and motivations, the resources they hold, their effectiveness in using these resources, and the sites at which decisions will be made. During the problem definition stage this information might be compiled in checklists so that relevant central actors and decision sites are considered; as decision trees so that the interrelation of actors, decision sites, and sequence of events is revealed; and as scorecards or impact tables so that the relative importance of issues to actors, and the preferences of actors for various alternatives, can be specified. A scorecard prepared during the problem definition stage can be expanded during later stages to reveal possible political problems, potential supporters and opponents, areas of compromise, new alternatives to consider, existing alternatives that might be modified to gain supporters, and steps to enhance opportunities for implementation.

Test Policies through Demonstrations and Experiments

Full-scale controlled experiments have revealed useful policy information and helped decide whether to continue or expand a program. Demonstration projects, in contrast, have been criticized because they have often been felt to be political compromises that did not really test the policy or provide useful policy information. However, the rapid pace of policy development often makes a true experiment impossible, and a demonstration project may be useful because the administrative bugs can be worked out on a small scale before a large program is begun (Williams 1975b). This approach, unlike an experiment that is intended to test various alternatives, is limited to learning whether the program can be administered, whether it is politically viable, and whether changes need to be made to facilitate implementation. This is not to suggest that experiments should not be undertaken, because they can provide useful information for designing policies in the future, but to suggest that once a policy is selected for implementation, a small-scale demonstration can help fine tune the policy and increase the chance for successful implementation.

Incorporate Policy Maintenance and Policy Monitoring Efforts

Experts involved in efforts to implement policy point out the many details that must be addressed, but the task is so complex that they also advise others to assume that various tasks will not be carried out as planned and that feedback procedures should be built into the implementation process (Gramlich and Koshel 1975). Consequently, the prospects for successful policy implementation can be enhanced by incorporating policy maintenance and monitoring activities into the policy development process. The basic need is to keep policies on track so they have a reasonable chance to be tested.

As part of the policy design, therefore, we should specify the steps to monitor the policy once placed into effect and the individuals responsible for collecting in-process data, the types of data to be collected, the analyses to be conducted with these data, the persons responsible for taking policy maintenance actions, and the possible actions to be taken. Policy monitoring and maintenance activities add to the cost of policies and are likely to be overlooked or eliminated during analysis. Yet to ensure that policies are properly implemented, these steps should be explicitly recognized and delegated as part of the policy development process.

Lead, Follow, or Get out of the Way

Someone has to take charge of implementation. "Almost everyone assumes that specification and implementation are somebody else's task. Higher-ups see implementation as being a lower-level responsibility; but the lower-levels look to higher echelons for specification and guidance" (Williams 1975a, p. 549). Steiss and Daneke (1980, p. 194) point out that it is a mistake to regard the implementation of policies as purely a management function beyond the purview of the policy analyst. They believe that too often policymakers assume that if someone can design it, someone can implement and manage it and that too often public policies are adopted with little knowledge of what will be necessary to implement them. They argue that implementation feasibility should be assessed before policies are selected. They suggest that each alternative should be analyzed in terms of the degree of consensus among the individuals or groups involved in or affected by the program and the magnitude of change the alternative represents. Steiss and Daneke provide the guideline that programs having high consensus/low change present few problems in implementation; whereas those with low consensus/high change or low consensus/low change may require further assessment of implementation feasibility. Degree of consensus, they suggest, can be based on an evaluation of the attitudes of the actors, including the target group, political leaders, administrators and bureaucrats, community and interest groups, and other interested parties such as evaluators and analysts.

Rosenbaum (1981) writes about the importance of considering both the amount of change sought and the extent to which individuals or groups support the policy. He believes that a well-crafted statute is a necessary condition to successful implementation, that the policy should be clearly specified so the change required is unambiguous, and that the policy should be enforceable. Major changes will require strong enforcement measures, including both bureaucratic cooperation and private compliance. Implementing agencies can be encouraged to comply by restricting their discretion through review and oversight and through rewards and penalties. Private compliance is more likely to be brought about by penalties and sanctions, although tax breaks have been used as an incentive (Rosenbaum 1981).

The importance of legislators and policy formulators in effective implementation has been shown by numerous studies. These actors can help ensure that statutes incorporate elements that facilitate acceptance of the policy, that skilled personnel are available to implement the policy, and that adequate funding is available to support implementation maintenance (Sabatier and Mazmanian 1979).

Management must want implementation (Williams 1975a), and leadership must be present (Levin 1981; Nakamura and Smallwood 1980). Policy professionals also have an important role to play. They can respond positively to policy initiatives by either taking the lead in implementation, or they can support the actions of others. The effective policy analyst will take steps to ensure that the recommended policy is implemented by developing a political strategy. Behn (1981) argues that an analyst has an obligation to maximize the chances for adoption if honest analysis revealead one or more preferable alternatives. Although some analysts eschew the advocacy approach and do not take a direct role in policy implementation, the greater obstacle may be that analysts too often get caught up in day-to-day activities, data collection, report writing, and other activities and unintentionally block effective implementation.

Conclusion

Although much has been written about the individual components of the policy implementation process, little work has been undertaken to put these parts together in a way that permits generalization about the policymaking process (Mazmanian and Sabatier 1981). This chapter is an effort to collect some of what we have learned about the implementation of policies in the framework of the policy analysis process, to identify the basic reasons why policies fail, and to indicate the many places in the policy development process where implementation must be explicitly considered if policies are to achieve their goals. Ideas about how to implement policies effectively are presented as a set of tips for analysts.

Chances for successful implementation can be improved if we identify real problems, devise alternatives that can be implemented, and seek clear solutions. We should incorporate political factors into analysis, test policies through demonstrations and experiments, and incorporate policy maintenance and monitoring into the process. We also should take an active role in enhancing the political prospects for implementation.

Above all, effective implementation requires attention to technical and political issues. Beginning with problem definition, the analyst should determine both the technical and political goals and objectives of the client, determine whether the issue is a technical or political problem or both, and uncover the nature of any political analysis being conducted. For example, the analyst should determine whether the political analysis is intended to cause the public to recognize the problem, to have the client accept the analysis, or to garner votes from constituents. The analyst can play an active role throughout the analysis. This assumes that the client seeks political advice from the analyst, but sometimes the client may be highly skilled in politics and will perform the political analysis. Even in these cases, the analyst or planner should collect and display political factors along with the technical and economic issues that bear on the alternatives.

In practice, implementation analysis is a continuing process. Things change; anticipated consequences may not occur; unanticipated ones may arise; and predictions of policy consequences are often wrong (Edwards and Sharkansky 1978). The policy analyst who engages in implementation analysis should be prepared to modify alternatives, to reconsider attitudes about favored options, and to recognize that even if favored alternatives are accepted, their implementation will depend on numerous actors in the policy process over whom the analyst has little control. The appropriate response is to consider policy implementation issues throughout the entire policy continuum and to devise politically astute implementation strategies.

References

Bardach, Eugene. 1980. On Designing Implementable Programs. In *Pitfalls of Analysis,* Giandomenico Majone and Edward S. Quade, eds. Chichester: John Wiley & Sons.

Behn, Robert D. 1981. Policy Analysis and Policy Politics. *Policy Analysis* 7:199–226.

Berman, Paul. 1978. The Study of Macro- and Micro-Implementation. *Public Policy* 26:172–79.

Brooks, Michael P.; Carl V. Patton; and Merlin A. Taber. 1978. *An Evaluation of the Service Access System Element of the Illinois Institute for Social Policy's Tri-County Project.* Urbana: Bureau of Urban and Regional Planning Research, University of Illinois.

Bullock, Charles S. 1981. Implementation of Equal Education Opportunity Programs: A Comparative Analysis. In *Effective Policy Implementation,* Daniel A. Mazmanian and Paul A. Sabatier, eds. Lexington, Mass.: D.C. Heath and Company, Lexington Books.

de Leon, Peter. 1983. Policy Evaluation and Program Termination. *Policy Studies Review* 2:631–47.

Derthick, Martha. 1972. *New Towns in Town: Why a Federal Program Failed.* Washington, D.C.: The Urban Institute.

Edwards, George C., and Ira Sharkansky. 1978. *The Policy Predicament: Making and Implementing Public Policy.* San Francisco: W.H. Freeman.

Elmore, Richard F. 1975. Lessons From Follow Through. *Policy Analysis* 1:459–84.

Gramlich, Edward M., and Patricia Koshel. 1975. Is Real-World Experimentation Possible? The Case of Educational Performance Contracting. *Policy Analysis* 1:511–30.

Greenberg, David; Al Lipson; and Bernard Rostker. 1976. Technical Success, Political Failure: The Incentive Pay Plan for California Job Agents. *Policy Analysis* 2:545–75.

Hargrove, Erwin C. 1975. *The Missing Link: The Study of the Implementation of Social Policy.* Washington, D.C.: The Urban Institute.

Hatry, Harry; Louis Blair; Donald Fisk; and Wayne Kimmel. 1976. *Program Analysis for State and Local Governments.* Washington, D.C.: The Urban Institute.

Haywood, Ian, ed. 1979. *Implementation of Urban Plans.* Paris: Organization for Economic Co-operation and Development.

Jacoby, Henry, and John Steinbruner. 1973. *Clearing the Air.* Cambridge, Mass.: Ballinger.

Kaufman, Herbert. 1973. *Administrative Feedback: Monitoring Subordinates' Behavior.* Washington, D.C.: The Brookings Institution.

Levin, Martin A. 1981. Conditions Contributing to Effective Implementation and Their Limits. In *Research in Public Policy Analysis and Management: Basic Theory, Methods and Perspectives,* John P. Crecine, ed. Greenwich, Conn.: JAI Press.

Mazmanian, Daniel A., and Paul Sabatier, eds. 1981. *Effective Policy Implementation.* Lexington, Mass.: D.C. Heath and Company, Lexington Books.

Meltsner, Arnorld J. 1972. Political Feasibility and Policy Analysis. *Public Administration Review* 32:859–75.

Nakamura, Robert T., and Frank Smallwood. 1980. *The Politics of Policy Implementation.* New York: St. Martin's Press.

Palumbo, Dennis J.; Stephen B. Fawcett; and Paula Wright. 1981. *Evaluating and Optimizing Public Policy.* Lexington, Mass.: D.C. Heath and Company, Lexington Books.

Patton, Carl V., and David S. Sawicki. 1986. *Basic Methods of Policy Analysis and Planning.* Englewood Cliffs, N.J.: Prentice-Hall.

Pressman, Jeffrey L., and Aaron B. Wildavsky. 1973. *Implementation.* Berkeley: University of California Press.

Rosenbaum, Nelson. 1981. Statutory Structure and Policy Implementation: The Case of Wetlands Regulation. In *Effective Policy Implementation,* Daniel A. Mazmanian and Paul A. Sabatier, eds. Lexington, Mass.: D.C. Heath and Company, Lexington Books.

Sabatier, Paul, and Daniel Mazmanian. 1979. The Conditions of Effective Implementation: A Guide to Accomplishing Policy Objectives. *Policy Analysis* 5:481–504.

Steiss, Alan Walter, and George A. Daneke. 1980. *Performance Administration.* Lexington, Mass.: D.C. Heath and Company.

Stockman, David A. 1975. The Social Pork Barrel. *The Public Interest* 39:3–30.

United Nations. 1975. *Urban Land Policies and Land-Use Control Measures. Volume VII. Global Review.* New York: United Nations Department of Economic and Social Affairs.

Van Horn, Carl. 1978. Implementing CETA: The Federal Role. *Policy Analysis* 4:159–83.

Weikart, David P., and Bernard A. Barnet. 1975. Planned Variation from the Perspective of a Model Sponsor. *Policy Analysis* 1:485–510.

Weiss, Carol H. 1972. *Evaluation Research*. Englewood Cliffs, N.J.: Prentice-Hall.
Williams, Walter. 1975a. Editor's Comments. *Policy Analysis* 2:451–58.
———. 1975b. Implementation Analysis and Assessment. *Policy Analysis* 2:531–66.
———. 1980. *The Implementation Perspective*. Berkeley: University of California Press.
Zeleny, Milan. 1982. *Multiple Criteria Decision Making*. New York: McGraw-Hill.

8

Participatory Research and Community Planning

L. David Brown

ommunity planning is often conceived as a comprehensive rational analysis of issues and alternatives that integrates interests to provide a blueprint for future community action. For some purposes, this picture of planning is quite appropriate, but for others, the blueprint conception of community planning is inappropriate or problematic (Friedmann 1981; Korten 1980). Two problems particularly affect this approach to planning: (1) the limited applicability of comprehensive rational analysis and (2) the restrictions on information and influence caused by concentrations of community wealth and power.

This chapter focuses on the implications of participatory research for solving these problems. It considers the problems of comprehensive community planning, describes participatory research with examples from practice, and relates participatory research to community planning as a process and to community planners as actors. It finally raises dilemmas implicit in community planning that are often made explicit by participatory research.

Problems of Planning

Many planners aspire to a comprehensive rational community planning process. This approach ideally combines analysis of community problems, participation by relevant parties in problem definitions and solutions, and systematic analysis of alternative solutions and consequences to produce plans whose logic compels widespread support for implementation.

However, the practice of community planning often deviates from this ideal. Analysis may be limited by lack of relevant information and knowledge. Participation may be restricted to a few relevant parties whose interests carry disproportionate weight in decision processes. The search for alternative solutions may be limited to a few incrementally different alternatives because of shortcomings of vision or political constraints. Decisions may be based on incomplete understanding of consequences or ignorance of potential outcomes. Such deviations from the ideal are not universal, but they are especially common when the decisions to be taken are nonroutine, involve high stakes, and generate considerable controversy.

One cause of problems is the application of comprehensive rational planning models to inappropriate situations. Investigators of public decision making suggest that planning is often incremental rather than comprehensive, short term and iterative rather than long term and systematic, and adopted by bargaining among parties with conflicting interests rather than by consensus on expert solutions (Lindblom 1959, 1979). Even in private corporations— ostensibly more able than communities to plan effectively—strategic decisions tend to be made incrementally when information is not available or when agreement about ends and means is lacking (Mintzberg 1978; Quinn 1980). Comprehensive planning may be feasible for routine allocation decisions, but strategies that allow incremental adjustment to new information or that enable participation by diverse stakeholders are more appropriate for novel challenges or conflicts of interests (Freeman 1984).

Several processes can produce planning decisions. Thompson (1974; Thompson and Tuden 1959) argues that the appropriateness of decision processes varies with agreement among participants on cause-effect relations (means) and desired outcomes (goals). When parties agree about both means and ends, rational computation to choose among alternatives is the appropriate decision process. When parties agree about ends but not causes and effects, majority judgment based on discussion and persuasion among experts with equal collegial influence should bring the most resources to bear on choosing the best means for attaining shared goals. When parties agree about causes and effects but disagree about desirable outcomes, bargaining among representatives of interest groups allows consideration and balancing of diverse interests. Finally, when parties disagree about both means and ends, decisions may result from inspiration in which parties trust a leader or a decision process in spite of their differences.

This argument suggests that comprehensive rational planning is appropriate when information is available and when affected parties agree on means and ends. But when parties disagree, comprehensive analysis and computational decisions are less appropriate. When more information about cause and effect is needed, planning processes that generate new information and promote collegial judgment by experts may be desirable. When affected parties have conflicting interests or disagree about goals, planning procedures that enable constructive bargaining among representatives of diverse groups may be required. When agreement is lacking about both means and ends, effective planning may require a generally accepted—even charismatic— leader, a common objective that is shared by all parties, or a decision process that has widespread legitimacy in spite of uncertainties about ends and means. Choosing planning processes to fit the community situation can reduce discrepancies between aspirations and performance.

Another cause of problems for community planning lies in community power distributions. Planning by judgment, bargaining, or inspiration each requires interaction among various parties to generate information, test alternatives, and negotiate support for implementation. Pluralistic give-and-take is a central feature of planning processes that respond to elements of a complex community. But concentrations of community wealth and power can systematically distort or exclude contributions from some parties with legitimate interests in planning outcomes. Low-power groups may be unaware of the planning process, unable to communicate their concerns in terms that are meaningful to planners, or incapable of influencing decisions. Even when planners actively seek information and ideas from all parties, some parties may have more or less influence than others.

Lukes (1974) argues that three different dimensions of power differences shape community decision making. At one level, decisions are openly contested in public arenas, and choices are made on the basis of the resource control of different parties. This pattern is the well-known pluralistic decision making, beloved of democratic theorists and incremental planners. Dahl's (1961) classic study of New Haven is an example of community decision making in which many different groups exerted influence on public policy formulation. Planning decisions in this model depended on the balance of power that emerged from contests among supporters of alternative solutions.

At another level, some groups are aware of their interests in decisions but lack the power to move issues to explicit consideration. Decisions are made by agenda control, and some issues never gain status as topics for debate. For example, Crenson's (1971) study of the "unpolitics of air pollution" illustrates how pollution from steel making appeared on the community agenda in Gary, Indiana, a one-company town, thirteen years after its equally polluted but multicompany neighbor, East Chicago, cleaned up its air. Planning decisions in this model were determined by the mobilization of bias and other uses of power that shape the public agenda.

At still another level, groups adopt the ideologies and explanations of those with more power, do not recognize their own interests in decisions, and accept as legitimate plans that directly contradict their interests. Thus, decisions (and nondecisions) may be shaped by awareness control, intentionally or unintentionally used by powerful groups to exploit the less powerful. Gaventa (1980) shows how powerful corporations, mine owners, and union officials controlled the awareness and activities of Appalachian miners and local residents for decades. Power differences thus shape consciousness as well as public agendas and outcomes of decisions. The more wealth and power are concentrated in a community, the more likely it is that some groups will have difficulty recognizing their interests or making their voices heard.

Even when interactive and incremental processes are used to develop community plans, some groups may participate less than others. Good intentions are not enough to create genuinely interactive and pluralistic planning processes. Even when planners actively seek involvement, social forces may limit the scope and quality of information from all groups affected by decisions.

This chapter focuses on participatory research as a strategy for enlisting less wealthy and less powerful participants in planning. Such a strategy can help develop better information, wider support, and innovative energy for community planning in an uncertain and multivalued world.

Participatory Research in Communities

The participatory research tradition has emerged from work with oppressed peoples in developing areas. For example, Freire (1970, 1974) has developed widely influential concepts for adult education and "conscientization" of the urban and rural poor in Latin America by engaging adults in critical analyses of the causes of their powerlessness and impoverishment. Similar approaches have been developed in projects in Africa and Asia (Hall 1981), although problems of communication and contact among investigators have delayed recognition of common concepts and methods.

Participatory research brings outside researchers and local participants together in a process of inquiry, education, and action on problems of mutual interest. Ideally, all parties become learners; they share control over the research process; they commit themselves to constructive action rather than detachment; and their participation promotes empowerment as well as understanding (Hall 1981). Outside researchers who undertake participatory research projects join with local participants to define problems, design data collection methods, analyze results, and utilize research outcomes. Outsiders and locals together learn about the forces operating to create local problems, organize to take collective action, and examine alternative strategies for improving the situation. In this way, people become aware of common interests and mobilize other actors in planning processes and decisions that affect the local community.

Participatory researchers sometimes sacrifice rigorous control for pragmatic utility (Susman and Evered 1978). They are committed to constructive change and work with people (for example, oppressed groups) on issues (conflicts with powerholders) according to values and ideologies (empowerment, equality, self-reliance) that may place them in opposition to current distributions of power and resources in society (Brown and Tandon 1983). Participatory research can help participants generate information that would not otherwise be available for community planning. It can help participants clarify their perspectives and interests, analyze the forces that oppress and befuddle them, and organize themselves to change the situation.

Mobilizing the Powerless: Organization-Building in India

Participatory research can increase the awareness and capacity of less power-ful groups to participate in community planning. The following example illustrates the impact of a participatory research project on small farmers in rural India and indicates how outside researchers can act as catalysts for new energy and activism in previously quiescent groups (see Tandon 1981; Tandon and Brown 1981).

Outside researchers from a private rural development agency began participatory research workshops with small farmers in rural Indian villages by posing questions (Why are you poor?) rather than providing answers. Responses were initially sparse—five minutes of silence followed the first question in the initial workshop—because participants were inexperienced with such dialogues and awed by the high status of the outsiders. The re-searchers were uncomfortable for different reasons. Outsiders and farmers lived together on equal terms during the workshop, and researchers felt dis-oriented by the lack of familiar facilities such as toilets and running water as well as by the initial passivity of workshop participants. Initial conversations left both parties with questions about the utility of the workshop.

Previous workshops with these farmers provided information for improving crop yields and quality but produced relatively little change and no new initiatives. The participatory research differed from previous workshops in several ways: dialogue encouraged participants to take initiatives in anal-ysis, discussions clarified agreements and common concerns among partic-ipants, and problem-solving exercises required participants to work collec-tively so they learned by experience about skills required for joint action. Villagers and outsiders together developed better understandings of village problems and discussed strategies for dealing with issues of high priority to them.

Outcomes of workshops were assessed in follow-up visits to villages and in systematic analysis of journals kept by group leaders. Initiatives to solve local problems by participating groups increased dramatically in comparison to past performance and to groups from other villages. Groups started local schools, increased school enrollments, and elected new representatives to local governments. Other villagers observed the success of participant groups and began to emulate them. The agency decided to train the rest of its staff in participatory research skills so the impacts of the project could be extended to other villages.

This project dramatically changed participant perceptions of community problems and expanded their capacity to act on those views. A short partic-ipatory research workshop with outsiders produced new farmer organiza-tions, increased levels of community-based initiative, and elicited positive responses from other villages and government agencies. The participatory research project created an aware and active constituency, enhanced community understanding of issues, and developed skill and energy for planning and implementation.

Generating New Awareness: Land Ownership in Appalachia

Participatory research can lay the foundation for community cooperation or conflict by identifying issues and raising awareness of problems among local groups or between local and external interests. An example of citizen group research on landholdings in Appalachia is instructive in this regard (Gaventa and Horton 1981).

Representatives of a coalition of citizen groups joined with the staff of a research and education center in a task force to propose a participatory research project on regional land ownership patterns in six states of Appalachia. The Appalachian Regional Commission was reluctant to support the project, preferring inquiry about land use to analysis of landownership, but eventually gave its support after the task force threatened a public confrontation.

Task force members held workshops in which researchers and citizens designed the research, prepared to collect data, and considered land reform strategies. They collected survey data on landownership in eighty counties and developed case studies of nineteen counties in six states. They wrote state and regional reports and worked with local groups to use the data to influence local and regional decision making. The analysis confirmed local expectations that landownership was highly concentrated. Absentee owners and outside corporations held most of the land and mineral resources, and their holdings were greatly underassessed for tax purposes in comparison to their value.

These results confirmed in overwhelming detail local perceptions that had long been denied by regional policymakers. The regional commission refused to issue task force case studies ("unscientific") and overviews ("too subjective") and delayed disseminating their other reports, so task force members independently disseminated their findings to news media and citizen groups. They shared skills in data collection and analysis with other citizen groups in areas with unanalyzed ownership patterns and developed networks of contacts across the region to link future action projects with each other.

This project produced knowledge about regional patterns of landownership that was previously available only at great costs. It succeeded in organizing citizen participants for coordinated inquiry into forces affecting their daily lives.

The project also demonstrated the potential political consequences of participatory research. Initial disputes over whether the project should focus on land use or landownership reflected concern with distributions of power and ultimate control over the land. The task force wanted to examine ownership control, while the commission preferred the less controversial focus on land use. The initial definition of the research problem shaped much of the subsequent inquiry process. The focus on fundamental distributions of power and control raised questions about the ways in which different stakeholders contributed (or failed to contribute) to local communities and so clarified the conflicts of interest between citizens and absentee owners. The project highlighted not only the potential for gaining new information from participatory research but also the political implications such information may hold for interested parties. Since the history of the area was one of political quiescence and lack of awareness (Gaventa 1980), it was understandable that those who benefitted from the status quo regarded the project with considerable suspicion.

Organizing Multiconstituency Decisions: Lending in Urban Heights

It is important that groups present perspectives and participate in planning decisions. But when groups have very different interests, like in the Appalachian project, planning may require special efforts to articulate different perspectives and to develop procedures that enable agreement. The struggles of citizen groups, municipal officials, and business interests over housing policies in a suburban city illustrate both problems and possibilities of participatory community planning by multiple conflicting interests (Gricar and Brown 1981).

Citizen groups in Urban Heights, an upper-middle-class residential community undergoing racial change, became concerned about possible financial disinvestment in the community by local lending institutions. There were indications that lenders were restricting home mortgage lending, called redlining, because of the city's age, racial composition, and proximity to deteriorated neighborhoods in other cities. Citizen groups, with advice from local social scientists, analyzed data on mortgages in the community over previous years and found evidence that some lending institutions were disinvesting from the community.

Citizen group representatives presented their analyses to lending institutions. The lenders denied disinvesting, and the citizen groups considered launching a public campaign in response. The city manager convened a Committee on Residential Lending, which was composed of citizens, lenders, realtors, city administrators, and elected municipal officials, and charged it with promoting reinvestment in the city.

Initial committee meetings produced little agreement on either committee goals or explanations for generally recognized problems. The city manager chaired meetings, set agendas, invited presentations, facilitated discussion of important topics, and sought to prevent escalation of conflict. Committee members gradually came to appreciate the complexity of issues and established subcommittees to deal with important issues in more depth. Subcommittee members developed rapport with each other, and their discussion gradually moved from analysis of causes of disinvestment to strategies for its prevention. They developed rapport in spite of initial antagonism as discussion revealed the complexities of problems they initially had viewed in simple and judgmental terms.

Subcommittees presented their analyses of underlying causes and possible action strategies to the committee as a whole. Over several years the committee influenced the city council and federal agencies to adopt policies favorable to local reinvestment. The committee conceived programs for commercial development and for rehabilitating mortgage foreclosed houses and began to branch out into other housing problems.

The initial participatory research project in Urban Heights involved citizens concerned about financial disinvestment in the city. Their analysis of patterns of mortgage lending at least partly confirmed their initial suspicions and gave them credibility among both city officials and business interests in the community. Many people initially viewed the committee as a fragile vehicle, created by the city manager and likely to fail if excessive conflict developed and disrupted discussions. The committee managed to avoid the Scylla of boredom by dealing with serious issues. It evaded the Charybdis of excessive conflict through the management skills of the city manager, the structural arrangement of subcommittees, the commitment of members to the city, and the discovery of common values and shared explanations for problems. In the course of its deliberations, the committee evolved from a collection of diverse representatives that focused on conflicting interests to a cohesive group of advocates of policies to promote urban revitalization.

In the later stages of the committee's evolution, participatory research projects were undertaken jointly by former antagonists, now linked in a common appreciation of the complexity of the problems they sought to solve. From a community planning point of view, the committee became a source of information and ideas about city development, a linkage to outside agencies like the Federal Housing Authority and the Veteran's Administration, and a sophisticated actor on the local government scene.

Implications for Planning

These cases were selected to represent the use of participatory research in diverse cultural and economic settings, on different questions, and at different stages of community planning and change. This section considers some of the implications of these experiences for community planning and community planners.

Participatory Research and Community Planning

Planning models that focus primarily on technical and analytic tasks such as problem definition, analysis and diagnosis, generation and selection of alternatives, and implementation design, monitoring, and outcomes may overlook factors that are crucial to planning and implementation. There are genuine problems in the technical aspects of community planning, of course, and plans that are technically poor are less likely to produce the desired outcomes. But the participatory research projects sketched in the preceding section suggest at least two community planning elements that critically affect outcomes: (1) forming preplanning activities that enable previously unheard groups and individuals to participate in analyzing problems and inventing solutions and (2) organizing and managing the interface among participants to make constructive use of diverse perspectives.

Participatory research projects emphasize the crucial impact of activities that define and prepare previously unheard stakeholders for community planning. Small farmers in India, citizen groups in Appalachia, and residents in Urban Heights all ordinarily had little voice in planning for their respective communities. Participatory research with these groups created the awareness, skill, and organization necessary for them to join and influence the process.

In the Indian case, rural village groups identified problems and possible solutions, essentially creating a community planning and implementation process where no local planning capacity had existed before. This case emphasizes the kinds of information, energy, and resources for community planning that may be mobilized as participants become aware and organized to improve their communities. Previously unorganized local farmers learned to act collectively and so became major forces for change in their villages and eventually in the region.

The recognition of financial disinvestment as a problem in Urban Heights was a direct result of citizen investigations of lending practices. The citizen challenge to lending institutions encouraged the city manager to convene the committee. Committee members would not have invested the time and energy required to develop common goals and strategies without the initial citizen concern.

Thus, participatory research projects can mobilize participants to provide diverse perspectives, shape definitions of problems, contribute previously unavailable information, and offer new alternative solutions. Participatory research projects potentially enrich the information and resource base of community planning.

This enriched base of information and energy has costs, however. New participants with diverse interests can make community planning decisions more difficult. An important issue in planning supplemented by participatory research is the need to manage conflicts among parties that have different perspectives and interests. When parties disagree in the planning process, judgment, bargaining, or inspiration can replace rational computation of generally accepted solutions as the dynamic of decision.

When Indian village groups developed coalitions of several villages to elect their candidates to local government bodies, they quickly drew hostile attention from supporters of incumbents. As village organizations acted to influence government agencies and village elites, they took on still other opponents. Initiatives by newly organized parties automatically set the stage for new negotiations, conflicts, and potential tensions with previous power-holders.

Problems with other agencies were highly visible in the Appalachian case. The task force and the regional committee clashed over research questions, funding, and dissemination of findings. Discussions among local citizens and absentee landlords involved still more conflict. Mutually acceptable plans for such diverse parties require carefully designed and managed decision making, and it is too easy for discussions to end in deadlocks or imposed solutions (Brown 1983).

Participants in the Urban Heights Committee on Residential Lending began discussions with widely divergent perspectives and interests. As a result of extensive discussion, carefully managed by the city manager, they developed common objectives, shared understandings of complex problems, a climate of mutual respect, and organizational arrangements that enabled cooperation despite initial differences.

The capacity of community planning to handle differences in perspective or conflicts of interest constructively depends in part on the organization developed in early interactions. Struggles over perspectives and interests in early phases can lay a groundwork of appreciation and respect (or antagonism and distrust) that enable (or disable) subsequent evolution of common understandings, shared solutions, and implementation agreements.

Experience with participatory research suggests that community planning should be conceptualized as a multiphase process like that diagrammed in figure 8–1. The initial phase involves work with groups that have important stakes in or contributions to make to decisions. These groups can identify problems, analyze underlying causes, consider alternative solutions, and formulate plans to influence decisions. The circular arrangement of the steps represents an iterative process of participant analysis. Participatory research can increase group awareness of problems and opportunities, expand their perceptions of alternatives, and empower previously unheard participants to join the planning process.

Participatory research can increase the number and diversity of groups

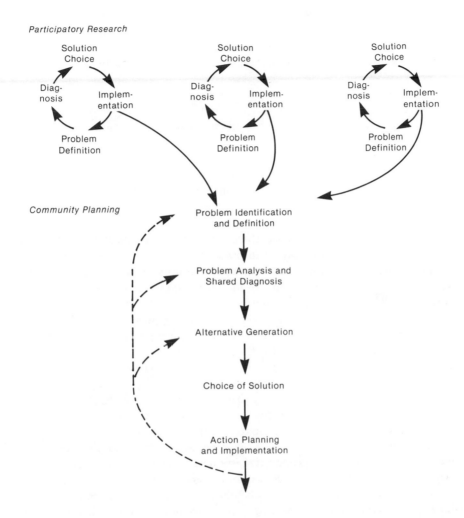

Figure 8–1. Two Phases of Community Planning

participating in community planning and thus make conflict more likely. The second phase of figure 8–1 requires managing diversity at each step. Diverse problem definitions must be integrated into a shared definition that enables focused analysis. Action plans must be chosen from a variety of alternatives. Implementation requires agreement on concrete and specific steps. New information and alternatives generated by implementation may call for further planning.

Participatory research can mobilize new participants early in community planning, and so enrich planning information, energy, and alternatives. But these diverse contributions must be constructively handled if they are to benefit rather than disrupt later stages of the planning process.

Participatory Research and Community Planners

Community planning often requires planners with technical and analytical skills for solving complex problems. The view of planning described here demands that planners apply the skills of participatory researchers to promote participation in a more interactive process. Planners as participatory researchers can expand awareness of community groups, enhance their ability to make themselves heard, and increase the extent to which planning reflects plural interests. Participatory research thus requires skills for building trust with diverse groups, helping them formulate their analysis of problems, and enabling them to gain access to decision-making processes. Many planners have little training or experience that prepares them for such activities.

Participatory researchers in the Indian villages were disoriented by the lack of familiar facilities and patterns of discussion in spite of their willingness to work in strange settings and their skills for promoting participation. Participatory researchers in the Appalachia project organized citizens, trained them to collect data, negotiated with the Regional Commission for financial support, and disseminated their findings to interested parties. Citizen organizations in Urban Heights needed help in recognizing problems, collecting and analyzing data, and presenting their results to skeptical or hostile audiences. Participatory research can make varied demands on community planners who want to promote wider participation in the planning process.

Community planners who engage in participatory research must recognize groups relevant to community problems, make contacts and mitigate initial suspicions, help people collect and analyze data, and help them utilize their findings. Planners may call on other participatory researchers to promote participation since the necessary skills are not often included in planner training. The point is that research can increase the resources available for planning.

Interactive planning requires that planners manage diverse perspectives and interests. Discussions can easily deteriorate into avoidance of conflict or suppression of critical issues, deadlocks or escalation over differences, or shortsighted compromises that resolve current problems at the expense of the future. The skills required depend on the nature of the disagreements (Thompson and Tuden 1959). When agreement exists on both means and ends so that computation is appropriate, bureaucratic structures are appropriate. Planners in such situations need analytic skills and bureaucratic authority, and decisions are made by experts on the basis of analysis.

When parties disagree about causes and effects, decisions by judgment are required and collegial decision-making structures are appropriate. In such circumstances, planners need skills to persuade peers, facilitate consensus, explore alternatives, identify mutual benefits, and articulate agreements (Brown 1983; Filley 1979; Fisher and Urey 1981). In the later stages of the Urban Heights Committee on Residential Lending, for example, the city manager and other participants became adept at facilitating discussions of alternative strategies for attaining shared goals.

When parties agree about causes and effects but disagree about preferred outcomes, bargaining processes are appropriate for decision making. Bargaining requires planners to develop skills to articulate and mediate differences, to control escalation, to manage restricted or distorted information, to create compromises and face-saving agreements, and to invent standards for fair resolution of disputes (Brown 1983; Fisher and Urey 1981). The Regional Commission and the task force in Appalachia, for example, bargained over many issues, including the research questions and the dissemination of results. Relations among the parties in this case might have benefitted considerably from more sophistication among planners about strategies for managing differences of interest.

When parties agree about neither causes and effects nor preferred outcomes, inspiration is appropriate for decision making (Thompson and Tuden 1959). Issue avoidance is likely in such situations, but charismatic leaders or innovative solutions can unite parties in spite of their differences. In the early period of the Urban Heights Committee, for example, parties disagreed on both preferences for committee goals and explanations of problems, and the dissolution of the committee was very likely. The city manager's ability to manage those differences was instrumental to the continuation of the committee.

Most community planning involves some combination of computation, judgment, bargaining, or inspiration. These elements may evolve from one to another over time—as did the decision-making process within the Committee on Residential Lending. Interactive planning with diverse parties requires skills for facilitating judgmental problem solving, mediating political negotiations, and using or supporting charismatic leadership in addition to traditional technical or analytical skills.

This chapter identifies community planning problems related to the limited applicability of comprehensive rational analysis and to restrictions of information and influence caused by concentrations of wealth and power. It argues that participatory research can expand the base of information, increase participation by less powerful groups, and develop structures and skills that yield better decisions and more commitment.

This approach is consistent with democratic values for widespread participation in community decisions. It can remain flexible in the face of uncertainty and allow adjustments as new information becomes available. It can increase the amount and quality of information and expand the energy and creativity of community members to develop and implement plans that affect them. Constructive conflict among alternative interests can generate more searching analysis, broaden the range of alternative solutions, and produce decisions that benefit diverse interests rather than a few. It also can build relationships among interests, enable them to share perspectives, and foster cooperation for the future.

This approach to planning is neither simple nor without costs, however. Analyses of conflict suggest that opportunities for benefit from interaction and participation exist. But constraints may limit the perception of mutual benefits in many situations, and resulting conflicts may be destructive for one or both parties. Community planners who promote interaction among unequally powerful parties can set in motion forces over which they have little control. They may be viewed by elites as allies of the poor, by the poor as allies of elites, or by all parties as meddlers. In situations polarized over power differences, it is often difficult to remain independent or credible with both sides.

Community planners ideally coordinate rather than control interactive planning and provide resources that enable different groups to participate meaningfully in shaping the future of their community. Planners may have to educate simultaneously the powerful about incentives for listening to others and empower the powerless to articulate their interests effectively. But when planners successfully expand participation in planning, the resulting plans reflect the interests of a larger public, and the planning process mobilizes resources for effective implementation.

References

Brown, L.D. 1983. *Managing Conflict at Organizational Interfaces*. Reading, Mass.: Addison-Wesley.

Brown, L.D., and R. Tandon. 1983. Ideology and Political Economy in Inquiry: Action Research and Participatory Research. *Journal of Applied Behavioral Science* 19:277–294.

Crenson, M.A. 1971. *The Un-Politics of Air Pollution: A Study of Non-Decision-making in the Cities*. Baltimore: The Johns Hopkins University Press.

Dahl, R.A. 1961. *Who Governs? Democracy and Power in an American City*. New Haven: Yale University Press.

Filley, A. 1979. *Interpersonal Conflict Resolution*. Glenview, Ill.: Scott, Foresman.

Fisher, R., and W. Urey. 1981. *Getting to Yes*. Boston: Little, Brown.

Freeman, R.E. 1984. *Strategic Management: A Stakeholder Approach*. Boston: Pitman.

Freire, P. 1970. *Pedagogy of the Oppressed*. New York: Herder and Herder.

Freire, P. 1974. *Education for Critical Consciousness.* New York: Seabury.

Friedmann, J. 1981. *Retracking America.* Emmaus, Pa.: Rodale.

Gaventa, J. 1980. *Power and Powerlessness: Quiescence and Rebellion in an Appalachian Valley.* Urbana: University of Illinois Press.

Gaventa, J., and B.D. Horton. 1981. A Citizens' Research Project in Appalachia, U.S.A. *Convergence* 14:30–42.

Gricar, B.G., and L.D. Brown. 1981. Conflict, Power and Organization in a Changing Community. *Human Relations* 34:877–893.

Hall, B.L. 1981. Participatory Research, Popular Knowlege, and Power: A Personal Reflection. *Convergence* 14:6–17.

Korten, D. 1980. Community Organization and Rural Development: A Learning Process Approach. *Public Administration Review* 40:480–510.

Lindblom, C.E. 1959. The Science of Muddling Through. *Public Administration Review* 19:79–88.

Lindblom, C.E. 1979. Still Muddling, Not Yet Through. *Public Administration Review* 39:517–526.

Lukes, S. 1974. *Power: A Radical View.* London: MacMillan.

Mintzberg, H. 1978. Patterns in Strategy Making. *Management Science* 24:934–948.

Quinn, J.B. 1980. *Strategies for Change: Logical Incrementalism.* Homewood, Ill.: Irwin.

Susman, G.I., and R.D. Evered. 1978. An Assessment of the Scientific Merits of Action Research. *Administrative Science Quarterly* 23:582–603.

Tandon, R. 1981. Dialogue as Inquiry and Intervention. In *Human Inquiry: A Sourcebook of New Paradigm Research,* P. Reason and J. Rowan, eds. Chichester: Wiley.

Tandon, R., and L.D. Brown. 1981. Organization Building for Rural Development: An Experiment in India. *Journal of Applied Behavioral Science* 17:172–189.

Thompson, J.D. 1974. Social Interdependence, the Polity, and Public Administration. *Administration and Society* 6:3–21.

Thompson, J.D., and A. Tuden. 1959. Strategies, Structures and Processes of Organizational Decision. In *Comparative Studies in Administration,* J.D. Thompson et al., eds. Pittsburgh: University of Pittsburgh Press.

9

Governing and Managing Public Organizations

John E. Tropman

People, money, and ideas are essential to any public organization. People are fundamental to organizational existence, and even the most roboticized firms have individuals who operate machinery and exert judgment at crucial times. People are the board and staff who make the organization run, the clients who use it, and the community around it. They are the politicians and professionals who influence the context in which the organization operates. They are the staff who are knowledgeable, trained, or developed in the job and without which no organization can function. Vogel (1979), in his discussion of the Japanese public service, makes this point and argues that it accounts for the high quality of their governmental organizations.

Money is the generalized resource that helps an organization accomplish its ends (Drucker 1983). Money pays for the product and staff and generates whatever surplus is possible. Organizations spend a tremendous amount of time pursuing money. Public organizational funds are likely to be heavily based on tax revenues, although fee income is substantial in some instances. Public organizations seem perennially short of the funds needed to do the job. It is almost axiomatic that any budget submission will request an increase and that any decrease or retrenchment will be opposed. Regulations often require public organizations to return unexpended monies to funders at the end of the year, which may lead to so-called terminal programming, with program initiatives using funds from accessible accounts in the remaining days of the fiscal year.

Ideas are also crucial to an organization. The most powerful ideas include the organizing myth or ethos that defines and sustains the organization's mission and purpose (Erikson 1970; Ouchi 1982; Peters and Waterman 1982). The notion of culture as a form of organizing ideas (which is what *ethos* means) is becoming a preferred form of explanation for events, as represented by Weber's (1956) Protestant ethic, Wilson's (1963) concepts of public regardingness versus private regardingness, Reich's (1983) idea of civic culture, or Ehrenreich's (1983) breadwinner ethic. Work on Japanese management by Ouchi (1982) and Pascale and Athos (1981) emphasizes organizational culture.

One subset of important ideas involves organizational goals. Naisbett (1982) asks organizations to think about their goals by asking the question, What business are we in? Public organizations are not exempt from such a question. Conceptual difficulties are part of the problem since it is not always clear what business the public organization is in. Thus, Naisbett suggests a second question, What business would it be useful for us to think we are in? The first question asks the organization to think about what it is doing; the second asks what the organization should be doing.

Other kinds of ideas are less global than these—such as, for example, ideas about how to manage, about the community context and ways to adjust to it, about organizational form and its implications for carrying out of daily activities, and about governing and managing the organization. And what of the policies and procedures that provide the daily guidance for the organization? In this case, they are ideas that have been written down and made legitimate by a city council, executive board, or some other organizational authority and that have legal force for the organization and its clientele.

Without ideas, then, people are undirected and money is wasted. But while much organizational energy is spent on securing people and money, very little is spent on securing and processing ideas. As a result, many organizations have a conceptual deficit as well as a personnel shortage or a fiscal shortfall.

In this chapter, I argue that ideas are a central resource for any organization and thus must be sought after, cared for, and developed through the organizational process. Ideas do not arrive ready for implementation. Each one needs to be taken from the initial suggestion stage through a process of development until it emerges in final organizational form—as policy. I also argue that the person who has responsibility (or who should have responsibility) for energizing and coordinating this process of search and development from idea to policy is the policy manager. The policy manager concept is relatively new. Daft and Bradshaw (1980) call them idea champions, Frankfather (1981) calls them entrepreneurial managers, and Moore (1982) refers to them in his work on why policy managers need policy analysis. Although the role of policy manager is new and the notion of idea management is a long way from acceptance, they represent important skills that promise more effectiveness at the workplace.

Policy management is important to human service organizations and other public or private agencies (Tropman 1984). It is especially important to public organizations because they often face special problems, such as conceptualizing their overall mission, that are different from and more serious than those of private agencies. The purpose here, however, is to introduce the notion of policy management as it applies to public organizations.

Policy and Practice

Policy is a ratified written idea that guides and sometimes prescribes action. A set of organizational policies provides the governing constitution or charter for an organization. Ideas emerge from the organizational context and follow a course through the organization, sometimes to emerge as policy. In many public organizations, that course is episodic, idiosyncratic, and largely unattended. The policy manager organizes and orchestrates this process so that there is an adequate supply of good ideas and so that the good ideas are not lost in the organizational process.

It is often thought that written organizational policy does not relate to what people do in the organization. Instead, one might be told "the way we do things around here—our policy—is to . . . ." The focus of this observation is on what I call *organizational practices*. Practices are what people actually do. Policy is what they should be doing. When the gap between policy and practice becomes too wide, when organizational policy becomes irrelevant to the day-to-day operations of the organization, then it is time to ask Naisbett's (1982) question, What business are we in anyway? Practice is an important dynamic of organizational life. No set of organizational policies is ever completely conclusive or anticipates everything. Practice is a way to work out in action the ideas that look good on paper, but when interstitial arrangements and practical responses to specific events provide the main source of organizational direction, then organizational policy needs reformulation. One task of the policy manager is to monitor the gap between policy and practice and to use that information to direct attention to areas that need policy reformulation. Areas where the gap is wider will require more urgent attention.

Ideas and Policy:
Steps in the Transformation Process

What does *attention* mean in this context? The first step is to ensure an adequate supply of ideas and other resources. Just as the financial officer seeks to ensure an adequate supply of money flowing into the organization and the personnel manager an adequate supply of potential employees, so does the policy manager seek an adequate supply of ideas. There are many ways to find a good supply of ideas, such as circulating new papers from colleagues and other organizations; providing speakers; and using idea seminars, retreats, and brainstorming sessions, among others. It is important to create a climate conducive to the generation and reception of new ideas and new approaches. Organizations represent a stock of available or potential ideas waiting to be used, just as a bank account represents a supply of money waiting to be spent or a personnel roster represents available people ready to be assigned. It is more difficult, but not impossible, to think of an organization as an idea pool. Working papers that propose alternative futures, methods of organization, or scenarios that raise environmental possibilities can activate the process. The policy manager thus seeks to ensure the supply, quality, and relevance of ideas to get them started in the policy process.

The second step is to provide structure. It is one thing to ask, Wouldn't it be interesting to . . . ? and quite another to propose an idea for review by affected individuals and groups. Structure represents a crucial aspect of idea and policy development. Good ideas can be structured in a way that renders them inoperable, and bad ideas can be written in a style that gives them a feasible appearance. Conceptual chemistry can help package an idea by linking it with other related ideas and approaches. Sometimes an idea by itself makes little sense or contribution, but an idea combined with or bonded to another can become a powerful force. The policy manager structures ideas and packages them for consideration and possible ratification.

Ratification is the third step. Ideas should be approved and given legitimacy by a mayor, governor, or other executive or by a state government agency, city council planning commission, or other authoritative body. Approval does not happen by accident but results from work, documentation, and movement through the approval process. The policy manager assists in this activity.

The fourth step is to develop working guidelines in preparation for operations. Even after the substantial work involved in developing, structuring, and ratifying an idea, the ratified document still needs to be translated into operational guidelines with both general and specific instructions. Federal agencies recognize these as federal regulations, but most public organizations have local counterparts.

The final step of the policy management process is to make operational the activity prescribed in the guidelines. Policy managers are not necessarily involved in operations but may monitor, assess, and evaluate the process to judge whether it solves problems and meets needs. The information developed from observation becomes part of the so-called policy loop, an aspect of the process that takes the problems from operations as equivalent to a demand for new ideas and begins the process again. This is a haphazard process in many public organizations because of the difficulties of public sector management.

The presentation of the process from idea to policy in logical steps does not mean that each step is completed in sequence or that other steps are not needed. It is a dynamic, feedback-oriented process, not a linear step-by-step one, although the sequential mode can contribute to understanding. For example, anticipated issues in the operational phase can inform structure and ratification. Feed-backward operations and feed-forward procedures can be simultaneous. Most new ideas can be fit into a changing organizational process. The organization can be slowed while it is fitted or retrofitted with new policies. Hence, the policy manager in the public sector must take special care to design policies that recognize a dynamic rather than a static situation.

Policy Management Difficulties of Public Organizations

Public management is really harder than private management (Curtis 1980). A public organization faces difficulties and constraints that are not routinely found in a private profit-making business, nonprofit organization, or charitable agency. There are issues of value conflict, problem definition, and organizational structure.

Value Conflicts

Policy managers may experience value conflicts in proposing ideas and making plans. The idea of a policy value conflict has been developed in detail by Edelman (1977), Hirschman (1982), and Tropman (1984). This approach views the value system as being made up of conflicting commitments that are linked together and shared by the public as well as the policy manager. Public agencies are, perforce, at the nexus of serious policy value conflicts, and the following sections describe these.

Adequacy versus Equity. Should the policy manager emphasize the equity or the adequacy of programs? On the one hand, most Americans are committed to equity in public programs. People should be able to benefit from such programs in proportion to what they contribute to society. On the other hand, Americans are also committed to adequacy in public programs. There should be a maximum above which benefits do not rise and a minimum below which they do not fall. The problem is that values of adequacy and equity conflict each with the other in most public programs.

Public versus Private. Should the policy manager foster public or private responsibility with respect to the provision of benefits? U.S. society has historically been privatized, with the public sector playing a residual role. Since the 1930s, however, the public sector at all levels has played an increasingly important role. Although the scope of the public role is presently uncertain, it likely will remain important while the conflict in society continues (Lipset and Schneider 1983). But questions continue to arise about whether a function should be served by a public or private body.

Personal versus Family. U.S. society emphasizes personal achievement and accomplishment on the one hand, family orientations and commitment on the other. This conflict poses a complex challenge. For example, in considering programs for the older adult, should the manager emphasize programs in which the family provides a basic level of resources beyond which the public provides the remainder, or should the public provide basic services and the family provide the remainder? How much should the public contribute?

These are not the only policy conflicts that face public organizations, but they do suggest some of the difficulties of policy formulation. The policy manager should anticipate such difficulties, expect opposition that may develop, and prepare for the kinds of questions that may be asked. Good ideas are never without their detractors, and the notion of policy value conflict should alert policy managers to possible challenge. Some attacks can come from unexpected quarters, like, for example, the proposal for a mandatory automobile seat belt law that some groups oppose as an infringement of personal liberty. Simon, Smithburg, and Thompson (1956) argue that effective policy should be linked to values. But if there are many values, and they come in juxtaposed sets, the problem becomes more complex. Policy managers are only beginning to get suggestions about how to deal with the problem of policy value conflict (Tropman 1984).

Problem Definition

Policy managers face other difficulties related to the nature of public problems. Rittel and Webber (1973) offer ten reasons why some problems are "wicked." These reasons can be consolidated for our purposes as follows.

No Definitive Formulation. There is no definitive formulation for problems faced by the policy manager in the public sector. Each problem is different and has alternative ways to explain causation. One result is that the policy manager is continually beset by alternative ways to define the particular problem at issue. Policy management thus sometimes seems like a game where the players always return to the start after a series of openings and never get beyond the initial moves to achieve results.

No Options. There are no clear sets of options in difficult problems. For many routine problems that face planners, there is a range of options that has some reasonable scientific assessment behind them from which the planner can select, and there are procedures that make it possible to narrow action possibilities down to a reasonable few. However, other public problems do not have this repertoire available. All manner of options are possible and selecting some workable ones from a very large list is an extremely difficult job. Every solution tends to seem unique and it is very hard to develop a set of repeatable operations on the basis of experience.

No Stopping Rule. There is no stopping rule for these tough problems. At what point does the policy manager stop making an effort? This difficulty can be exacerbated in the case of human services because of the potentially disastrous human consequences that can result from stopping efforts to solve problems that seem to produce others or resist solution.

No Right to Be Wrong. Rittel and Webber (1973) assert that the practitioner has no right to be wrong. This difficulty can be intensified in human services because it may affect people with special needs. For example, a mistake in pursuing a child abuse complaint could result in the death of a child.

In short, policy management in a public context really is harder (Curtis 1980). However, the difficulties increase the need for policy management that can ensure an adequate supply of new ideas into the organization. Public planners, managers, administrators, and other practitioners also often operate as policy managers in their concern with ideas, although they may never have viewed themselves or been viewed in this way. But to the extent that they seek both to create a supply of ideas and to guide their development, they serve the policy management function.

Organizational Structure

Curtis (1980) argues that the structure of U.S. public organizations can cause problems. Such structure can have positive value in one context and lead to difficulties in others.

Separation of Powers. Management of public interests is divided into four key arenas—executive, legislative, judicial, and the civil service or standing government. Policy proposals may involve most, if not all, of these sectors, each of which may face different demands and interests. The purpose of the separation of powers was to prevent too much influence from accumulating in a single arena. The idea of checks and balances was to prevent misapplication of power and the implementation of bad ideas. Such structures can help ensure that democratic participation does not become mob rule, but they also can challenge the policy manager.

User-Provider Gap. This gap involves the separation between the buyer and the consumer of service. In private business, the buyer of service is also the consumer, and the consumer decision to buy represents important feedback to the business organization. In public services, however, the consumer of service is only indirectly (although very definitely) the provider of funds. The actual providers of funds are the legislators and the allocation committee members. Public service employees are likely to focus on funding sources, in some cases to the detriment of the consumer. Drucker (1983) calls this process "misdirection by the budget." Proper direction should come from consumer preferences, but it is very difficult to find a useful and direct way to express consumer preferences in public organizations. The vote is not as flexible as the dollar; its message is more moot and expressed through elected officials rather than directly. This is not to suggest that business organizations always respond to the information given to them by the market. The stubborn refusal of U.S. automobile companies to attend to problems of fuel economy and product quality is a major factor that has permitted foreign car makers to take over a substantial fraction of the U.S. market, but the problem of insufficient information is different from the problem of denial.

Spoils System. Individuals appointed to offices within the standing government may have little interest or competence in the particular service being offered by the agency or department in question. This lack of interest or competence can create substantial problems for the public manager who might otherwise look to these individuals for leadership or support.

Public Eye. Curtis (1980) describes the difficulties of managing in the public eye. While some people do best under direct scrutiny, it is often necessary to have privacy during the process of developing and shaping ideas. Yet others might say that is exactly what they do not want: people developing and trying out ideas in private without public input. It is possible both to agree with this sentiment and to recognize the difficulty of new idea exploration in the glare of publicity. That is a time when policy managers may play a conservative game and stick with tradition to avoid looking foolish. Constant public scrutiny creates problems for the policy manager and challenges him or her to develop and apply special techniques to foster an open process while retaining measures of privacy needed to generate ideas.

Difficulty of Assessment. Other difficulties may be added to those outlined by Curtis (1980). Outcomes within the public realm are hard to assess. Will a physical plan for an area be successful? It may take years, if ever, before the answer is known. The American tendency to press for immediate results may mean that projects that require more time to mature are less likely to be appreciated or funded. In contrast, the Japanese orientation to the longer term may make it more possible to tolerate some ambiguity while the project is developing (Ouchi 1982).

Multiple Interests. The public manager must serve multiple interests, unlike the private business executive who can often select a target sector or market sector to service. It is no surprise that the public manager often finds himself or herself thrust into a situation of irreconcilable perspectives and demands.

Pressure of Human Need. Pressure represents another source of stress for public managers, especially those involved in human services. For many people, the government is the last source of hope and help. Citizens often fail to realize that government, like other bureaucratic organizations, may do better with planning and foresight. Government public housing offices are not always prepared to deal with emergency housing needs, coming as they often do at a moment of crisis. Social service departments or welfare offices may find it difficult to respond to emergency needs and yet also share a sense of obligation to respond when a person in need walks into the office. This pressure tends to emphasize the importance of skills and techniques to provide immediate assistance. New ideas are often longer range in nature and must lack this sense of immediacy with respect to current problems.

Pressure on Staff. Faced with client pressure to do something and the desire to help, staff of public human service organizations feel considerable pressure to act. However, the action orientation often contrasts with a more contemplative orientation (Hirschman 1982). These two orientations are not completely opposed, but most managers of public human service organizations are aware that the staff feel the pressure of urgency from the clients, and many managers also contribute to that pressure from their motivation. Part of the reason people come to work for a public human service organization is to help. When staff find their ability to help truncated by bureaucratic procedures and other organizational difficulties, they may experience restiveness and disappointment. Somehow, being where the ideas are is something that is often thought of as not being where the action is. There is an inherent sense of satisfaction in being in the center of activity. This is what Peters and Waterman (1983) call "bias for action." Excellent companies are characterized by doing and should support such action as long as it is thoughtful and guided. For this, one needs ideas.

Policy Management Techniques

Given the difficulties of policy management in general and policy management in public organizations in particular, several techniques are useful to practice.

Recognition of a Policy Management Function

It is important to recognize that ideas—their supply and guidance—are a crucial element in the successful operation of public organizations. It is more difficult to recognize when an organization has a conceptual deficit because an absence of ideas is less tangible and palpable than missing money or people. Nonetheless, one must begin with the recognition that policy management is important.

Appointment of a Policy Manager or Policy Management Function

It is important to recognize that policy management requires some kind of personnel and financial commitment. This commitment typically emerges by appointing someone to the role of policy manager or asking someone to serve the policy management function as a part-time assignment. There are a number of ways this can be done. Some large organizations have departments that undertake this role, although an individual or two can provide a start. But there should be more than a simple recognition that ideas are important. This recognition should be made concrete by creating positions and hiring people.

Use of Policy Science

Individuals who perform policy management can benefit from policy science, including recognition of the importance of the stages of idea development. Problem definition, proposal development, policy ratification, program planning, and program operation are crucial to the process. Each has particular characteristics that together contribute to the whole. Policy science can provide policy managers with perspectives and knowledge about the elements of the system as means to improve practice.

Knowledge of Policy Groups and Decision Quality

Most important decisions in the public and private arenas are made in groups. The function and integrity of decision-making groups, as well as the articulation and quality of decisions they make, are often dependent on the group process. It is not possible to make good decisions with bad information, but it is possible to handle good information so badly that its utility is destroyed. Cohen (1972) anticipated this possibility and outlined the conditions under which it is likely to occur in his work on the garbage can model of decision making. The stages of policy development are almost always stages of group process. Policy proposals may move from a group that defines the problem to other groups that develop proposals, to still others that ratify, plan, and administer the program.

The policy manager should be aware of the shifts in group dynamics, issues, and value conflicts from one stage to another. For example, the policy ratification stage is often an open or quasi-open decision-making situation, especially in the public sector where legislation or regulation requiring openness is in force. Hence, public conflicts and current concerns are likely to surface even if they have not been visible in more private or less open phases of problem definition and proposal generation. It might be politically necessary for the policy manager to include some material in the policy proposal that he or she knows will directly respond to emergent issues. He or she also might assume that once the policy moves into planning and design, those same concerns may have a much different priority.

The policy manager not only should be aware of varying group dynamics in stages of the policy process but also should understand the characteristics and peculiarities of the different groups. There are advisory groups of every shape and size, many mandated by federal and state government regulations. There are city councils, planning commissions, human services boards, and other kinds of voluntary boards of directors with whom the policy manager will have contact. Each of these groups makes decisions that are important for the policy manager to understand. For example, an advisory committee may make a decision to advise a person, organization, institution, or the public at large. They may lament the fact that they do not have the authority to produce results. Groups with formal authority, however, may spend a good bit of time avoiding its use. The roles and responsibilities of policy managers, particularly if they are involved in or assigned to assist in group decision making, may vary considerably from one group to another.

The policy manager should be concerned with the quality of group decisions and seek to structure and provide information to promote effective action and innovative response. He or she should help guide the flow of ideas in a way that avoids applying pressure to or developing distance from participants. In the former case, action may result in a precipitous and thoughtless manner; in the latter case, action may not result.

Writing Skills

Another way in which the policy manager in public organizations can improve the supply and processing of ideas is through written communication. Policy usually is written, and hence, the ability of the policy manager to write policy is crucial. However, more than policy must be written. Memos, reports, announcements, press releases, and other media that include analysis and discussion are part of the written work of the policy manager. Although the writing demands of the policy and planning professions are high, professional education and training tend to neglect writing skills. Report writing is a skill that needs attention, and the ability to communicate persuasively in writing can extend the influence of the policy manager (Booher 1984; Holcombe and Stein 1981).

Conclusion

Public organizations need to give more systematic attention to ideas as a part of their daily routine—new ideas about what their mission and role should be and then how to accomplish them. However, public organizations tend not to assign individuals explicitly to this task, and the process of new idea development is haphazard and lackluster.

Idea development, however, even if it were an organizational priority, would not be sufficient. It would be only the first step in a process called policy management. In this process, new ideas that enter the organization are considered, refined, shaped, and finally emerge as policy and plans that guide the organization in daily practice.

This policy management function requires a formal role and responsibility designation. That role is the policy manager, an individual who specializes in providing a supply of new ideas to the organization and who works at their processing and implementation to ensure that these ideas are functioning to solve the problems they were designed to address. The policy manager, like the fiscal and the personnel manager, occupies a crucial role in the organizational structure.

But public organizations face problems that are different from and often more difficult than what private organizations face. These difficulties involve value dilemmas, conflicts in the definition of problems, and structural and organizational complexities.

Despite difficulties, skills and techniques are available to the policy manager to facilitate his or her work. These include skills of policy analysis, policy science, policy writing, and group management. Each skill requires the recognition of this function and the assignment of the policy manager role as a first step. Ideas are too important an organizational resource to be left to chance.

References

Booher, Diana. 1984. *Send Me a Memo.* New York: Facts on File.

Curtis, Donald. 1980. Management in the Public Sector Really Is Harder. *Management Review* 69:70–74.

Daft, Richard L., and Patricia J. Bradshaw. 1980. The Process of Horizontal Differentiation: Two Models. *Administrative Science Quarterly* 25:441–456.

Drucker, Peter F. 1980. The Deadly Sins in Public Administration. *Public Administration Review* 40:103–106.

———. 1983. Managing the Public Service Institution. *The Public Interest* 33: 43–60.

Edelman, Murray. 1977. *Political Language: Words that Succeed and Policies that Fail.* New York: Academic Press.

Ehrenreich, Barbara. 1983. *The Hearts of Men.* New York: Anchor Doubleday.

Erikson, Kai. 1970. *Everything In Its Path.* New York: Simon & Schuster.

Frankfather, Dwight. 1981. Welfare Entrepreneurialism and the Politics of Innovation. *Social Service Review* 55:129–146.

Hirschman, Albert O. 1982. *Shifting Involvements: Private Interest and Public Action.* Princeton, N.J.: Princeton University Press.

Holcombe, Mary A., and Judith K. Stein. 1981. *Writing for Decision Makers*. Belmont, Calif.: Wadsworth.

Lipset, Seymour Martin, and William Schneider. 1983. *The Confidence Gap: Business, Labor, and Government in the Public Mind*. New York: Free Press.

Moore, Mark H. 1982. Policy Managers Need Policy Analysis. *Journal of Policy Analysis and Management* 1:413–418.

Naisbett, John. 1982. *Megatrends: Ten New Directions Transforming Our Lives*. New York: Warner.

Ouchi, William. 1982. *Theory Z: How American Business Can Meet the Japanese Challenge*. Reading, Mass.: Addison-Wesley.

Pascale, Richard T., and Anthony Athos. 1981. *The Art of Japanese Management: Application for American Executives*. New York: Warner.

Peters, Thomas, and Robert Waterman. 1982. *In Search of Excellence*. New York: Harper & Row.

Reich, Richard. 1983. *The Next American Frontier*. New York: Times Books.

Rittel, W.J. Horst, and Melvin M. Webber. 1973. Dilemmas In A General Theory of Planning. *Policy Sciences* 4:155–169.

Simon, Herbert; Donald Smithburg; and Victor Thompson. 1956. *Public Administration*. New York: Knopf.

Tobin, Sheldon; Stephen M. Davidson; and Ann Sack. 1976. *Effective Social Services for Older Americans*. Ann Arbor: Institute of Gerontology, University of Michigan.

Tropman, John E. 1984. *Policy Management in the Human Services*. New York: Columbia University Press.

Tropman, John E.; Harold R. Johnson; and Elmer J. Tropman. 1979. *Essentials of Committee Management*. Chicago: Nelson-Hall.

Vogel, Ezra. 1979. *Japan as Number One: Lessons for America*. Cambridge: Harvard University Press.

Weber, Max. 1956. *The Protestant Ethic and the Spirit of Capitalism*. New York: Scribners.

Wilson, James Q. 1963. Planning and Politics: Citizen Participation in Urban Renewal. *Journal of the American Institute of Planners* 29:242–249.

10
Developing Coalitions in the Face of Power: Lessons from the Human Services

Milan J. Dluhy

The literature on coalition building has seen major theoretical and conceptual development in recent years, including game theoretic, social psychological, and political or power models (Murnighan 1978). While there have been a few descriptive studies of coalition formation, there is a virtual absence of empirical research on the behavior of coalitions in practice (Stevenson, Pearce, and Porter 1984). This chapter tries to fill this gap by presenting case studies of coalition behavior to develop a typology of coalitions in the human services. This typology is then used to derive practice principles to guide individuals and groups who seek to exercise influence over the public agenda beyond what they could accomplish alone.

The practical necessity of using coalitions to achieve common objectives in the human services has been discussed by others (Dluhy 1984; Humphreys 1979; Roberts 1984; Weisner 1983). Since the austerity policies and budget cutbacks of the 1980s will likely continue in the near future, however, concerned planners will need to know how and when to use coalitions to achieve their objectives. Studies indicate that an environment of scarce resources and a decentralized political structure will result in constantly changing and reformulated coalitions (Bacharach and Lawler 1980). Contemporary circumstances thus stress the importance of understanding the dynamics of coalition formation for the years ahead.

Concepts and Definitions

In its simplest terms, a coalition represents a convergence of interest on the part of a number of actors, both individuals and organizations, and an interaction around furthering these common interests (Warren 1977). This chapter focuses on political coalitions—that is, coalitions whose primary purpose is the achievement of political objectives in the public policy process (Dluhy 1981). Political coalitions may also serve secondary purposes such as providing social experiences for its members, disseminating information in an educational way to its members, and allowing people in the coalition to make contacts and find new jobs.

The origins of coalitions vary from one case to another, but all political coalitions are socially constructed groupings that emerge from common interests in a community or society (Bacharach and Lawler 1980). Many political coalitions form because of external issues that generate a crisis and response by a community or society. Once the issue is raised, these common interests need to be mobilized. Charismatic leadership can facilitate mobilization of interests, but community meetings, public hearings, or professional gatherings might be instrumental as well. At this point, some individuals or groups may determine whether they can maximize their gains by joining a coalition or by acting alone (Gamson 1962, 1968). A rational approach would seek to maximize the gain, while minimizing the effort. Thus, a minimal expenditure of individual or group resources that maximizes a substantial gain is usually the most prudent strategy.

Individuals or groups join political coalitions to maximize gains in the public policy process, but why do some coalitions succeed while others fail? Why are some coalitions temporary while others become permanent organizations? Coalition behavior involves a temporal dimension of stability or duration that represents one of the central themes in the literature on coalitions (Hinckley 1979) and receives analysis in the case studies that follow. Of particular interest is the set of circumstances that leads to permanence. Many coalitions form merely to raise issues; others develop solutions to pressing problems; and still others push for adoption of specific solutions by the public sector. Throughout this process of agenda setting, different kinds of coalitions emerge.

Coalitions that deal with politically salient issues as well as those led by adroit and charismatic leaders have greater chances of becoming stable over time. In addition, coalitions that are able to tap into a sufficient resource base as well as develop an effective communication network are likely to achieve more stability.

Another dimension of coalition behavior is its horizontal or vertical nature. A horizontal coalition represents a broad set of actors at the community or societal level. These actors may represent groups such as minorities, women, businesspeople, laborers, or professionals, but they band together in a particular geographic setting, like a community, state, region, or country, to respond to a crisis or solve a problem. In contrast, a vertical coalition represents a narrower set of interests that bands together simultaneously at all geographic levels, community, state, region, or country. Thus, a broad-based group of actors in a community who join together to oppose school desegregation policies is an example of a horizontal coalition, while a group of concerned scientists from a number of places who band together to oppose nuclear war represents a vertical coalition. Horizontal coalitions are usually community based, while vertical coalitions are more narrowly organized according to sectors or professional groups.

Of additional importance to understanding coalition behavior is whether the various actors who join coalitions share similar broad-based goals or ideology or whether they share functional goals. In this context, a number of groups in a community may share the fundamental goal of eliminating teenage pregnancy, but these same groups may have different functional goals. Thus, a planned parenthood organization may advocate the use of birth control devices, but a particular church may condemn that goal and promote another. It is important for potential coalition members to examine the compatibility of underlying broad goals or ideologies and the functional goals of other individuals and groups. One of the most critical aspects of coalitions is the diversity of functional goals among the members. It is often easy to mobilize individuals or groups who share an underlying ideology, but it is harder to keep these members participating at a high level if their functional goals are in conflict. The trick is to appeal to this underlying set of values while minimizing conflict among functional goals. Coalition members will continue to participate as long as they perceive a direct benefit from participation while at the same time concluding that their participation is not unnecessarily detracting from or conflicting with any of their functional goals.

As mentioned earlier, many coalitions form because of an external issue or crisis. Group action is fundamental because no single individual or group can deal with the issue alone, and therefore it requires an organized public response. The critical factor, however, is that coalitions are issue oriented. The actors share common objectives or goals even though they may have different functional goals or divergent motives for participation.

In sum, political coalitions form to enhance policy objectives. External issues or problems usually generate a crisis that demands a response. The decision to join a coalition is normally made to improve one's gains while minimizing one's input of resources. Some coalitions have a short duration, while others adapt and accommodate over time. In some cases, they may even begin to take on the features of a more permanent, unitary organization. Even though some coalitions are horizontal and others are more vertical in their organization, all coalitions face the fundamental question of whether the broad goals of the coalition are compatible with the functional goals of its individual members.

Coalitions in the Human Services

The success of a political coalition is best understood in the context of coalitional dynamics. This section draws on four different case examples to illustrate these dynamics.

Table 10–1 summarizes some of the background characteristics of four coalitions in the human services in which the author has been a participant-observer for several years. These coalitions were chosen specifically because they illustrate many of the dimensions of coalitions discussed previously. Of particular interest is the fact that the four coalitions range from temporary to permanent, illustrate coalitions with both goal conflict and consensus, and demonstrate the differences between horizontal and vertical types of coalitions. A brief sketch of each coalition sets the stage for a more generalized typology and discussion of coalitions. The coalition labeled "homeless" was a community-based coalition organized to help homeless individuals in a medium-sized community. After two cold winters and numerous newspaper accounts, concerned citizens and clergy met to discuss how to get homeless people off the streets as quickly as possible. While there was broad consensus on this objective, the functional goals of many members of the coalition were not the same. For example, some wanted to purchase a shelter, others advocated setting up a referral system that would place people in foster homes, and still others thought giving the homeless housing vouchers to stay at local hotels would work. Coalition members met irregularly, kept no minutes, and argued continuously. In the end, they were able at least to get the issue on the formal public agenda, and city officials finally allocated money to purchase a shelter for the homeless. The coalition did not provide the solution to the problem but exerted the necessary pressure on others to solve the problem. The coalition then disbanded, and even though the community is still struggling with issues of the homeless, the coalition has never met again. In terms of coalitional dynamics, this coalition formed rapidly in a rather unplanned way, but when it got the issue on the formal public agenda and officials responded, it appeared to lose its purpose and finally disbanded. It is questionable whether this same coalition will ever form again.

The coalition labeled "aging" represents a second case. For several years, fifty program directors who managed community-based programs throughout a midwestern state met for professional in-service training. These program directors managed volunteer programs that involved older adults in community-based projects. While some individual programs received federal money, most relied on state money and local fund raising. Training sessions provided skills in areas such as supervision, staff development, and fund raising and allowed directors to interact informally and become aquainted. When the state experienced severe fiscal problems, the directors began to meet to discuss how they could collectively influence the state budget and their program's appropriations. They recognized their common problems of agency survival and agreed to cooperate to maintain or increase their funding. They elected officers, drafted bylaws, and developed a formal newsletter that was sent to all members. The coalition was successful in maintaining funding in its first year and in increasing funding in its second. The coalition

Table 10–1
Characteristics of Four Coalitions in the Human Services

Characteristics	Homeless	Aging	Youth	Youth and Family
History	Formed out of a crisis by charismatic individual (horizontal)	Formed as a result of professional training and periodic meetings (vertical)	Formed to help with upgrading of training (vertical)	Formed as reaction to passage of federal legislation (vertical)
Membership	Broad-based, from different segments of community	Limited to program directors and professional staff	Limited to program directors and professional staff	Open, but heavily program directors
Level of conflict or agreement	Consensus on broad purposes	Consensus on specific issues	Consensus on specific issues	Mixture of consensus and conflict
Functional goals of coalition members	Very different	Narrow set	Narrow set	Mixture
Information and communication flows	Informal, irregular	Regular	Regular	Regular and formalized
Internal issues	Personality clashes	Propriety of members	Propriety of members	Division of responsibility and representation
External issues	Buy or lease a shelter	Increase funding base	Impose licensing and regulation	Strengthen youth programs

then reached a crossroad. Coalition leaders recognized success and wanted to turn attention to other pressing issues in the aging field. However, other members felt they had become too political already and might compromise their professional status in their home communities, while others urged a broader and more visible political agenda and discussed possibilities of hiring a part-time lobbyist and establishing an office in the state capitol. The coalition remains viable today, meets regularly, and maintains communications. The question is whether it should adapt to a new set of issues, reformulate toward stronger political action, or disband.

The third coalition, labeled "youth," represents a group of professional social workers who administered residential programs for youth in a southern state. They formed an association, adopted bylaws, elected officers, and met quarterly to discuss issues such as licensure and regulation of professionals. Association members appeared to agree on a broad set of professional goals, especially the outcome of proposed changes in licensing and regulation in that state. When the state experienced budget cutbacks, however, association members considered the possibilities of taking more powerful political positions on issues. Since then, the association has successfully lobbied for maintaining funding for youth programs in the state and has seriously considered more political activity. However, some members oppose involvement beyond professional areas of concern. They advocate continuation of the earlier record of success rather than to reformulate the organization with a new, more political membership. Meanwhile, the communications system has become more formalized, with a newsletter, phone bank, and written position statements on issues. The association employs a professional fundraiser and discusses possibilities of hiring a paid executive director and student intern in the state capitol.

The fourth coalition represents "youth and family". This coalition is a national organization of 800 individuals and organizations interested in a broad range of issues affecting youth and their families. The coalition has been involved in issues relating to juvenile justice, runaway and homeless youth, missing children, and youth rights. While the coalition formed initially in reaction to the passage of federal legislation that funded delinquency prevention programs for juveniles, it has become involved in a wider variety of issues. While the membership is diverse in composition, the predominant number of members runs residential programs for youth. However, the coalition has numerous factions whose functional goals conflict with positions taken by the national body. No issue has split the group or forced members to join other coalitions. With success has come bureaucratization—formal bylaws, officers, paid staff in Washington, D.C., computer-based telecommunications systems for the members, quarterly newsletters, and an annual policy symposium adopting formal and written policy positions. Resources are available so the coalition can expand its activities. Despite internal factional conflicts, the coalition has survived for years and appears to be headed toward permanence. However, the success of the coalition and the stabilization of its organization and resources have set a more conservative agenda in Washington. Therefore, bureaucratization may alter its short-term ability to respond to a crisis or pressing issue.

The typology presented in table 10–2 can be illustrated through the four case examples. Clearly the homeless coalition was temporary, loosely organized, and limited to raising a single issue within a community. It did not become permanent because no single person emerged as a charismatic spokesperson and because the coalition was too diverse to agree on a single solution to the problem. Individual members pursued incompatible functional goals. While all agreed there was a problem that needed to be solved, the solutions offered were too varied, making consensus impossible. In contrast, the aging coalition was able to be more focused than the homeless coalition. Members of the coalition easily agreed that maintaining and increasing their funding base was desirable. This consensus on goals not only provided incentives for participation but also extended the life of the coalition since funding cycles were repetitive. Only when the coalition considered issues other than funding did the membership raise some objections. Time and the choice of issues beyond funding will determine the future viability of this coalition.

The youth coalition exhibits many of the same features as the aging coalition. Both could be labeled *associational* (see table 10–2), while the homeless coalition is clearly *ad hoc*. The youth and family coalition is the most advanced. It does have internal conflicts, but goal consensus has been sufficient to guarantee longevity and the leadership has been able to keep popular issues continually in front of the membership while minimizing issues that have created conflict. The youth and family coalition can be characterized as a *network*. The major difference is that the youth and family coalition has become bureaucratized, while the other coalitions have remained more informal and less structured. In sum, on a continuum, the homeless coalition is the most temporary, the aging and youth are more permanent, and the youth and family is the most permanent. In terms of organizational structure, the continuum is quite similar. The homeless coalition is informal and loosely structured; the aging and youth coalitions are more formal and tightly organized; and the youth and family coalition is the most formalized and tightly organized.

Therefore, each of these coalitions shows an organized set of interests that can be analyzed on a continuum where the major dimensions include organizational stability and structure. *Ad hoc* coalitions are single-issue, loosely structured and organized, volunteer staffed, and mainly horizontal in composition. *Associations* and *federations* represent more permanence and structure but still have a limited agenda or number of issues. Only the *network* represents a coalition with the permanence to respond to a broad set of changing issues. Some observers might argue that when an organization of

Table 10–2
Typology of Coalitions Based on Stability and Structure

Characteristics	Ad Hoc	Association	Federation	Network
Selection and recruitment of membership	Haphazard, loose	Professional credentials and identification required	Professionalism and direct economic incentive required	Ability to contribute to legitimacy/credibility of organization required
Ideology/Conflict	Broad ideological consensus	Consensus on professional goals	Consensus on economic issues	Mixed consensus and conflict
Resources	Limited	Moderate	Moderate/substantial	Substantial
Staff	Volunteers only	Volunteers and interns	Volunteers and limited paid staff	Volunteers and paid staff
Communications	Irregular and informal	Infrequent but formal	Frequent, both formal and informal	Extensive
Longevity	Short term	Moderate	Long term	Long term
Issues	Single issue	Professional or nonpartisan	Fiscal and legislative	All types
Organizational structure	Loose, informal	Bylaws and officers	Bylaws and officers	Very formalized
Degree of success	Varying degrees of success	Limited success in professional areas of control	Success can be broad based	Success can be broad based

interests takes on the characteristics of a network, it ceases to be a coalition and becomes a unitary organization (Warren 1977).

As planners think about political coalitions and their dynamics, they should examine the properties that make a coalition *ad hoc, associational, federational,* or like a *network.* The reality of power is that political bases become stabilized and structured so that configurations of common interests can regulate the nature and extent of conflict as well as the ultimate resource distribution in a community or society (Bacharach and Baratz 1962). At this point, they may become the power structure, not a temporary coalition seeking to influence the public agenda.

One question of coalitional dynamics as represented through the typology is whether the social concerns of planners are better served by a political environment in which coalitions temporarily form and respond to changing issues or in which they form more permanently and can move from one set of issues to another. The answer may reflect the views of a democratic system and how it operates. For example, one view of how the system operates has been called "a policy issue network" (Heclo 1979). This view involves dynamic practice and periodic regroupings of common interests in ways that are strikingly similar to the *ad hoc* coalitions described earlier. Another view has been referred to as the "Iron Triangle," in which a stable set of participants coalesces to control fairly narrow issues that are largely in their direct economic interests (Kirst 1984); this view resembles the *network* coalition. Planners might decide which of these views fits their assessment of democratic practice.

Lessons from Practice

Coalitions represent responses to changing political environments in which common interests coalesce. Some coalitions have impressive external legitimacy and political appeal. Coalitions that promise to keep the homeless off the streets, bring professionalism to the treatment of troubled youth, actively involve the elderly in volunteer community projects, or return missing children to their families can have timely and popular appeal. Therefore, it is critical that coalitions gain legitimacy by presenting their case in a politically appealing way. The broader public must see the coalition's issue as compelling (Dluhy 1981).

Successful coalitions need adequate resources, sensitive leadership, effective communication channels, organizations capable of delivering a message or exerting influence, and the means to motivate members to remain and participate actively in the issues. Planners can benefit from coalitions but should learn lessons drawn from practice when entering the political environment through participation in a political coalition.

For example, leadership is critical to coalition success. The leader of a coalition becomes a principal spokesperson and, therefore, an individual who establishes the legitimacy and appeal of the coalition. Collective leadership is possible but charismatic spokespersons are often more effective. Leaders are also largely responsible for responding to individual members. Payoffs for members should be made clear so that the trade-offs between common coalition objectives and the functional goals of members are not forgotten. As such, issues dealing with funding, professional standards, and cost effectiveness often appear to be relatively easy issues around which human service workers can mobilize, but more controversial positions taken by the coalition may cause some members to question their participation. Leadership should constantly cut issues in ways that are attractive to members. Single-issue coalitions can die because the leadership fails to help identify issues that appeal to the members. Thus, another lesson is that skillful leaders must emerge or be recruited if the coalition is to be successful.

Also, coalitions need resources to survive, but the challenge is to combine material and intangible or symbolic resources that can be used to influence the public agenda. The lesson is that members of coalitions have different resources and that assembling them efficiently is crucial. Some members may fall short on their dues, but they may be the first to testify or the first to help publish the monthly newsletter. Here, leadership can help again by being sensitive to the use of a broad array of resources.

Finally, coalitions need resources to produce, but they also need the organizational capability to deliver. For example, this may mean a communication system that keeps members informed, solicits their opinions, and directs them to persons or groups who need to be contacted and influenced. Telegrams, letters, phone calls, personal visits, and public testimony may be required. Without an effective communication network, coalitions may find it hard to deliver their message (Dluhy 1984). In time, organizations can become more highly structured, but the lesson is to become more structured without loosing the ability to respond to changing and emerging issues. Again, sensitive leadership helps to maintain this balance.

Conclusion

Coalitions play a fundamental role in political environments, and planners should be more sensitive to their use. While the literature provides conceptual and theoretical insight, empirical analysis through case studies can offer more practical advice. While some coalitions are episodic, others become more permanent. Planners should consider whether participation in the *ad hoc, association, federation,* or *network* type of coalition provides more benefits for them while minimizing their costs. Collective action can be effective if viewed realistically and practically in terms of individual and group resources. It is important to weigh all the decision costs involved in joining a coalition so that the short-term need to win does not obscure the long-term need to be successful in the larger political environment (Adrian and Press 1968). In the end, coalitions provide one of the most effective vehicles for planners to achieve their objectives when faced with power configurations that might otherwise appear intimidating. The typology of coalitions offered in this chapter illustrates not only the types of coalitions that operate in practice but also the characteristics that distinguish these types. One virtue of political pluralism is that coalitions can take different forms and that each form can have different degrees of success. There is no ideal type of coalition but a variety of types on which planners can draw to be successful.

References

Adrian, C., and C. Press. 1968. Decision Costs in Coalition Formation. *American Political Science Review* 62:556–563.

Bacharach, P., and M. Baratz. 1962. Two Faces of Power. *American Political Science Review* 56:947–952.

Bacharach, S., and E. Lawler. 1980. *Power and Politics in Organizations*. San Francisco: Jossey-Bass.

Chesler, M. 1981. Creating and Maintaining Interracial Coalitions. In *Impacts of Racism on White Americans*, B. Bowser and R. Hunt, eds. Beverly Hills: Sage.

Dluhy, M. 1981. *Changing the System: Political Advocacy for Disadvantaged Groups*. Beverly Hills: Sage.

Dluhy, M. 1984. Moving From Professionalism to Political Advocacy in the Human Services—How to Organize A Successful Statewide Political Effort in Youth Services. *Journal of Sociology and Social Welfare* 11:654–684.

Gamson, W. 1962. Coalition Formation at Presidential Nominating Conventions. *American Journal of Sociology* 68:157–171.

Gamson, W. 1968. Coalition Formation. In *International Encyclopedia of the Social Sciences*, D. Sills, ed. New York: Macmillan and Free Press.

Heclo, H. 1979. Issue Networks and the Executive Establishment. In *The New American Political System*, A. King, ed. Washington, D.C.: American Enterprise Institute.

Hinckley, B. 1979. Twenty One Variables Beyond the Size of Winning Coalitions. *Journal of Politics* 41:192–212.

Humphreys, N. 1979. Competing for Revenue Sharing Funds: A Coalition Approach. *Social Work* 24:14–18.

Kirst, M. 1984. Policy Issue Networks: Their Influence on State Policy Making. *Policy Studies Journal* 13:247–264.

Murnighan, J. 1978. Models of Coalition Behavior: Game Theoretic, Social Psychological and Political Perspectives. *Psychological Bulletin* 85:1130–1153.

Roberts, M. 1984. Building a Political Organization to Support A Coalition's Policy

Position. Paper presented at the Annual Symposium on Community Organization and Administration, Detroit, Michigan.

Stevenson, W.; J. Pearce; and L. Porter. 1984. The Concept of Coalition in Organization Theory and Research. Unpublished paper, Irvine: Graduate School of Management, University of California.

Warren, R. 1977. *Social Change and Human Purpose*. Chicago: Rand McNally.

Weisner, S. 1983. Fighting Back. A Critical Analysis of Coalition Building in Human Services, *Social Service Review* 57:291–306.

11
Roles for Planners in Community Development

Neil S. Mayer

P lanners can have powerful impacts on neighborhood revitalization by working within community development corporations (CDCs).[1] These corporations—private, nonprofit organizations created by the residents of troubled neighborhoods—have emerged as potential leaders in the revitalization process. They have planned and implemented projects in various fields, including housing rehabilitation and construction, economic and commercial development, and provision of community facilities in addition to human service delivery, social advocacy, and neighborhood organizing. They have produced visible results in a growing number of urban areas.

CDCs have many strengths in social commitment, community leadership and involvement, and sensitivity to pressing local needs. But they often lack expertise and experience in designing effective strategies to address needs, formulate plans, and implement specific community development projects. Trained planners can help CDCs develop capacity and skills to carry out their difficult work. At the same time, CDCs offer opportunities for planners with social commitments to help people of limited means and power to respond to their problems and revitalize their neighborhoods.

This chapter analyzes the scope and quality of efforts of CDCs, with an emphasis on the factors that affect revitalization success and on the roles for planners in improving their record of accomplishment. It draws on the author's research on more than 100 CDCs practicing neighborhood revitalization in cities today.

Scope and Quality of Development

Virtually every major U.S. city, growing or declining, contains neighborhoods with serious social and economic problems. While these neighborhoods differ in the extent of their inadequate incomes, insufficient job opportunities, deteriorated housing, and declining economic base, they face similar obstacles to effective revitalization.

The characteristics of these neighborhoods and their residents, together with the reluctance of outsiders to invest in them, form a circle of cause and effect that has proved difficult to escape in the quest for revitalization. Neither the private nor public sector has been successful in solving the problems of these troubled communities. In the immediate sense, disinvestment decisions by private profit makers — including business, lending institutions, and real estate operators — have created many of the conditions that confront the neighborhoods. Whether these decisions are based on accurate assessments of economic risks or on other factors, the same conditions that have caused disinvestment in the past persist in many cases today. Only rarely is for-profit action leading to revitalization of troubled neighborhoods, and then it is often designed to serve higher-income newcomers rather than long-time residents. To some extent, residents have disinvested in troubled neighborhoods as well, losing the belief that their resources and efforts can have any impact.

Public policy also has not been highly successful in stabilizing and revitalizing neighborhoods with serious problems. Government programs have sometimes demolished rather than rebuilt these communities, provided inadequate or piecemeal assistance, directed public facilities and services to less distressed areas, or supported incentives to the private sector that have been costly and inefficient. In each case, government often has shown limited knowledge of and sensitivity to neighborhood priorities.

CDCs represent a set of institutions that, in neither the conventional private nor public mold, focuses attention on community revitalization as a central objective. CDCs are created and controlled by community residents and thus need not be cajoled into focusing efforts on distressed neighborhoods. Their projects are more likely to serve current residents than to produce improvements that benefit other people. Ideally, they bring special sensitivity to neighborhood needs and have the capacity to involve other residents directly in the revitalization process. Despite sporadic support and many obstacles, a number of CDCs have increased their capacity and skills to make substantive improvements in their communities.

CDCs are extremely diverse in their experience, scale, and focus. For example:

The Watts Community Labor Action Committee in Los Angeles, California, has been the beneficiary of continuing large-scale support from labor union, private foundation, and federal government sources. Its employees number in the hundreds and are organized into divisions, working on a broad range of housing, economic development, and social service projects in some of Los Angeles' most distressed black neighborhoods.

The Inquilinos Boricuas En Accion, in Boston, Massachusetts, has a substantial track record of developing housing for the Hispanic area in which it operates. It has developed about 800 housing units and diversified into new commercial development and rehabilitation within its immediate area.

The Renigades Housing Movement, Inc., in New York City, was an early leader in the movement for self-help in the rehabilitation and management of badly deteriorated multifamily housing. Renigades has a small staff, continues to struggle to make housing improvements, and attempts to extend its impact by bringing job-generating activities into unoccupied buildings in its Harlem neighborhood.

The St. Clair–Superior Coalition in Cleveland, Ohio, was founded as an advocacy organization in an ethnically diverse neighborhood. It has moved into development but with careful concern that its advocacy functions not be sacrificed in the process. It gained early experience with the rehabilitation of a few single-family houses and created a separate development unit for the purpose of avoiding dominance by the development function.

The East Bay Asian Local Development Corporation in Oakland, California, was born in an effort to save a single, vacant, large commercial structure in Oakland's Chinatown. Over several years, it has renovated the building and made it a center for public and private services to the Asian community. The organization has built on its experience and diversified its work to housing and other areas.

The literature reports many examples of CDC accomplishments but very little comprehensive assessment of whether they achieve their goals.[2] This author's research at the Urban Institute provides an extensive analysis of performance by a large number of CDCs, examining the experience of ninety-nine organizations and their specific HUD-funded Neighborhood Self-Help Development (NSHD) projects from 1980 to 1982.[3] The overall record is one of significant success, as judged by key CDC and societal objectives, despite difficult circumstances.

The NSHD study collected information on the ninety-nine CDCs' basic characteristics and histories, their project plans in terms of tasks to undertake and expected results, their project outcomes, and their accomplishments in leveraging NSHD funds. These data were drawn from a study of program documents submitted by the grantees, from follow-up phone calls, and from two site visits to each sample of thirty CDCs. The site visits were used to gather information on topics more difficult to assess from a distance, including project performance in terms of the distribution of benefits and the role of resident self-help, CDC capabilities such as staff skills and board participation, the effect of internal capabilities and external factors on performance, and the process of capacity building.

The CDCs in the study completed nearly two-thirds of the project tasks they set for themselves. Direct outputs were substantial both on an absolute scale and relative to plans. Table 11–1 reports on projects that were complete by the time research ended. It compares their outputs to the levels CDCs originally proposed, with the results that nearly all intended weatherizing and solarizing of homes took place; over 80 percent of goals for housing rehabilitation, by far the most common project type, were reached; and roughly four-fifths of proposed community facilities were completed (not shown in the table). New housing and commercial space rehabilitation projects produced about half their intended outputs despite the withdrawal of important federal subsidies between times of project planning and implementation,[4] and economic development projects to create permanent jobs and enterprises and to assist existing business reached nearly 40 percent of expectations, despite the onset of serious recession and high interest rates and suspension of federal funding.[5]

CDCs also were successful in assembling other private and public sources to leverage their NSHD grants—a widely heralded policy goal in urban development efforts in recent years. The median CDC generated other monies of roughly three times the amount of NSHD funding.[6] Despite a deteriorating funding environment, CDCs garnered almost exactly the funding levels they initially anticipated. And even in projects planned before 1980, the private sector provided a quarter of all funds, and a private institution was the largest

Table 11–1
Ratios of Actual to Planned Outputs for Completed Projects

Project Type	Average Ratio of Actual to Planned Outputs[a]
Housing rehabilitated	.831
New housing built	.538
Commercial space rehabilitated	.458
New commercial space built	.093
Businesses assisted	.367
Permanent economic development jobs formed	.394
Housing units weatherized	.971
Housing units solarized	1.000

[a]Averaged across the actual to planned output ratios for each CDC with a completed project of that type.

single funder for one-third of the projects. Furthermore, CDCs effectively promoted self-help—that is, direct resident participation in planning and carrying out revitalization work. Residents took active roles on CDC volunteer boards of directors, as paid staff and construction crews, and in improving their own homes and neighborhood facilities. Free labor alone accounted for perhaps one-tenth of total project resources.

CDCs were systematically successful in directing project benefits to neighborhood residents and businesspeople of limited means. They deliberately designed their projects to reach this objective, and they reached it consistently even when it involved increased complexity and cost. New and rehabilitated housing was occupied and controlled by local people at costs they could afford. Jobs generated went to neighborhood residents, especially inexperienced youth. While this finding is not surprising given CDC goals, it represents an important departure from many other public and private revitalization efforts. The CDCs' performance in serving their citizens in very troubled neighborhoods was a unique success.

Still, CDC performance was market by wide variation among organizations. Some projects made very little progress by any of the preceding standards. And even successful projects and organizations often had only limited impacts on CDC neighborhood needs for revitalization. Many factors affected these outcomes. But the involvement of trained planners in CDC efforts could aid significantly in improving their performance and in expanding their capacity to solve neighborhood problems.

Factors Affecting Success

Many factors affected the success of individual CDC projects studied. Among internal characteristics—those residing in organizational staff, board of directors, experience, and structure—the significant contributions included the following:

A broadly skilled executive director who was familiar with the community development process and effective in a diverse set of other roles involving directing and lining up resources for such projects;

A key staff member with specific experience in and knowledge about development projects;

An understanding of issues of project financial feasibility and of their importance;

A track record of accomplishments in development and related neighborhood work that attracts outside support and helps provide other needed skills and experience;

A competent, dedicated staff team with balance among skills;

Doing good homework—that is, maintaining contact with funders, making good proposals and presentations, following correct procedures for handling money and reporting progress, and the like;

Clear division of project responsibilities and avoidance of staff overload;

Careful financial record keeping;

Cooperative participation by the board of directors.

CDC success also depended heavily on the participation, support, and cooperation of other individuals and groups. The key factors included the following:

Active community support and involvement in shaping projects, gathering political and financial support, and conducting the project;

Good relations with local government, both political decision makers and potentially cooperative city staff;

Access to competent technical assistance;

Key links to private actors, especially lenders and foundations;

Success in finding early, risk-taking project supporters;

Good continuing relationships with funders.

While CDCs have at least some significant ability to influence and shape their internal capacities and relations with others, external factors beyond their control have also played central roles in project performance:

Cutbacks in federal funding,

Rising private market interest rates and an economy in recession,

Limited incomes and markets within their communities,

Direct obstacles such as bad weather and strikes,

Abrupt changes in local government.

CDCs varied in their ability to respond effectively to these external conditions, depending on internal capacity and relations to outsiders. Indeed, many combinations of factors affected performance, as did the relationship between types of projects and such factors.

Staff trained in development were extremely important in determining the success or failure of CDC projects, especially the staff member serving the key role of project director.[7] Table 11–2 demonstrates the importance of this planning and management function in NSHD programs. The table assesses CDCs' success in completing half or more of their project tasks, given the level of staff development capability. A standard chi square test was used to test the significance of observed differences in performance. CDCs that had a staff member—either the executive director or more often another person—directing the project who had at least some development expertise had a much higher likelihood of success in their project work than did those with no in-house staff expertise. Seventy percent of projects under the direction of such staff were more than half-completed, compared to little more than one-third of those led by people without expertise. Table 11–3 shows the importance of staff skill in fund raising in development. The table indicates that CDC success in obtaining the level of non-NSHD funds they originally anticipated was greatly increased by the presence on staff of technical development expertise.

Where trained staff were absent, CDCs often felt their way through the definition of project work and sometimes stumbled over self-imposed delays, extra costs, and similar difficulties. Problems in ordinary project implemen-

Table 11–2
Staff Development Skills and Project Success

Presence of In-House Development Expertise	Percentage of CDC Project Work That Is Complete	
	0–50	Greater than 50
No expert	0.63	0.37
Key staffer with some or substantial expertise	0.30	0.70

Note: Based on sample with chi-square significant at the .05 level.

Table 11–3
Staff Development Skills and Success in Leveraging Funds

Presence of In-House Development Expertise	Ratio of Actual (Non-NSHD) Funds Obtained to Funds Planned	
	0–50	Greater than 50
No expert	0.57%	0.43%
Key staffer with some or substantial expertise	0.27	0.73

Note: Based on sample with chi-square significant at the .05 level.

tation included failing to meet city code or zoning requirements, causing extensive project holdups; neglecting to establish rehabilitation budgets for specific buildings leading to internal disagreements over expenditures; lacking knowledge of how to move funding applications through federal agencies, resulting in lost or postponed resources; or failing to recognize needs for outside technical assistance in a specialized area until crises arose. CDCs — often underfunded, operating in difficult environments, and serving low-income people — needed technical staff capable of avoiding unnecessary problems. External conditions certainly did matter in CDC performance and could be dominant, but trained staff strongly affected the likelihood of success under any given set of conditions.

This finding was exemplified in particular by the impact of staff expertise in the fields of feasibility analysis, financing mechanisms, and market analysis and marketing on the level of CDC project success. One-half of the CDCs with limited skills in these areas clearly suffered some significant project problem as a result, and others lacked important capabilities for work they hope to take on in the future. One important problem for several organizations was failure to recognize the need to assess financial feasibility during the early stages of project consideration. Some CDCs spent substantial money and effort on projects without making the preliminary analyses that later showed, for example, that project costs dictated rents for commercial space well beyond prevailing market levels. Or they pursued projects that turned out, on belated assessment, to hinge narrowly on the availability of financing on improbably advantageous terms — financing that then did not materialize, leaving them without realistic options. Other projects suffered from cash shortages stemming from incomplete cost estimates or failure to assess impacts of the timing of revenues and expenditures.

The performance effects of staff financial planning expertise were felt principally in commercial and economic development projects. Table 11–4 shows the dramatic impact of financial skills on the success of those projects, while table 11–5 demonstrates the lack of a comparable role in housing and a few other projects. This difference in effects is natural given the greater market dependence of the commercial and economic development projects. Housing subsidies, together with strong housing demands in CDC neighborhoods, can ensure project feasibility,[8] while economic and commercial development efforts depend more on the ability to sell goods and services produced or to attract firms to space provided in distressed areas, at prices set by CDC costs. What is interesting is that commercial and economic development projects were the same kinds of efforts that resulted in more frequent CDC project failures and were more negatively affected than housing projects by worsening economic conditions and reduced federal funding of relevant programs.[9] While outside influences were especially important for these types

Table 11–4

Financial Marketing Skills and Project Success: Commercial and Economic Development Projects

	Percentage of CDC Project Work That Is Complete	
Presence of Substantial Skills	*0–50*	*Greater than 50*
No (for part or all of project)	0.68	0.32
Yes	0	1

Note: Based on sample with small cell sizes; chi-square test not appropriate.

Table 11–5

Financial Marketing Skills and Project Success: Housing, Community Development, and Energy Projects

	Percentage of CDC Project Work That Is Complete	
Presence of Substantial Skills	*0–50*	*Greater than 50*
No (for part or all of project)	0.38	0.62
Yes	0.41	0.59

Note: Based on sample with chi-square not significant at any reasonable level.

of projects, skilled staff simultaneously made a marked difference. It is clear that staff financial and market skills have a major impact on CDC project success, even in the face of powerful forces beyond CDC influence.

It should be noted that increasing project success was not a narrow contribution to the overall work of neighborhood-based development organizations. A track record of successful project work, besides yielding its own concrete results, was a principal catalyst in building support from community members and in attracting the interest and participation of funders for CDC activities.

It is important to emphasize the value of development expertise by staff rather than by external sources of technical assistance. Technical assistance providers, especially those with extensive experience with CDCs along with their technical skills, provided valuable aid to these organizations. And technical assistance was of value even in key areas such as program planning and financial analysis. But ultimately it was important that the skills be held in house and not only borrowed. The continuing shifting of project planning and implementation specifics was clearly handled better by a full-time staffer who was continuously available to respond to problems and carry out project plans. Lack of financial and market staff skills made it difficult for CDCs to do the quick assessments that could help shape choice of projects or respond promptly to changing financial conditions by quickly recognizing and pursuing feasible alternatives. Only the coupling of in-house staff and outside technical assistance skills made possible the assembling of large-scale, complex projects and financing packages. At least somewhat skilled development staff were also better able to define needs for and efficiently select, use, and learn from technical assistance than were others.

Further, technically skilled staffers are critical to the future prospects of CDCs. A clear precondition to substantial expansion of such organizations, based on observation of many CDCs in various stages of growth, was the addition of strong project directors or overall community development directors. Even the most talented executive directors could not put together and manage multiple large-scale projects—as well as provide overall organizational direction, management, and links to community and to outsiders—without recruiting and training other people to take on primary project responsibilities. For NSHD grantees, the opportunity to add new project directors and give them experience was a central component of the capacity building generated by the program. Addition of financial and market skills appears specifically important to CDCs' future success in a changed public policy and economic environment. Reductions in federal grant funding, continuing high interest rates, the complexities of tax incentive schemes to encourage private investment and reduce project costs, and CDCs' increased efforts toward partial self-sufficiency and profit making all intensify the need for appropriate analytic skills on staff. Similarly, a difficult national environment will make strategic planning and project selection skills still more highly valuable. And these conditions increase the overall vulnerability of CDCs and their projects, making serious technical work that reduces unnecessary problems an even higher priority.

Roles for Planners

CDCs are affected by very difficult neighborhood conditions, by internal limitations and complex relationships with external sources of support and funding, and by local and national economic and political changes—circumstances that could overcome organizational staff in many situations. By examining CDC characteristics, capabilities, and shortcomings, it is possible to identify potential contributions by planners in more detail.

Most CDCs need additional staff to implement extensive development projects. Many have few staff members of any kind. The median number of staff members among the organizations in our study was only eleven and 25 percent had five or fewer employees.[10] Executive directors were highly dominant in their organizations. While these leaders showed a great talent in shaping program direction, gathering community and political support, and raising funds, more than half of those observed had limited proven capability in development and few had extensive training and experience when NSHD projects began. In addition, executive directors were often overloaded with critical tasks other than planning and implementation of specific projects.

Most CDCs designated a separate project director for their NSHD projects and for other major projects they had undertaken in the past. But trained, experienced project directors were difficult to attract to small, insecurely funded organizations that pay modest wages. Over a quarter of the project directors we observed had very little development experience, and another half had only limited background. Skilled staff for development projects are much needed by CDCs. Such positions could be filled, to CDC advantage, with well-trained planners.

A particularly important role to be played in CDC work is in the process of project planning. This process requires people with enough knowledge to facilitate the basic steps, sequencing, and processes for conducting housing, economic development, or similar projects; to identify tasks to be performed, allocate responsibilities, and establish realistic schedules; and to respond to new information and changes as they arise. This basic capability was frequently lacking in CDCs, at least at the start of NSHD projects, because key staff were neither trained in the development process nor experienced in the kinds of projects they were expected to guide. In two-thirds of observed CDCs, either program planning skills were noticeably weak or CDC staff as a whole gave inadequate attention and priority to program planning. If people with academic training, and especially with at least some limited experience, in planning for development had been available, they could have supplied a skill clearly in short supply, as well as an understanding of the need to do program planning early and well, even if a first-guess plan needed to be repeatedly revised as circumstances changed or were clarified. This skill need not be highly technical, involving complex financial packaging, architectural and engineering capability, or the legalities of tax syndications. A clear understanding of the tasks necessary to carry out a development project, their level of difficulty and the requirements for outside assistance, and experience-based realism about costs and timing would mark a boost in expertise for many CDCs.

CDCs also were short of staff skilled in analyzing the financial feasibility of development projects, determining the financing and other conditions needed to make them workable, and outlining business plans and marketing strategies. Two-thirds of the CDCs for which we had clear assessments lacked appreciable staff expertise in financial planning and marketing, and again, many failed to recognize its value. Some CDCs have little specific knowledge about the components of financial projections—for example, the cost elements of a given type of project or the initial capital required. A good number could not develop a project pro forma on their own. Even a planner with modest financial analysis abilities, along with cognizance of its import, could fill some of the often ample room for improvement in CDC skills in this area. A technically well-trained planner, able to assess complex financing alternatives in terms of which ones make projects feasible or might be modified to do so, would be still more valuable.

In addition, CDCs have shown only limited progress in developing strategic neighborhood plans, designating the set of projects that would potentially meet their goals and the critical links between them, and the preconditions for their success. To a significant extent, this situation is a realistic response to conditions. Most CDCs have little, if any, assurance that they can obtain the continuing and flexible funds that would allow them to pursue in any orderly way the key projects they identified. Instead, CDCs by necessity pursue targets of opportunity, as they arise, that fit within broad organizational objectives. Still, skilled planners could help assess which opportunities to seek and priorities to pursue, with special understanding of the interactions among projects and between them and neighborhood conditions. They might be even more valuable to CDCs in seeing how past CDC projects create the opportunity for future projects, as both planners and other clever CDC staff have already been doing in many instances.

Finally, planners could take broader leadership responsibilities in CDCs and serve them well as executive directors or deputy directors with broad direction-giving and resource-gathering functions. Continuity of commitment and other characteristics are critical there, although a planning perspective can certainly be of general value. Identifying goals and promising projects, and putting together the people and the financial resources to implement them, are roles that planners who have also established roots in their communities can effectively play.

Key Skills for Practice

The best prepared project or development directors were knowledgeable and experienced in conceptualizing a project; assessing its financial feasibility, market potential, and capital needs; identifying an appropriate financial structure and funding sources; outlining the steps to completion; supervising the bricks-and-mortar components of the project; managing the efforts of other staff, crews, contractors, and technical consultants; and responding with ingenuity to crises. But the practicing planner willing to make a CDC commitment need not be intimidated. In many instances, some familiarity with and limited experience in several components of such work could make a significant contribution to CDC capability, especially if the background were with the same type of project in which a CDC is engaged.

The best training for CDC work is somewhat different from past traditions of public sector, land-use-oriented planning education. Training and experience, even at lower levels of responsibility, in the actual implementation of a housing or economic development project is the best basis for serious project planning. Specific quantitative analytic skills, especially in computing project feasibility given projected revenues, financing alternatives, and operating costs, are very much needed. But many planners may be equipped with such skills by academic training and early professional work, equal to or beyond the skills available within many CDCs. Nonexpert CDC staff can gain such skills through experience with CDC projects and with technical consultants. But such experienced staff always are in short supply and sometimes are lacking altogether in an organization run by a talented but overtaxed community leader.

Technical skill is by no means sufficient for productive work in a CDC environment. Most CDCs are committed to their communities' definitions of needs and priorities. Many give serious attention to informing and consulting with their boards of directors, even when such processes might delay a project or lead to choices that conflict with experts' advice. A CDC planner clearly needs a genuine willingness to work with community residents to chart project direction. This willingness applies not only to selection of project priorities but also to specifics of implementation. For example, community people may have strong views about who should be served by a housing project, with implications for financing needs, ownership patterns, and architectural design. This might mean more work for staff and delays in implementation, while subsidies are obtained to serve lower-income people. Members of the community also may expect to participate in resident selection and the establishment of operating rules.

CDC planners also need sensitivity to neighborhood priorities and community politics. Practitioners interested in living within CDC neighborhoods have a better opportunity to gain community sensitivity. But the turf of some CDCs provides wide latitude of residence, and many CDC staff live beyond the immediate neighborhood and learn about the community on the job. It is not ultimately personal residence but the skill to translate community desires into identified project opportunities and then feasible plans that distinguishes the practitioner.

Basic to these skills is a commitment to CDC goals of revitalizing distressed communities and of benefiting disadvantaged residents within them. In most cases, CDC work involves long hours, inelegant working conditions, lower pay than is available elsewhere,[11] and fragile funding conditions that sometimes threaten job security.

There are many benefits of CDC work, however. CDC practitioners quickly find themselves in positions of substantial project responsibility. They participate in governance and management, control financial operations, and face pressures of regular decision making and immediate crises. This capacity building through project experience can benefit the CDC as a whole and offer major learning opportunities for individual practitioners. In NSHD-funded projects, project directors with planning degrees but limited hands-on experience repeatedly described their first CDC projects, or first projects of a given type, as important contributors to their capabilities. Furthermore, responsibility also can provide special opportunities for accomplishment. CDC staff took great personal price in the renovated homes or newly built buildings enjoyed by residents as a result of their work. Many also gained respect and appreciation from community members.

Because CDCs offer them immediate opportunities for responsibility, even young planners can gain professional visibility by CDC work. In many cases they may become well known to city, state, or federal government staff members, private lenders and developers, and members of CDC boards. Innovative projects that confront difficult problems can earn great respect in cities across the country. Indeed, CDC staff that produce good projects can too often be stolen away by higher paying firms and institutions. Planners must make sufficiently long commitments to CDC work to ensure that both they and the community benefit from their learning experiences.

CDCs can provide supportive environments for working and learning. In the best cases, new project directors with limited expertise were joined by support teams dealing with many dimensions of their work. Board members or paid outsiders provided assistance on technical matters, trained bookkeepers or financial managers provided project financial controls, executive directors aided with project management and helped make initial political and funding contacts, and local government staff guided practitioners through bureaucratic processes. Planners considering CDC work might assess the availability of such support mechanisms in a given organization.

CDCs also offer significant opportunities to develop leadership skills beyond specific project roles. Many practitioners automatically become directors for development activities, responsible for taking a lead in pursuing new projects as well as implementing those already begun. Some may gradually take political and funding source contact responsibilities and share the responsibilities of dealing with board members, although many prefer to leave those activities to others, and executive directors sometimes want to retain control of them. Planners with real links to their communities may become CDC executive directors.

Conclusion

CDCs can be effective in generating neighborhood revitalization where other types of groups have failed, in achieving important social goals, and in serving people of limited means and power. And planners with training and experience in development can be of great value to CDCs in helping them to plan and implement their projects successfully and in enabling them to expand the scope and scale of their work. Their revitalization efforts provide opportunities for both planners and CDCs to build skills and produce results in otherwise difficult conditions.

This process of mutual benefit has been made substantially more difficult by recent federal cutbacks that have reduced funding for CDCs and for the programs they make use of in their work. Planners may have to take somewhat greater risks, during such a period, to help CDCs develop projects that can then obtain needed funds. Planner skills will need to be honed in new directions to develop ventures in concert with private for-profit actors and otherwise to take advantage of shifts in the CDC environment. But the potential for planners to make a difference has likely grown under the more difficult circumstances. And the further maturing of many CDCs born in the 1970s, as well as the continued turning by activists to local levels of action, provides an expansion of valuable opportunities.

If the federal government continues to withdraw support for urban revitalization, CDCs' fragile successes may be interrupted and the momentum of capacity building may be lost. But if policymakers provide at least the modest funding necessary to sustain basic CDC staffing and projects, then planners can continue to make significant contributions to CDC growth and success.

Notes

1. CDCs are also called neighborhood development organizations or community-based development organizations.

2. See, for example, Bratt, Byrd, and Hollister (1983); National Commission on Neighborhoods (1979); and New World Foundation (1980). The previous studies that most systematically assess the experience of large numbers of community organizations in the development field are National Center for Economic Alternatives (1981) and Abt Associates (1973). For a useful look at changes in the CDC environment and responses to it, see McNeely (1982) and Cohen and Kotler (1983).

3. Each organization was the recipient of an NSHD program grant from HUD in 1980 for a specific project (a program since eliminated by the Reagan administration). For a full report of this research, see Mayer (1984).

4. These cutbacks were found especially in Section 8 housing.

5. Economic Development Administration funding in particular was suspended.

6. A small number of highly successful cases lifted the average leverage ratio to nine.

7. This key person could also be the overall director of development activities.

8. This finding holds at least over the relatively short term our study could observe.

9. Much CDC housing work was protected by continuing federal community development funding or advance commitments of Section 8 funds.

10. The NSHD program deliberately selected as grant recipients CDCs that had at least some paid staff and program experience but that were not uniformly the country's largest and most sophisticated. Grantees therefore constitute quite a representative middle range of currently working CDCs.

11. The extent of this differential varies widely.

References

Abt Associates. 1973. *An Evaluation of the Special Impact Program.* Cambridge, Mass.: Abt Associates.

Bratt, R.G.; J.M. Byrd; and R.M. Hollister. 1983. The Private Sector and Neighborhood Preservation, mimeographed. Cambridge, Mass.: Neighborhood Research.

Cohen, R., and M. Kotler. 1983. *Neighborhood Development Organizations After the Federal Funding Cutbacks.* Washington, D.C.: Department of Housing and Urban Development.

Mayer, N.S. 1984. *Neighborhood Organizations and Community Development: Making Revitalization Work.* Washington, D.C.: The Urban Institute Press.

NcNeely, J. 1982. Self-Help Community Development: Life After Reagan. *Citizen Participation* 3:3–5.

National Center for Economic Alternatives. 1981. *Federal Assistance to Community Development Corporations: An Evaluation of Title VII of the Community Services Act of 1974.* Washington, D.C.

National Commission on Neighborhoods. 1979. *People Building Neighborhoods: Final Report to the President and the Congress of the United States.* Washington, D.C.: Government Printing Office.

New World Foundation. 1980. *Initiatives for Community Self-Help: Efforts to Increase Recognition and Support.* New York.

12
Feminist Advocacy Planning in the 1980s

Jacqueline Leavitt

C losing the gender gap can improve conditions for women and make planning more relevant to the larger society. Changing demographics, location of employment, wage levels, and other factors are affecting urban areas and causing problems for women. Women are increasingly likely to concentrate in central cities, head single-family households with sole responsibility for children, rely on mass transit and subsidized housing, and receive federal assistance of some type. They are experiencing problems of access to education, work, transportation, security, day care, and other services. Planning practitioners have responded to some of these problems in the past but have not always addressed women's needs explicitly. Interest increased in the 1970s when more women became planners and national issues such as equal rights provided a more receptive climate, but the gender gap remains. To close the gap, I argue that future planning practice around women's interests should apply a feminist advocacy approach.

What Are the Problems?

Women face problems of such significance in cities and society that gender can no longer be ignored in planning practice. These problems include the shift away from traditional nuclear family households, the presence of women in the labor force, and the feminization of poverty. Consider the following:[1]

Studies project that by 1990, the increase in total number of households will be attributed to a proportionately smaller number of married couples with children; there will be a rise in married couples without children and unattached individuals with and without children.

During the 1970s, there was an increase in single-parent families; by 1979, there was an 81 percent increase in mothers with one or more children in the home, compared to a 51 percent increase in female-headed households, and a 12 percent increase in family formation.

In 1980, of the little more than 30 million families with children under 18, 5.34 million were headed by women; 92 percent of the 12 million children living with one parent were living with their mother.

More than half the nation's children have mothers who work away from home; in 1981, 8.2 million, or 44.9 percent, of all preschoolers had mothers in the labor force.

By 1978, almost 60 percent of all women were in the paid labor force; by 1990, it is predicted that this figure will rise to 68.3 percent, with 70.1 percent married women with children older than six and 55.3 percent with children under six.

Occupational sex segregation continues; in both 1969 and 1979, about one-half of all working women were employed in fewer than 30 percent of the detailed census occupations and in occupations in which 30 percent or more of the employees were women.

Through 1978, women working full time earned about 60 percent as much as men.

The median income for all women, families, and individuals, in 1980 was $4,920.

The median income of $27,744 for two-earner families in 1980 was about a third higher than for families where only the husband worked and nearly triple the income of families maintained by women; women who headed households were the largest group of poor in the country.

Among the elderly, about 2.8 million women over the age of 65 live in poverty, as compared to 1.1 million men.

Women are more likely to be concentrated in central cities, rely on mass transit, live in public housing, and receive Section 8 assistance. Unlike other discriminated groups, women's access to education, occupations, transportation, housing, and security can be controlled by the availability of child care. Given their average low income, the consequences of no child care have the effect of reducing women's life options. What happens is that women elect not to have children, or not to work, or husband/wife families often work on split shifts so that at least one parent can be available. In other cases, people conform to rather rigid time schedules, and while this occurs for women and men of other classes, for the majority of low- and moderate-income women, the returns are low pay and complicated schedules with kin networks. The most prevalent form of child care remains reliance on friends and relatives.

Women's roles as wives, mothers, child rearers, and nurturers place them in a uniquely disadvantaged position. From cradle to grave, women are held responsible for the young and the elderly, in work unacknowledged by pay, in the limbo of conditional liberation.

There is naturally a companion set of figures for men, and as women's roles are transformed by participation in the labor force, men's roles are also undergoing decisive changes. Structural unemployment will have an impact on men's self-image in a society where their masculinity has been measured by the worth of their paid labor. There has been an increase in the number of households of single men; their median salary is below that of two-earner families, as well as below that of nuclear families with wives at home. There has been an increase in the number of men who are single parents.

Race also affects women and men. Among women, blacks and those of Hispanic origin earn less than white women whose median income, in turn, is lower than men's. Among men, black male workers are likely to suffer the worst, particularly in service industries where they have not shared in its growth. As conditions change, blacks do worse than whites.

Poverty is a critical problem for women. The feminization of poverty, a phrase first used by Pearce (1979), describes those at the lowest end of the economic spectrum in society. It is not surprising that these people are increasingly women given their dual oppression: subordination to men and economic discrimination. Other factors, such as the capacity to bear children and de facto child-rearing responsibilities, further contribute to uneven subjection of women.

As Ehrenreich (1983) writes:

> In 1980 two out of three adults who fit into the federal definition of poverty were women, and more than half the families defined as poor were maintained by single women. In the mid-sixties and until the mid-seventies, the number of poor adult males actually declined, while the number of poor women heading households swelled by 100,000 a year prompting the National Advisory Council on Economic Opportunity to observe that: "All other things being equal, if the proportion of the poor in female householder families were to continue to increase at the same rate as it did from 1967 to 1978, the poverty population would be composed solely of women and their children before the year 2000."

To work on issues of the poor and fail to recognize that two out of three adults in poverty are women is to avoid what should be a critical component of any plan.

My aim is not to neglect the problems of men. By focusing on women as a group, however, I highlight their particular characteristics. Any study needs to go further and consider distinctions and similarities among gender, race, ethnicity, class, and age. Nonetheless, it is important to recognize that new initiatives are needed to broaden the field to incorporate issues related to women.

Perspectives on Feminist Advocacy Planning

Feminist advocacy planning builds on an earlier tradition of advocacy as an approach to planning. In the 1960s, Davidoff (1965) argued that planners should openly advocate particular group interests or become advocates for what they deem proper in society. He believed that any group that has interests at stake in the planning process should have those interests represented and that planners should work with specific groups to improve their conditions and enhance participatory democracy. Advocate planners applied knowledge and skills on behalf of poor people and minorities in urban ghetto areas, in public agencies responsible for comprehensive planning, and in community organizations developing programs and services at the neighborhood level. If advocate planners were not typical of most professionals in the field or were criticized for failing to accomplish genuine social change (Heskin 1980), they provided a precedent for practitioners who identify with feminism and want to take action within the planning profession (Welch 1984).

Feminist advocacy planning broadens earlier advocacy planning by incorporating issues related to women. One component is to approach planning from a feminist perspective. Some people argue that any step that brings visibility to women's issues or offers technical assistance to a group comprised primarily of women is a step forward. For example, any plan or program that betters women's conditions—increasing available jobs, affordable housing, accessible transportation—is to the good. Others argue that this is not enough, that the plan must do more than merely identify women as beneficiaries or increase their jobs or housing, but instead must transform the economic and patriarchal systems. In this, women's equality with men must become part of but is not the whole program. Power relationships must change. Women thus become not just planning targets or objects, but their needs and strengths become an integral part of the planning process. This is the approach emphasized here.

Bunch (1981, p. 196) proposes five criteria that enable a person to evaluate whether reforms are progressive or not and that can be applied to feminist advocacy planning:

1. Does this reform [that is, plan] materially improve the lives of women, and if so, which women, and how many?
2. Does it build an individual woman's self-respect, strength, and confidence?

3. Does it give women a sense of power, strength, and imagination as a group and help build structures for further changes?

4. Does it educate women politically, enhancing their ability to criticize and challenge the system in the future?

5. Does it weaken patriarchal control of society's institutions and help women gain power over them?

The key is the extent to which the planner identifies with or considers women's issues important and incorporates women's needs in planning.

It should be noted that being a woman does not necessarily mean being a feminist. A female planner has to make a conscious choice about her professional identification. Those who do may be labeled as feminists and perceive that their professional standing is under attack. Men who make a conscious decision to be feminist or supportive of women's issues have far less to lose by that choice. In the planning profession, to be a feminist or interested in women's issues is to reject explicitly much of the professional socialization in one's training. Reluctance to identify as a feminist is compounded because of the relative newness of women's tenure as planners—ten years compared to about seventy for men—and because planners' identities are unclear anyway.

It also should be noted that identification as a feminist is easier in some cases than in others. The determination of where and how best to introduce women's issues can be relatively easy when the issue concerns women primarily, as with government agency staff working on battered women's shelters or with a neighborhood group surveying community needs as a basis for funding for a battered women's shelter. Any location, any client relationship will do.

In the case of other issues that inherently, but less obviously, concern women or where there is no direct relationship with female clients, advocacy has to begin by first identifying gender as an important variable. For example, women are the major recipients of federal housing assistance in Section 8 and public housing, the major users of mass transit, and the majority of single parents and the elderly. Yet it is not surprising to find city or national planning reports on these subjects that either do not call attention to this issue or, having done so, go no further with the findings (Engler 1982; Drury et al. 1978). The opportunity exists to make gender visible by drawing explicit attention to it.

Another component of feminist advocacy planning is to analyze urban structure and community process from a feminist perspective. Women are more likely to be concentrated in central cities. Unlike other discriminated groups, women's access to education, occupation, transportation, housing, and security can be affected by the availability of child care.

It is thus necessary for planners to develop approaches that consider the totality of people's lives—their homes, family relations, living arrangements, and work—and to analyze the spatial consequences. It should no longer be the spatial ordering that is central to urban planning, for example, but rather the complexity of ways in which human beings behave—the division of labor between men and women, the relationship of labor in the home to paid labor at an off-home work site, the varying demands and needs through the life cycle—within the spatial context of a neighborhood, city, suburb, or rural area.

For example, when examining a site for a residential neighborhood, planners typically look at physical data, but even when they analyze cultural data (Lynch 1962), issues arising from the division of labor within the household are neglected, if not ignored. If the division of labor were to be treated as a variable, issues about accessibility to commercial and public facilities might reveal whether the physical plan either facilitates or exacerbates domestic labor. Similarly, if the division of labor and work within the household were analyzed as to density and privacy, more weight might be given to issues of building massing and scale. If, at the same time, or independently, women's labor force participation outside the home were analyzed in relation to urban impacts of displacement and gentrification, differences among women's earning power and the implications for neighborhood change might be sharpened. Interesting class and gender issues arise over whether the increased earnings of some women lead to poorer women and their families being an at-risk population and displaced (Downs 1977).

Yet another component of feminist advocacy planning is to identify gender variables in all aspects of practice. For the planner not working directly with women—who may be alone in her or his interest in women's issues, overloaded with a more pressing assignment, or doubtful about how to integrate women's issues in the work at hand—it may be sufficient simply to raise questions and circulate memos. A staff person could circulate a memo about a women's conference or publication to the appropriate departments, calling attention to the significant issues, or suggest a proposal about further analysis using gender as a variable. For example, the late Joyce Skinner of the U.S. Department of Housing and Urban Development's (HUD) Women's Policy and Program staff analyzed the resolutions from International Women's Year as they related to further actions HUD executives could take (Leavitt 1980a). Evelyn Mann of New York City's Planning Department was willing to receive proposals about how data could be incorporated into the next census to facilitate analyses by gender. A Los Angeles County commission supervisor hired Professors Dolores Hayden and Ena Dubnoff to present plans and architectural drawings for single-parent housing units after reading an excerpt from Hayden's book (1984). In each example, conditions existed that provided receptivity to the memo and women were understood to be the subject under study. In Skinner's analysis of the resolutions, the visibility of top women executives in the Carter administration was important. HUD involvement included reworking data, original research, nationally sponsored competitions, and establishment of a women's section. In the New York case, Mann attended a seminar sponsored by Donna Shalala and run by Eugenie Birch on women and housing. Shalala had formerly advocated women's issues as head of HUD's Office of Policy Development and Research and has used her role as president of Hunter College to further the issues.

Women are increasing in number as planning staff members and directors, but the profession is still dominated by men who are affected by the male ethic and view of the world (Gilligan 1982). Planning assumes a value set that is inherently and historically masculine. The nature of the planner-client relationship is to establish a hierarchy in which the planner is expert. Direction for planning comes from policymakers, explicitly politicians and implicitly economic interests. While planners have relative autonomy and hearings may provide a forum for the public-at-large, the overriding goals and objectives are more likely to be shaped by men than women politicians, male corporate heads rather than female.

But the gender gap may have an impact on who shapes policy (as more women may be in decision-making positions) as well as on the policies (as women's needs become more prominent). As perceptions of the importance of the gender gap increase and the climate becomes more supportive, women planners might feel more comfortable choosing to adopt feminist advocacy strategies.

The National Congress of Neighborhood Women (NCNW), a community-based women's organization with a central office in Brooklyn, New York, offers one innovative case study of how women can adopt feminist strategies. Since 1974, under NCNW's auspices, a nationwide grass-roots women's group has grown to deal with housing, education, economic development, and employment at the local level. The Brooklyn group began with a neighborhood-based college-accredited program for local women returning to school and has moved increasingly toward comprehensive community planning. One of their projects is a proposal for intergenerational housing for a city-owned, abandoned hospital in their neighborhood. This proposal grew out of an identification of the needs of women and will affect single parents, older women, working mothers, and residents in public as well as private housing.

Since 1982, NCNW has been planning for a national institute that would bring women together to elaborate women's positions on a variety of issues, including housing, employment and economic development, health, child care, education, and community planning (Feit and Peterson 1984). The agenda is set by the organization. The majority of board members is neighborhood leaders. The grass-roots women's expertise has developed from firsthand experience as well as from formal training. They thus have knowledge of the issues and a perspective that is often more pragmatic than that of the so-called experts.

The leadership technique used by NCNW in developing its network of low-income women involves professionals in a personal and immediate way. This technique draws on peer counseling, consciousness raising, and the re-evaluation counseling movement. Meetings begin by breaking into small groups and responding to questions that elicit personal responses. People are not allowed to be self-destructive or critical of others but are directed toward enabling everyone to listen to what others are saying. In this way participants are encouraged to understand racial, ethnic, and class biases and to see other women as allies. Empowerment is central to the NCNW planning and organizing model, and specific issues are thus viewed as means and not ends. For example, housing is not seen solely as a commodity that improves material well-being but as a vehicle for empowerment.

The New Jersey Bergen County League of Women Voters housing advocacy project offers another case study of practitioners working directly with women. League members discovered that people seeking housing assistance were either single parents who could not find affordable shelter or elderly who were house rich but could not afford the upkeep. The league sponsored several workshops, one of which focused on the housing needs of single parents. Since single parents and the elderly are mostly women, the feminist issue was related to the feminization of poverty.

The league organized its workshop along more traditional lines than the NCNW. Participants worked with an architect and planner to develop a prototype house to accommodate single parents and their children. That design has continued to evolve by incorporating suggestions from potential users. Although the collaboration did not lead to a built project, the ideas were published, circulated, and presented in conferences (Petitt and Glassman 1983).

Advocacy with both the NCNW and the league occurred outside government and through direct contact with women constituents. Both the NCNW and the league are explicitly women's groups; women's needs and values were directly stated, and intervening barriers between the women and professionals were reduced.

There are distinctions between NCNW and the league, however. Based on Bunch's (1981) earlier criteria, one could conclude that the outcome of the league project on single-parent housing, a relatively clear-cut program, would materially improve conditions. How the project fared with the other four criteria—whether individual women would gain in personal attributes, whether women who live in the single-parent house would go on to build other institutions, whether they were educated politically or with a heightened ability to criticize and challenge the system—is less clear. The housing proposal does not ensure that personal and structural changes would occur, but it would provide shelter and services, and changes in material conditions could lead to larger changes. A woman who no longer struggles to get decent housing or who joins the company of other women from similar circumstances might engage in more political efforts. Also, the organization of a single-parent house could weaken patriarchal control by reducing a woman's dependence on a mate and providing her with the space and time to find a better job and become more active politically and in other ways she desires.

NCNW is more explicit in its planning and organizing. Process is integral in its efforts. Individual grass-roots women are given space in which to ask questions and overcome intimidation by professional jargon. The very act of organizing a dialogue in the form of a national institute begins to give women a sense of power and strength. The institute becomes an alternative way of arriving at policy. Since most public policies appear almost preordained by government, the institute provides a vehicle for discussing and formulating ways to challenge economic, patriarchal, and other aspects of current or proposed policy. It would be ideal for the feminist advocacy planner to work directly with women. But such jobs are not always available or remunerative. It is more likely that the practitioner will find herself or himself in government, where opportunities may exist to relate to women's groups outside the job. In Minnesota, for example, there is a Women's Economic Action Plan (Minnesota Women's Consortium 1984); in California, a Women's Economic Agenda (Chelnov, Ewell, and Vrois 1984). Nationally, the National Low Income Housing Coalition has developed a woman's platform around housing issues (Vogel-Heffernan and Cook 1984). The scope and quality of opportunities should increase in the years ahead.

Education and Research for Change

Planning education could serve as a resource for developing knowledge, skills, and attitudes conducive to feminist advocacy planning. The continual incorporation of new areas of expertise into planning education might lead to the idea that any subject could be included in the field. This is not so. Since the 1970s, advocates for women's issues have been tugging at the edges of planning practice and education. A breakthrough may be imminent, however.

Until now, those women's issues that emerged in planning paralleled what was happening in the country since the 1960s through the latest phase of the women's movement. The most widely known issue of this movement began with achieving equal rights, the centerpiece of ratification of the Equal Rights Amendment (ERA). Despite the setback in the early 1980s with the defeat of the ERA, the struggle continues for equal pay for equal work, equal access to education, maternity benefits, and child care on the job. Within the planning profession these issues surfaced in the 1970s within the national planning organizations. Although women planners have not achieved parity with men, there has been a significant gain in women's entry and graduation from planning programs, from 46 in 1968 to 775 in 1978, from 7.5 to 31 percent.

In the middle 1970s, women and some men, practitioners and educators, lobbied for and were successful in establishing the technical division, Planning and Women, within the American Planning Association. Subsequently, HUD funded a bibliography on women and planning and a competition on proposals and projects benefiting women. The bibliography was published by the Council of Planning Librarians, and the publication of the competition results may be published independently of HUD. Both fell victim to Reagan cutbacks.

Courses or concentrations of study on women's issues in planning programs did not follow or, if given, did not become standard fare in curriculum planning. There are no joint degree planning programs with women's studies, as in other fields such as social work, public health, and law, although students may elect to do independent study or master's theses. Interests appear divided between issues affecting women planners and issues of women's needs. What is also happening is that some of the issues are being integrated into courses rather than remaining isolated as a separate sector. This trend toward assimilation may be a handicap in the development of feminist analysis as applied to planning.

New initiatives are needed to broaden planning courses about women. Although much of what people learn comes from day-to-day activities on the job, the prior development of knowledge about women's issues can lead to better practice. The importance of prior training involving both exposure to materials and discussions of various strategies and their effectiveness cannot be underestimated. At the University of California at Los Angeles, for example, feminist planners and designers in the Graduate School of Architecture and Urban Planning initiated a student-run course on feminist theory and its application to planning. In collaboration with the minority students' caucus, they also held a Women in Poverty conference and sponsored a conference on domestic violence and planning. At Hunter College, a two-year seminar on women and housing has been given in which leading women practitioners in New York City had an integral part. The practitioners included the college president as well as many members of the metropolitan-based Women in Housing and Finance group. Student exercises included the financial analyses of actual projects of their impact on women and the development of a position statement on housing introduced to the Democratic party's platform committee (Birch 1985). At Columbia University, students wrote master's theses on women's issues. Fung (1984) analyzed the supply and demand of housing units for single parents in Nassau–Suffolk, Holley (1984) interviewed planners in southern California about whether and how planning departments integrated issues about child care into their work plans, and Granby (1980) studied women in the work force.

Revisions in curricula with women's issues in mind are overdue. The question is whether to develop a segregated women's sector or to integrate the issues into all courses (UCLA Feminist Planners and Designers 1984). This question touches on the interdisciplinary nature of planning, a familiar subject in planning education.

Also, planning educators are in positions to encourage a more realistic appraisal of what women do. What is needed now is to start with the complex ways in which people organize their lives around their home, family relationships, and work and to analyze the spatial consequences. The interdisciplinary nature of planning education is traced to its beginnings at a time when architecture, landscape architecture, and engineering exerted a major influence. Now, as perhaps no time since the 1930s, that physical imprint needs to be expanded to understand not only economic and social implications but implicitly to incorporate issues about women. The dramatic shifts in women's roles and the attendant consequences for men and children deserve no less.

The link to planning could begin by acknowledging women's unpaid domestic labor, their connection to the neighborhood, their multiple roles as wife-mother-worker, and their preference for denser areas where activities can be concentrated. The neighborhood school concept should be updated, with the optimum use of land based not on maximum return to the business community but in enhancing the ability of people to perform several roles well. Closed schools can be recycled as child care learning centers; remote office centers using communications technology can be located in neighborhoods where workers are close to children and home; and shared housing with collective kitchens and dining areas can be viable options.

These are but a few ideas. Closing the gender gap, with its spatial implications, can be one way in which planning education retains its timeliness and relevance to the larger society.

Conclusion

Planners have largely forsaken the development of master plans with a long time dimension, but those interested in forming strategies about women's issues might benefit from a look to the future. The feminization of poverty and the gender gap both affect and are affected by outcomes in the economic and political sphere. Women now constitute a third of the students granted planning degrees and should increasingly take positions of relative authority. This authority, buttressed by a shift in planning curricula, can help them set research agendas, sanction studies, and provide general leadership in women's issues. I have argued elsewhere that numbers alone do not mean that women can make a difference in defining planning content; there also has to be a feminist consciousness (Leavitt 1980a). Women's self-consciousness about their needs has been growing, and they are more willing than ever to go public. The 1980s should be a time of exploring issues, building coalitions in which women play a central role, and regrouping. The 1990s should be a time for implementing the benefits in much the same way as the 1980s work has built on the past.

Note

1. See U.S. Department of Commerce, Bureau of the Census, Current Population Reports, P-23, no. 107, *Families Maintained by Female Householders 1970–79,* by Steve W. Rawlings (Washington, D.C.: Government Printing Office, 1980); U.S. Department of Commerce, Bureau of the Census, Current Population Reports, P-20, no. 305, *Marital Status and Living Arrangements: March 1980* (Washington, D.C.: Government Printing Office, 1980); U.S. Department of Commerce, Bureau of the Census, Current Population Reports, P-20, no. 366, *Household and Family Characteristics: March 1980* (Washington, D.C.: Government Printing Office, 1980); U.S. Department of Labor, Bureau of Labor Statistics, "Half of Nation's Children Have Working Mothers," In *News* (Washington, D.C.: November 15, 1981); Mary Rubin, "Women and Poverty: Research Summary," (Washington, D.C.: Business and Professional Women's Foundation, 1982); U.S. Department of Labor, Bureau of Labor Statistics, "Occupational Segregation and Earning Differences by Sex," by Nancy F. Rytina in *Monthly Labor Review* (Washington, D.C.: Government Printing Office, January 1981), pp. 49–53.

References

Birch, Eugenie Ladner, ed. 1985. *The Unsheltered Woman: Women and Housing in the 80s.* New Brunswick, N.J.: Center for Urban Policy Research.

Bunch, Charlotte. 1981. The Reform Tool Kit. In *Building Feminist Theory: Essays from QUEST,* Charlotte Bunch, Jane Flax, Alexa Freeman, Nancy Hartsock, and Mary-Helen Mautner, eds. New York: Longman.

Chelnov, Sandy, with assistance from Miranda Ewell and Linda Vrois. 1984. *Women's Economic Agenda: A Call to Action by and for California Women.* Oakland, Calif.: Women's Economic Agenda Project.

Davidoff, Paul. 1965. Advocacy and Pluralism in Planning. *Journal of the American Institute of Planners* 31:331–338.

Deal, Mary. 1984. Woman's Urban Innovations. *Women and Environments* 6: 21–22.

Downs, Anthony. 1977. The Impact of Housing Policies on Family Life in the United States since World War II. *Daedalus* 106:163–181.

Drury, Margaret; Olson Lee; Michael Springer; and Lorene Yap. 1978. *Lower Income Housing Assistance Program (Section 8): Nationwide Evaluation of the Existing Housing Program.* Washington, D.C.: U.S. Department of Housing and Urban Development.

Ehrenreich, Barbara. 1983. *Hearts of Men: American Dreams and the Flight from Commitment.* Garden City, N.Y.: Anchor Books.

Engler, May, with Roberta M. Spohn. 1982. *Housing and the Elderly: Older Renters in New York City in 1980.* New York: Department for the Aging.

Feit, Ronnie, and Jan Peterson. 1984. *Neighborhood Women Look at Housing.* Brooklyn, N.Y.: National Congress of Neigborhood Women.

Fung, Caroline. 1984. Housing for Female-Headed Single Parent Families in Suburbia: A Case Study of Nassau and Suffolk Counties, New York: Master's thesis, Division of Urban Planning, Columbia University.

Gilligan, Carol. 1982. *A Different Voice: Psychological Theory and Women's Development.* Cambridge: Harvard University Press.

Granby, Karen H. 1980. Bread, Roses and Respect, Too! Master's thesis, Division of Urban Planning, Columbia University.

Hayden, Dolores. 1984. *Redesigning the American Dream: The Future of Housing, Work and Family Life.* New York: Norton.

Heifetz, Robert J. 1971. Origins, Development, Case Studies and Critique of Advocacy Planning: Implications for Planning Education. Ph.D. dissertation, Division of Urban Planning, Columbia University.

Heskin, Allan David. 1980. Crisis and Response: A Historical Perspective on Advocacy Planning. *Journal of the American Planning Association* 46:50–63.

Holley, Deborah. 1984. Day Care and the Role of the Planner. Master's thesis, Division of Urban Planning, Columbia University.

Leavitt, Jacqueline. 1979a. Research Needs and Guidelines on Women's Issues: Planning, Housing and Community Development. Washington, D.C.: Office of Policy Development and Research, U.S. Department of Housing and Urban Development.

Leavitt, Jacqueline. 1979b. *Woman as Public Housekeepers.* New York: Division of Urban Planning, Columbia University.

Leavitt, Jacqueline. 1980a. Planning and Women, Women in Planning. Ph.D. dissertation, Division of Urban Planning, Columbia University.

Leavitt, Jacqueline. 1980b. There's More to Affirmative Action than Gaining Access: The Case of Female Planners. In *New Space for Women,* Gerda Wekerle, Rebecca Peterson, and David Morley, eds. Boulder, Colo.: Westview Press.

Leavitt, Jacqueline. 1984. The Shelter Plus Issue for Single Parents. *Women and Environments* 6:16–20.

Leavitt, Jacqueline. 1985. Aunt Mary and the Shelter-Service Crisis for Single Parents. In *The Unsheltered Woman: Women and Housing in the 1980s,* Eugenie L. Birch, ed. New Brunswick, N.J.: Center for Urban Policy Research.

Lynch, Kevin. 1962. *Site Planning.* Cambridge, Mass.: MIT Press.

Minnesota Women's Consortium. 1984. Minnesota Women's Economic Action Plan. St. Paul.

Pearce, Diana. 1979. The Feminization of Poverty: Women, Work and Welfare. *Working Women and Families* 4:28–36.

Petitt, Mary Lou, and Judy Glassman, eds. 1983. *Housing for Single-Parent Families.* Trenton: New Jersey Department of Community Affairs.

Piven, Frances Fox. 1984. Women and the State: Ideology, Power and the Welfare State. *Socialist Review* 14:11–19.

Steinem, Gloria. 1984. How Women Live, Vote, Think . . . *Ms* 8:51–54.

UCLA Feminist Planners and Designers. 1984. Presentation of Curriculum Recommendations to the Planning Assembly. Graduate School of Architecture and Urban Planning, University of California, Los Angeles.

Vogel-Heffernan, Mary, and Christine Cook. 1984. Background Information for Participants in the Second National Low Income Housing Conference. Washington, D.C.: National Low Income Housing Coalition.

Welch, Mary Beth. 1984. What Might Feminist Praxis Contribute to Planning Practice? Los Angeles: Graduate School of Architecture and Urban Planning, University of California.

13

Political Strategy for
Social Planning

Barry Checkoway

S ocial planning operates in an imbalanced political arena. Private groups blame government for economic problems and planning agencies for a variety of ills. They mobilize substantial resources, mount campaigns to shape attitudes, and elect representatives who target agencies with reductions and cutbacks. In the recent history of health planning, for example, American Hospital Association leaders pledged to "square off at the regulators" and "beat the system" (McMahon 1978, p. 113). American Medical Association leaders vowed to obstruct planning agencies and urged doctors "to roll up their sleeves and apply the political pressure of organized medicine" (Lipschultz 1980, p. 1). In Iowa and Texas, physicians and hospitals mobilized letter-writing campaigns against federal planning guidelines (Danaceau 1979). In Rhode Island, they aroused citizens and defeated plans for medical laborpower and hospital beds (Rosenberg 1980). In Illinois, they assigned staff to political campaigns, bussed voters from hospital wards to the polls, and elected slates to planning boards (Checkoway 1982a). Planners no longer expect to generate widespread support but instead may struggle for survival in the face of power.

It is thus no surprise that planning agencies may not implement their plans. Analysts have documented the impacts of power imbalance and problems of implementation for years (Barrett and Fudge 1981; Larson 1980; Lynn 1980; Mazmanian and Sabatier 1981; Palumbo and Harder 1981; Pressman and Wildavsky 1973; Thompson 1981). The surprise for many planners today is that the problem is neither power imbalance nor implementation alone but also their future in the community. Austerity policies and adversarial power challenge planners to recognize political change and develop capacity for the years ahead.

This chapter analyzes political strategy for social planning. It draws on research and practice in several fields and includes cases of planners and agencies that apply innovative methods to formulate strategy. It does not suggest that these planners are typical in the field, that these methods alone are sufficient to alter the context of practice, or that this approach contradicts the drive for efficiency or effectiveness. It does suggest that planning operates in a political context and that political strategy can serve as a source of power for planners who want to influence implementation.

Perspectives on Strategy

Social planning is a process to develop policies, plans, and programs for human services. Practitioners work in public or private settings; in functional areas such as health, housing, or welfare; and in territories ranging from neighborhood to nation. They play various analytical and interactional roles; espouse equity, justice, or other social values; and hold ideologies from conservative to progressive. Some analysts view social planning as means to assess the social impacts of land use and other planning decisions, others as means to create social change in society overall. These views are important to consider, although the emphasis here is on human services. It would be as much a mistake to place all burden for social impacts on social planners as it would be to excuse any planner from the responsibility of considering social values in his or her work. No single notion of planning characterizes all forms of practice.

Social planning practice is changing. Previous years of economic growth contributed to an increase in federal, state, and local planning agencies, in addition to regional and special purpose bodies with territorial or functional responsibilities. In times of growth, planning was viewed as a type of social engineering characterized by objective fact finding and the so-called rational model. Leading texts emphasized technical research and hard data, while government guidelines described scientific application of facts (Krueckeberg and Silvers 1974; Spiegel and Hyman 1978). Planners were akin to technical experts who analyzed data for people who considered alternatives and made decisions. If some planners criticized contradictions between the rational model and actual practice or used planning as a vehicle for power redistribution and social change, they were by no means typical in the field.

Today economic recession has replaced growth and reduced development, exacerbating conditions in central cities and metropolitan areas, some of which are slowing or declining in population and other measures of urban activity. Private groups mobilize against social programs and target agencies with reductions. Budget cuts have worsened conditions for poor people, minorities, and other disadvantaged groups who had depended on social programs because they perceived or knew of few other possibilities. Soup kitchens, housing shelters, and health clinics report requests for emergency services. The future of social planning is uncertain at a time when social programs are more important than ever (Hasenfeld 1983a).

Previous planning agency attempts to operate in a political context have tended to produce uneven results. Some agencies have advocated the interests of disadvantaged groups, but they have not always built sufficient support to withstand opposition and implement plans (Davidoff 1965; Heskin 1980; Krumholz 1982). Others have established programs to involve citizens in planning, but they have not always ensured the quality or desired impact of participation (Checkoway 1982b; Rosenbaum 1983), and yet others have adopted subarea programs to involve territorial subunits in planning, but this move has often deconcentrated functions without decentralization to local residents (Checkoway 1984). Some exceptional agencies have formulated strategy, but they are not typical.

Political strategy can serve as a resource for social planning at the community level. Strategy is the science and art of mobilizing resources toward goals. It involves choice and sequence, staging and timing, and some combination of roles and styles. Strategy shows commitment to think ahead, anticipate alternatives, and achieve results (Booth 1977; Bryson and Delbecq 1979; Staples 1984; Steiner 1979).

Corporate leaders formulate strategies with fervor. For example, the Chamber of Commerce (1979) publishes action plans to help members serve on planning boards. Medical construction, equipment, and supply industry trade associations join local interests to support legislation favoring expansion of facilities (Glenn 1979; McKinlay 1984; Relman 1980). Long-term-care industry provider organizations prepare legislation representing local operators and strategies advising them how to prepare for actions by reform groups (Norville and Modrow 1978).

Planners in public agencies tend not to think or act strategically. Studies suggest that although planners once may have emphasized broad strategy and long-range plans, many have become preoccupied with applying instrumental rationality and short-range expedience (Dyckman 1983; Marcuse 1983). They often train in schools in which strategy is not central and subsequently lack skills to operate strategically (Baum 1983b; Hemmens, Bergman, and Moroney 1978; Schön et al. 1976). Other studies suggest that some social administrators consider playing a more powerful political role, but others raise legal, ethical, or professional questions about practice (Alexander 1982; Stewart 1981). Increasing numbers of them do participate in politics but tend to lack influence in decisions (Mathews 1982; Wolk 1981).

However, there is evidence of increasing efforts to develop strategic social planning practice. For example, Bleiker (1978) instructs planners to develop support for plans that are difficult to implement. Bryson, Freeman, and Roering (1985) describe a health service, county government, and other agencies that formulate plans with implementation in mind. Gummer (1984), Hasenfeld (1983b), and Patti (1983b) cite literature on social administrators who recognize the importance of political influence in organizational relationships affecting effectiveness. Mahaffey and Hanks (1982) edit studies of strategy and politics with accounts by practitioners who run campaigns and win elections.

Should social planners formulate political strategy? Some analysts argue that public, nonprofit, or voluntary agencies are strategically weak and would benefit from strategy developed in business (Wortman 1981). Others warn against applying corporate models to agencies where strategy might violate norms or undermine the trust on which public practice presumably depends (Walker 1983). The issue is not whether planners should act more like business but whether they will develop any strategy. Meanwhile, corporate groups will continue to formulate strategy and influence agencies.

Skills in Political Strategy

Political strategy involves several skills that we can place and consider in sequence, although no single notion of process characterizes all approaches to practice. The following are not the only skills, but they are among the most important.

Set Goals

Goals are statements of general social concern toward which action is directed. They provide an expression of vision and a sense of direction. They provide a proclamation of domain and a platform on which to campaign in the community. They result ideally from a process that gives them legitimacy and represents those who participate in their formulation.

Goal setting can build support for plans as well as engender controversy and evoke opposition. In Winnetka, Illinois, citizens hold annual meetings to discuss issues, mail questionnaires with utility bills, and formulate platforms for public officials. In Dallas, citizens hold small group meetings to discuss problems, convene citywide conferences to set goals, and form committees to draft plans for implementation (Goals for Dallas 1982). In Alameda, California, committee members conduct interviews and surveys, organize task forces, and draft goals for implementation by officials. In Raleigh, North Carolina, city councillors used study groups, training workshops, and issue-balloting techniques to expand participation and set goals in a city dominated by development interests. The program was so influential that private power-holders formed an opposition group and elected representatives committed to private ends (Smith and Hester 1982).

However, goals often originate outside the community. They may come from earlier mandates, higher authorities, or emergency events that require quick action. The issue is not that such goals are necessarily inappropriate for local action but that they may limit the process in which people set goals for themselves. Goal setting can activate citizens, but this is not necessarily typical of practice today.

Identify Issues

Issues express specific social concerns and affect people in deeply felt ways. They appeal to particular constituencies with concrete proposals and provide tactical handles for practice. Which is the most salient issue? Who are the constituencies? What tactics apply? Booth (1977) instructs practitioners to "cut" issues in ways that relate to constituencies, although many planners produce plans with broad goals for some general public. Such plans may serve functions but diffuse constituencies and exacerbate implementation. Such goals may be valuable but too vague to move constituents to action.

How can planners identify issues that build support? Lancourt (1979b) challenges planners to consider salience in identifying issues for implementation. She assumes that people will act in the name of public responsibility when it is in their interest to do so. Roche (1981) describes planners who take goals from agency plans, list groups with identifiable stake and political strength, define issues in terms or target groups, and use media to make issues come alive to these groups. These planners engaged labor leaders by seeking their input and showing how plans would maintain wages and minimize disruption to employees. They did not justify esoteric formulas or sell rationality but appealed to labor leaders' interests and finally won their endorsement.

However, issues alone do not generate support. On the contrary, Krumholz (1982) describes planners who frame plans in terms of specific issues but still lack resources to overcome opposition in the community.

Develop Constituencies

Building an organization involves caring about those who are affected. Whose issue is it? What do they see as their stake? What power do they bring? Constituencies are those who are affected by issues and are potential supporters of an organization. They can provide a membership base and show strength in the face of power. Planners who represent the public interest rather than specific constituencies may do so at risk to themselves.

Planners usually do not view planning agencies as constituent organizations with a membership base. Instead, they often take the general public as their constituency, develop plans for all interests within their jurisdiction, or remain aloof from the influence of particular groups. However, agencies that try to represent the interests of everyone represent no one, reduce their accountability, and open themselves to dominance by those already organized in the community. Strategic representation of constituencies requires mechanisms of accountability, but many agencies lack such mechanisms and thus may benefit groups with concentrated interests and ongoing organizations over individual citizens representing no particular interest or some diffuse public interest (Marmor and Marone 1980; Pitkin 1967).

Who are the constituencies? There is reason to expect planners to engage constituencies with a commitment to planning. But planning has many participants who are skeptical of the enterprise. It would be ironic if agencies involved individuals or groups with relatively little commitment to the activity, although this happens in some communities.

Constituencies are not random relationships but may result from efforts to identify and develop them (Barkdoll 1983; Benveniste 1977; Lipschultz 1980). In one agency, for example, planners identify major constituency groups, invite them to select representatives to the governing body, and assist them in building support in the community. In another they create an independent constituency organization with business, labor, professional, and consumer group members who build support beyond the governing body (Checkoway 1981b). In yet another they analyze agency goals in terms of key individuals and then develop relationships and provide services to selected individuals in expectation of loyalty in return (Roche 1981). Successful politicians have long received rewards from responding to their constituents (Johannes 1984; Riordan 1963). Constituents are too important to withdraw from the matter or to leave them to traditional mechanisms of representation alone.

Select Tactics

Political strategy can involve a series of campaigns or planned activities in sequence that build on the success of the one before. Each campaign can involve a series of tactics or particular actions that focus on issues. Which tactics will work? What resources will they require? Where will they lead? Selecting tactics is a systematic activity informed by strategic objectives. These activities also can engender commitment from individuals who derive psychosocial benefits from involvement in them, but therapy is not usually a principal end of political strategy.

Private economic groups employ tactics to build power. Feldstein (1977) describes health associations that prepare legislation, provide information to regulators and legislators, and deliver benefits to their members. Pines (1982) describes business groups that send sample editorials to local newspapers for publication, conduct opinion surveys and legal analysis, pack hearings with witnesses and lengthy testimony, write speeches for legislators, prepare amendments and influence regulations.

However, planners often apply safe tactics without strategy in mind. Studies show that in citizen participation programs, planners distribute plans to libraries, publish legal notices of meetings in newspapers, conduct formal public hearings, publish newsletters, and convene boards and committees rather than apply more powerful methods. In political action, they play conventional roles in which they are more likely to discuss issues, write letters, and join political organizations rather than attend political meetings, participate in political campaigns, contribute money to candidates, or run for office (Mathews 1982; Wolk 1981). Exceptional practitioners may become political gladiators, but they are not typical in the field.

Tactics are not strategy but ideally flow from it. They can cause changes but they also can provoke countertactics that jeopardize the agency. The issue is not whether to select tactics but to assess the agency situation and select those that work.

Build Organizational Structure

Structure refers to institutional means that involve some combination of established policies and procedures, roles and responsibilities, mechanisms and methods toward goals. What structure and process will generate ideas and solve problems? How should participants make decisions, divide responsibilities, and implement plans? What are the roles of boards, committees, chairpersons, and staff members? The challenge is to fit structure to situation.

More research is needed on organizational structure for political strategy, but lessons can be learned from innovative agencies. These include an agency that centralizes governance in a representative board and forms an independent organization to expand participation; deconcentrates functions to subarea councils with staff and facilities to address local concerns; and forms committees and task forces to involve individuals and channel adversaries. Studies suggest that the organizational or structural correlates of practice in agencies include community leadership, executive management, staff skills, and resources in time and money in addition to sociopolitical context and commitment to goals (Checkoway and O'Rourke 1983; Mayer 1984; Tropman 1984). Structure is not strategy but can facilitate its practice.

Activate People in Planning

The benefits of citizen participation are well known. For agencies, participation can provide information, improve communications, and fulfill legislative mandates. It also can open up the political process, involve low-income and minority citizens, and develop community organization. For citizens, participation can offer opportunities to gain representation, exercise legal and political rights, and influence policy decisions. Done with knowledge and skill, participation can improve planning and build support for change.

Recent years have witnessed an increase in the participation methods employed by agencies, although the overall record has been uneven. Many agencies have expanded the scope of participation, and exceptional agencies have sought participation with fervor. But few have adopted strategic objectives for participation or employed methods that activate citizens. Analysts have criticized shortcomings of agencies that use participation to serve administrative ends rather than to transfer power to citizens but have not shown that support has been built (Checkoway 1981b).

Knowledge of participation has increased over time. Agency catalogues count more than fifty current or emergent methods; analyze selected methods according to function; and rationalize the design, implementation, and evaluation of practice (Advisory Commission on Intergovernmental Relations 1979; Community Services Administration 1978; U.S. Department of Transportation 1976). Analysts study methods and factors that influence the field (Burke 1979; Gil and Lucchesi 1979; Glass 1979; Rosenbaum 1983; Rosener 1975). Reflective practitioners provide lessons from experience. For example, Creighton (1981) describes programs to identify objectives and publics, formulate alternatives, assess internal and external resources, and match methods to purpose at each stage of planning. However, others suggest that formal methods alone do not ensure the quality or impact of participation, while other factors such as organizational leadership and commitment do foster quality participation (Checkoway and O'Rourke 1983; Schön 1983). Methods serve functions but alone appear insufficient to activate citizens or support agencies.

Find and Develop Leaders

Citizen leaders ideally show commitment to goals and develop a following in the community. They also attend board meetings and chair committees, but these are vehicles for leadership rather than being leadership. Many planners retreat from the process by which leaders are selected or developed. Instead they view leadership in the narrow context of committees or meetings, consider selection and representation process beyond their domain, or appropriate leadership by promoting people who hold positions in established institutions. However, leadership appropriation also may promote people who are unrepresentative of the community or too busy to give time to the agency. We should expect leaders to be committed to their agencies, but many participants in planning are skeptical of the enterprise. It would be ironic if agencies appropriated leaders with relatively little commitment to planning, although this happens in some communities.

How can planners develop leaders? Neven (1981) describes a process of searching for people with few credentials but with demonstrated capacity for personal initiative and community problem solving. Max (1973) describes steps to find persons who have shown talent for organizational activity but who never considered themselves as leaders. He directs staff to help create a context where individuals can recognize their abilities and view themselves as leaders. Bradley (1981) describes an agency that seeks to identify potential leaders and develop their skills. He assumes that any citizen can function well with proper support, that planners have a responsibility to foster development, and that if citizens are not acting like leaders, planners may not be doing their job properly. Dale (1979) and Leinberger (1978) describe curricula to teach board members how to consult with citizens to enlist their participation. There is no science of leadership development in planning, but if planners do not take responsibility, then who will?

Educate the Public

Citizens cannot be expected to support social planning without understanding their problems and their stake in the agency addressing them. Why is planning important? Whose interests does it serve? The challenge is not public relations but popular education and community development. An older conception of planning teaches planners to help people learn about themselves, the forces that affect their lives, and possible actions against their problems (Friere 1970; Goulet 1973; Michael 1973).

Private economic groups recognize popular education as a social force. They advertise to build their reputation and to persuade others of their positions. They prepare programs for the workplace and classroom, publish curricula and textbooks, and establish research centers for strategic analysis and dissemination throughout society (Pines 1982). Media officials respond to the most powerful inputs they receive, and these often come from private interests who may own or control information networks and communications channels. They thus may accept private notions of public planning, emphasize shortcomings of agencies, and present clients in a negative light. They can exert powerful influence on public understanding.

Planners also recognize the importance of popular education but often employ public hearings and other low-visibility approaches to inform the general public rather than specific constituencies (Texas Municipal League 1975; Winholz 1968). Others lack educational objectives or rely on obscure media like legal notices in newspapers, although studies show that these are among the least effective ways to communicate with the public (Rosener 1975; Sinclair 1977). Yet others use technical language that exacerbates difficulties in understanding and gives the impression that only professionals can present an adequate response (O'Rourke and Forouzesh 1981). Low-income and minority citizens may have particular problems in understanding (Mueller 1973). No wonder many people lack understanding of agencies, know little about the people served by them, or withdraw their support.

New initiatives are needed to expand public understanding of social planning. Who are the people to be reached? What issues will develop constituencies? What media and language will communicate? Joslyn-Scherer (1980) provides perspectives on problems and issues related to communications in the human services. Gordon (1978) formulates strategy for using newspaper, radio, and television media for social change. Brawley (1983) presents ways human service organizations can use mass media to communicate their message. Lauffer (1984) analyzes marketing methods for social agencies to sell services to target groups. Glenn (1947) describes agencies that produce planning exhibits for shopping centers and popular publications for mass distribution. Some innovative agencies provide direct mail and personal outreach by staff and board members, conduct education and leadership training programs, publish educational guides to activate citizens, and reach the public through newspaper columns and television and radio appearances (Checkoway 1981b). These agencies view public understanding as central to their mission and work to bring planning closer to the community.

Establish Relationships with Influentials

These key actors are able to influence decisions that affect the agency. Who are the influentials? What are their political resources? What is their place in various institutions? What are the possible paths of influence? These are not random relationships but result from a plan for establishing and maintaining them.

How can planners identify and develop relationships with influentials? Tait, Bokemeir, and Bohlen (n.d.) and Trounstine and Christensen (1982) describe positional, reputational, and other methods to identify influentials in the community. Roche (1981) analyzes ways to cultivate relationships through issue-based appeals to self-interest, special efforts to involve influentials in decisions, or priority responses to requests from government, business, and media. He describes planners who confer with influentials to explain their stake and who participate in elections for officials in return for support. There is no lack of published advice on how to win friends and influence others.

Strategic analysis and tactical research are forms of intelligence that produce knowledge for neither general reference nor academic study but for actual practice (Greever 1972; Katz 1980; Nix 1977). Planners respect research but few employ strategic analysis with implementation in mind. Traditional planning studies serve functions but contrast with strategic studies that may influence implementation (Henderson and Thomas 1980).

Build Coalitions

Coalitions are working relationships that unite individuals or groups around a common purpose. They may be short-term or relatively permanent, voluntary and occasional, or professional and staffed. They are important for individuals seeking to share resources and generate power beyond the reach of what each could accomplish alone (Dluhy 1981).

Coalition building varies from one case to another. On the local level, for example, an agency covering a large rural area applies coalitional planning among public officials and community leaders. Agency staff identify influentials and include them on governing boards as means to build support. Another agency creates councils that identify local problems, lobby legislators, and support implementation at the subarea level (Roche 1981). Yet another agency targets underserved groups and develops a coalition that has an impact on agency activities (Glenn, Lipschultz, and Sherry 1981).

On the state level, Dear and Patti (1981) show how groups build coalitions and influence legislation. Dluhy (1981) describes how professionals organize statewide political structure, take formal positions, and target bureaucrats and politicians. Berry (1981) analyzes how national coalitions conduct research for release to media, contact constituents, and advocate in legislative and administrative arenas. Coalitions face obstacles and have costs, but the costs should be weighed against the benefits during turbulent times.

Advocate for Political Change

Advocacy is the practice of representing interests in legislative, administrative, or other established arenas. It assumes that existing institutions are capable of serving interests in society, that some interests mobilize more resources than others, and that practitioners can compensate for political imbalance by representing less powerful interests rather than special economic ones.

There is nothing new about planning as a form of advocacy. Early twentieth century planners applied rudiments as part of social reform movements intended to improve conditions in large cities and poor neighborhoods. In the 1960s and 1970s, planners openly advocated the interests of poor people and minorities to give them a voice in the planning process. They worked with community groups, contended with adversaries in the political arena, and sought to overcome the effects of public and private institutional decisions. They represented clients against urban renewal, routes of proposed expressways, and intrusion of facilities into nearby areas.

Today practitioners apply diverse advocacy roles. Legislative advocates lobby legislators to see things their way in policy decisions. Administrative advocates hold agencies accountable for compliance with mandates and regulations. Legal advocates represent classes of people in judicial arenas. Educational advocates build arenas around practice through popular education and media campaigns. Electoral advocates educate and turn out voters through political appeals connecting social issues to specific constituencies and agency programs (Newman 1983).

There is growing knowledge of social practice as political advocacy (Patti 1983a). Bell and Bell (1982) describe ways to monitor the bureaucracies responsible for implementing social legislation. Dluhy (1981) and Whitaker (1982) analyze approaches to build coalitions to achieve social welfare objectives in the face of opposition. Salcito (1984) and Whitaker and Flory-Baker (1982) analyze methods to participate in political campaigns to elect representatives supportive of social values. Messinger (1982) describes her campaign for political office and service as an elected official in New York City. Mahaffey (1982) analyzes her role as a city councillor in establishing a new service in Detroit. Political participation is a practice skill that directly affects the context of planning, a lesson that private economic interests learned years ago.

What Are the Obstacles?

There are obstacles to political strategy for social planning at the community level, although describing them is not my primary purpose here. However, it is important to recognize reality while also embracing the possibility of change.

It is difficult to formulate political strategy when planning agencies lack legitimacy in the community. Private economic interests exercise power in planning decisions and resist efforts to share this power with others. Citizens may accept the notion of private power over planning for public intervention. Only a fraction of the general public perceive planning as an activity in which they could participate, know of the functions of planning agencies, or think that social programs work (Foley 1955; Lipsky and Lounds 1976; Riska and Taylor 1978). Citizens often receive information through networks influenced by private interests and hesitate to intrude in areas involving private power. The lack of public knowledge tends to lower expectations and reduce incentives for planning. This is not to suggest that public attitudes toward planning necessarily arise from some independent consciousness to be taken as given. On the contrary, it would be as mistaken to take public attitudes as given as it would be to ignore private efforts to shape them or to reject the possibility that new initiatives could alter the situation. Intervention can make a difference, as private interests have shown for years.

It also is difficult to formulate political strategy when planners lack knowledge, skills, or attitudes conducive to practice. Baum (1983b) finds only a minority of planners who regard their work as properly or inevitably political, a majority of straightforward technicians who believe they are or should be concerned with objective fact finding and rational analysis of information, and a substantial group who are ambivalent about acting politically and who tend to emphasize technical skills as a result of this ambivalence. There are exceptional practitioners who think and act politically, but they appear neither typical of practice nor influential in decisions (Mathews 1982; Wolk 1981).

This image has implications for planning education. First, most planners do not perceive themselves as political, a situation that could be defined as a problem for education to address. Second, a minority of planners are political, and their work could provide lessons for others. Third, a substantial group of planners is ambivalent and could be viewed as possible allies in changing practice. There is no a priori reason why planners could not develop skills to build political support in the community. Education could find excellent opportunities here.

But education does not always prepare people for effective practice. De Neufville (1983) contends that planning schools agree on no common literature, raise questions that have no answers, and provide poor instruction to make planning work. She argues that theory is inconsistent with experience, irrelevant to application, and frustrating to practitioners. Schön et al. (1976) find graduates who report that skills in negotiating, influencing, and consulting with clients are not usually available in planning curricula. Hemmens, Bergman, and Moroney (1978) find graduates who report that their jobs require skills not covered by training received in the schools. Some schools place students in political settings with elected officials and legislative representatives, but this placement has done little to strengthen subsequent political practice (Campfens and Loach 1977).

But it would be as much a mistake to blame scholars and educators for not bridging the gap between knowledge and action as it would be to excuse practitioners from their responsibility to apply knowledge that is available. The issue is not necessarily the continuing need to improve knowledge and education but whether practitioners are willing or able to apply what is known. Some planners have effectively influenced implementation, but others have opted to sit tight and wait for earlier times to return rather than to play a more active role. Despite technical innovations in planning, most planners have not adopted behavior conducive to agency survival.

In the final analysis, planning agencies face the power of private economic interests. Public participation has increased in scope and quality, and some citizens have organized around planning agencies, but private interests remain the most active, organized, and influential participants. They challenge planners to respond, but even exceptional practice would still operate in the face of this power.

Will Strategy Create Change?

Planning operates in a political context, and planners who want to influence implementation can benefit from political strategy. There are obstacles to political strategy for planning practice, but exceptional agencies show possibilities and provide lessons nonetheless. This does not suggest that the answer to implementation is in political strategy alone, because planning operates in an arena that requires more than the skills described here. Nor does it deny that this approach might engender controversy and arouse reaction by groups that may emerge as more powerful than before. Nor does it neglect that planning agencies offer only one of several means to act politically and create change in the community. There are other means, one or a combination of which may be better ways to create change. In the final analysis, political strategy for planning practice might not make much difference. But then again, it might.

References

Advisory Commission on Intergovernmental Relations. 1979. *Citizen Participation in the American Federal System.* Washington, D.C.

Alexander, Chauncey. 1982. Professional Social Workers and Political Responsibility. In *Practical Politics: Social Work and Political Responsibility,* Maryann Mahaffey and John W. Hanks, eds. Silver Spring, Md.: National Association of Social Workers.

Barkdoll, Gerald L. 1983. Involving Constituents in Agency Priority Setting: A Case Study. *Evaluation and Program Planning* 6:31–37.

Barrett, Susan, and Colin Fudge, eds. 1981. *Policy and Action: Essays on the Implementation of Public Policy.* New York: Methuen.

Baum, Howell S. 1983a. *Planners and Public Expectations.* Cambridge, Mass.: Schenkman.

Baum, Howell S. 1983b. Politics and Ambivalence in Planners' Practice. *Journal of Planning Education and Research* 3:13–22.

Bell, William G., and Budd L. Bell. 1982. Monitoring the Bureaucracy: An Extension of Legislative Lobbying. In *Practical Politics: Social Work and Political Responsibility,* Maryann Mahaffey and John W. Hanks, eds. Silver Spring, Md.: National Association of Social Workers.

Benveniste, Guy. 1977. *The Politics of Expertise.* San Francisco: Boyd and Fraser.

Berry, Jeffrey M. 1981. Beyond Citizen Participation: Effective Advocacy Before Administrative Agencies. *The Journal of Applied Behavioral Science* 17:463–477.

Bleiker, Hans. 1978. *Citizen Participation Handbook.* Laramie, Wy.: Institute for Participatory Planning.

Booth, Heather. 1977. *Direct Action Organizing.* Chicago: Midwest Academy.

Bradley, John. 1981. An Educational Approach to Health Planning. In *Citizens and Health Care: Participation and Planning for Social Change,* Barry Checkoway, ed. New York: Pergamon.

Brawley, Edward A. 1983. *Mass Media and Human Services: Getting the Message Across.* Beverly Hills: Sage Publications.

Brown, L. David. 1983. Organizing Participatory Research: Interfaces for Joint Inquiry and Organizational Change. *Journal of Occupational Behavior* 4:9–19.

Bryson, John M., and Andre L. Delbecq. 1979. A Contingent Approach to Strategy and Tactics in Program Planning. *Journal of the American Planning Association* 45:167–179.

Bryson, John M.; R. Edward Freeman; and William D. Roering. 1985. *Strategic Planning in the Public Sector: Approaches and Future Directions.* Minneapolis: Strategic Management Research Center, University of Minnesota.

Burke, Edmund M. 1979. *A Participatory Approach to Urban Planning.* New York: Human Sciences Press.

Campfens, Hubert, and Fred Loach. 1977. Political Placements in Social Work Education: The United States and Canada. *Journal of Education for Social Work* 13:11–17.

Chamber of Commerce of the United States. 1979. *A National Health Care Strategy.* Washington, D.C.: National Chamber Foundation.

Checkoway, Barry. 1979. Citizens on Local Health Planning Boards: What Are the Obstacles? *Journal of the Community Development Society* 10:101–116.

Checkoway, Barry. 1981a. Citizen Action in Health Planning. In *Citizens and Health Care: Participation and Planning for Social Change,* Barry Checkoway, ed. New York: Pergamon Press.

Checkoway, Barry. 1981b. Consumerism in Health Planning Agencies. In *Health Planning in the United States: Selected Policy Issues.* Washington, D.C.: National Academy of Sciences Press.

Checkoway, Barry. 1981c. The Politics of Public Hearings. *The Journal of Applied Behavioral Science* 17:566–582.

Checkoway, Barry. 1982a. The Empire Strikes Back: More Lessons for Health Care Consumers. *Journal of Health Politics, Policy and Law* 7:111–124.

Checkoway, Barry. 1982b. Public Participation in Health Planning Agencies: Promise and Practice. *Journal of Health Politics, Policy and Law* 7:722–733.

Checkoway, Barry. 1984. Two Types of Planning in Neighborhoods. *Journal of Planning Research and Education* 3:102–109.

Checkoway, Barry, and Thomas O'Rourke. 1983. Correlates of Consumer Participation in Health Planning Agencies. *Policy Studies Journal* 3:296–310.

Checkoway, Barry, and Jon Van Til. 1978. What Do We Know About Citizen Participation? A Selective Review of Research. In *Citizen Participation in America: Essays on the State of the Art,* Stuart Langton, ed. Lexington, Mass.: D.C. Heath and Company, Lexington Books.

Community Services Administration. 1978. *Citizen Participation.* Washington, D.C.

Creighton, James L. 1981. *The Public Involvement Manual.* Cambridge, Mass.: Abt Associates.

Dale, Duane, with David Magnani and Robin Miller. 1979. *Beyond Experts: A Guide for Citizen Group Training.* Amherst, Mass.: Citizen Involvement Training Project.

Danaceau, Paul. 1979. *The Health Planning Guidelines Controversy: A Report from Iowa and Texas.* Hyattsville, Md.: Health Resources Administration.

Davidoff, Paul. 1965. Advocacy and Pluralism in Planning. *Journal of the American Institute of Planners* 31:596–615.

Davies, James C. 1975. *Politics of Pollution.* Bloomington: Indiana University Press.

de Neufville, Judith Innes. 1983. Planning Theory and Practice: Bridging the Gap. *Journal of Planning Education and Research* 3:36–45.

Dear, Ronald B., and Rino J. Patti. 1981. Legislative Advocacy: Seven Effective Tactics. *Social Work* 26:289–296.

Dluhy, Milan. 1981. *Changing the System: Political Advocacy for Disadvantaged Groups.* Beverly Hills: Sage Publications.

Dyckman, John. 1983. Planning in a Time of Reaction. *Journal of Planning Education and Research* 3:5–12.

Feldstein, Paul J. 1977. *Health Associations and the Demand for Legislation: The Political Economy of Health.* Cambridge, Mass.: Ballinger.

Feshbach, Dan, and Takuya Nakamoto. 1981. Political Strategies for Health Planning Agencies. In *Citizens and Health Care: Participation and Planning for Social Change,* Barry Checkoway, ed. New York: Pergamon Press.

Foley, Donald. 1955. How Many Berkeley Residents Know About Their City's Master Plan? *Journal of the American Institute of Planners* 21:138–144.

Friedmann, John F. 1973. *Retracking America: A Theory of Transactive Planning.* Garden City, N.Y.: Anchor.

Friere, Paulo. 1970. *Pedagogy of the Oppressed.* New York: Seabury Press.

Gil, Efraim, and Enid Lucchesi. 1979. Citizen Participation in Planning. In *The Practice of Local Government Planning,* Frank So, ed. Washington, D.C.: International City Management Association.

Glass, James J. 1979. Citizen Participation in Planning: The Relationship between Objectives and Techniques. *Journal of the American Planning Association* 45: 180–189.

Glenn, John M., Lilian Brandt, and F. Emerson Andrews. 1947. *Russell Sage Foundation 1907–1946.* New York: Russell Sage Foundation.

Glenn, Karen. 1979. *Planning, Politics and Power: A User's Guide to Taming the Health Care System.* Washington, D.C.: Consumer Coalition for Health.

Glenn, Karen; Claire Lipschultz; and Susan Sherry. 1981. The Consumer Health Advocacy Project. In *Citizens and Health Care: Participation and Planning for Social Change,* Barry Checkoway, ed. New York: Pergamon Press.

Goals for Dallas. 1982. Goals for Dallas. Paper presented at the Annual Conference of the American Planning Association, Dallas.

Gordon, Robbie. 1978. *We Interrupt this Program. . . . A Citizen's Guide to Using the Media for Social Change.* Amherst, Mass.: Citizen Involvement Training Project.

Goulet, Denis. 1973. *The Cruel Choice: A New Concept in the Theory of Development.* New York: Atheneum.

Greever, Barry. 1972. *Tactical Investigations for People's Struggles.* Chicago: Midwest Academy.

Gummer, Burton. 1984. The Social Administrator as Politician. In *Human Services at Risk,* Felice Davidson Perlmutter, ed. Lexington, Mass.: D.C. Heath and Company, Lexington Books.

Harty, Sheila. 1979. *Hucksters in the Classroom: A Review of Industry Propaganda in Schools.* Washington, D.C.: Center for Study of Responsive Law.

Hasenfeld, Yeheskel. 1980. The Implementation of Change in Human Service Organizations: A Political Economy Perspective. *Social Services Review* 54:508–520.

Hasenfeld, Yeheskel. 1983a. The Changing Context of Human Services. In *Human Services at Risk,* Felice Davidson Perlmutter, ed. Lexington, Mass.: D.C. Heath and Company, Lexington Books.

Hasenfeld, Yeheskel. 1983b. *Human Service Organizations.* Englewood Cliffs, N.J.: Prentice-Hall.

Hemmens, George C.; Edward M. Bergman; and Robert M. Moroney. 1978. The Practitioner's View of Social Planning. *Journal of the American Institute of Planners* 44:181–192.

Henderson, Paul, and David N. Thomas. 1980. *Skills in Neighborhood Work.* London: George Allen & Unwin.

Heskin, Allan. 1980. Crises in Response: A Historical Perspective on Advocacy Planning. *Journal of the American Planning Association* 46:50–63.

Johannes, John R. 1984. *To Serve the People: Congress and Constituency Service.* Lincoln: University of Nebraska Press.

Joslyn-Scherer, M.S. 1980. *Communication in the Human Services.* Beverly Hills: Sage.

Katz, John. 1980. *Action Research: A Guide to Research.* New Orleans: The Institute.

Kimmey, James R. 1981. Technical Assistance and Consultation for Consumers. In *Citizens and Health Care: Participation and Planning for Social Change,* Barry Checkoway, ed. New York: Pergamon Press.

Klein, Ted, and Fred Danzig. 1974. *How to Be Heard: Making the Media Work for You.* New York: Macmillan.

Krueckeberg, Donald A., and Arthur L. Silvers. 1974. *Urban Planning Analysis: Methods and Models.* New York: John Wiley & Sons.

Krumholz, Norman. 1982. A Retrospective View of Equity Planning: Cleveland 1969–1979. *Journal of the American Planning Association* 48:163–184.

Lancourt, Joan. 1979a. *Confront or Concede: The Alinsky Citizen-Action Organizations.* Lexington, Mass.: D.C. Heath and Company, Lexington Books.

Lancourt, Joan. 1979b. *Developing Implementation Strategies: Community Organization Not Public Relations.* Boston: Boston University Center for Health Planning.

Larson, James S. 1980. *Why Policies Fail: Improving Policy Implementation.* New York: Praeger.

Lauffer, Armand. 1984. *Strategic Marketing for Not-for-Profit Organizations.* New York: Free Press.

Leinberger, Paul, ed. 1978. *How to Be a More Effective Commissioner or Public Board Member.* Berkeley: Continuing Education in Environmental Design, University of California.

Lipschultz, Claire. 1980. *Political Action in Health Planning: Building a Consumer Constituency.* Bethesda, Md.: Alpha Center for Health Planning.

Lipsky, Michael; and Morris Lounds. 1976. Citizen Participation and Health Care: Problems of Government Induced Participation. *Journal of Health Politics, Policy and Law* 1:85–111.

Lynn, Laurence E. 1980. *The State and Human Services: Organizational Change in a Political Context.* Cambridge, Mass.: MIT Press.

Mahaffey, Maryann. 1982. A Social Worker–Politician Creates a New Service. In *Practical Politics: Social Work and Political Responsibility,* Maryann Mahaffey and John W. Hanks, eds. Silver Spring, Md.: National Association of Social Workers.

Mahaffey, Maryann, and John W. Hanks, eds. 1982. *Practical Politics: Social Work and Political Responsibility.* Silver Spring, Md.: National Association of Social Workers.

Marcuse, Peter. 1983. The Feeble Retreat of Planning. *Journal of Planning Education and Research* 3:52–53.

Marmor, Theodore R., and James A. Morone. 1980. Representing Consumer Interests: Imbalanced Markets, Health Planning and the HSAs. *Milbank Memorial Fund Quarterly/Health and Society* 58:125–165.

Mathews, Gary. 1982. Social Workers and Political Influence. *Social Services Review* 58:617–628.

Max, Steve. 1973. *Four Steps to Developing Leaders.* Chicago: Midwest Academy.

Mayer, Neil S. 1984. *Neigborhood Organizations and Community Development.* Washington, D.C.: Urban Institute Press.

Mazmanian, Daniel, and Paul A. Sabatier, eds. 1981. *Effective Policy Implementation.* Lexington, Mass.: D.C. Heath and Company, Lexington Books.

McKinley, John B., ed. 1984. *Issues in the Political Economy of Health Care.* New York: Tavistock Publications.

McMahon, J. Alexander. 1978. The Perspective of the American Medical Association. In *Effects of Payment Mechanisms on the Health Care Delivery System,* W.R. Roy, ed. Washington, D.C.: Department of Health, Education and Welfare.

Mendeloff, James. 1979. *Regulating Safety: An Economic and Political Analysis of Occupational Safety and Health Policy.* Cambridge, Mass.: MIT Press.

Messinger, Ruth W. 1982. Empowerment: A Social Worker's Politics. In *Practical Politics: Social Work and Political Responsibility,* Maryann Mahaffey and John W. Hanks, eds. Silver Spring, Md.: National Association of Social Workers.

Michael, Donald J. 1973. *On Learning to Plan and Planning to Learn.* San Francisco: Jossey-Bass.

Mueller, C. 1973. *The Politics of Communications.* New York: Oxford University Press.

Neven, David. 1981. *Left-Handed Fastballers: Scouting and Training America's Grass-Roots Leaders 1966–1977.* New York: Ford Foundation.

Newman, Sanford. 1983. Project VOTE: Tapping the Power of the Poor. *Social Policy* 13:15–19.

Nix, Harold L. 1977. *The Community and Its Involvement in the Study Planning Action Process.* Washington, D.C.: Department of Health, Education and Welfare.

Norville, Jerry L., and Robert E. Modrow. 1978. Preparing for Potential Actions by Nursing Home Reform Groups. *Nursing Homes,* March–April, pp. 4–11.

O'Rourke, Thomas W., and Mohammed Forouzesh. 1981. Readability of HSAs' Plans: Implications for Public Involvement. *Health Law Project Library Bulletin* 6:23–26.

Palumbo, Dennis J., and Marvin A. Harder, eds. 1981. *Implementing Public Policy.* Lexington, Mass.: D.C. Heath and Company, Lexington Books.

Patti, Rino J. 1983a. Political Action. In *1983–84 Supplement to the Encyclopedia of Social Work.* Silver Spring, Md.: National Association of Social Workers.

Patti, Rino J. 1983b. *Social Welfare Administration: Managing Social Programs in a Developmental Context.* Englewood Cliffs, N.J.: Prentice-Hall.

Pines, Burton Yale. 1982. *Back to Basics: The Traditionalist Movement that Is Sweeping Grass-Roots America.* New York: William Morrow.

Pitkin, Hannah F. 1967. *The Concept of Representation.* Berkeley: University of California Press.

Pressman, Jeffrey L., and Aaron B. Wildavsky. 1973. *Implementation.* Berkeley: University of California.

Relman, Arnold S. 1980. The New Medical-Industrial Complex. *New England Journal of Medicine* 303:963–970.

Riordan, William L. 1963. *Plunkett of Tammany Hall: A Series of Very Plain Talks on Very Practical Politics.* New York: E.P. Dutton.

Riska, E., and J.A. Taylor. 1978. Consumer Attitudes Toward Health Policy and Knowledge and Legislation. *Journal of Health Politics, Policy and Law* 3: 112–123.

Roche, Joseph L. 1981. Community Organization Approach to Health Planning. In *Citizens and Health Care: Participation and Planning for Social Change,* Barry Checkoway, ed. New York: Pergamon Press.

Rosenbaum, Nelson ed. 1983. *Citizen Participation: Models and Methods of Evaluation.* Washington, D.C.: Center for Responsive Governance.

Rosenberg, Charlotte. 1980. These Doctors Head Off a Health-Planning Debacle. *Medical Economics* 27:33–35, 42, 47, 51.

Rosener, Judy B. 1975. Citizen Participation: Tying Strategy to Function. *Public Management* 12:16–19.

Salcito, Ramon M. 1984. Social Work Practice in Political Campaigns. *Social Work* 29:189–191.

Schön, Donald A. 1983. *The Reflective Practitioner: How Professionals Think in Action.* New York: Basic Books.

Schön, Donald A.; Nancy Sheldon Cremer; Paul Osterman; and Charles Perry. 1976. Planners in Transition: Report on a Survey of Alumni of MIT's Department of Urban Studies, 1960–1971. *Journal of the American Institute of Planners* 42: 193–202.

Sinclair, Michael. 1977. The Public Hearing as a Participatory Device: Evaluation of the IJC Experience. In *Public Participation in Planning.* W.R.D. Sewell and J.T. Coppock, eds. New York: John Wiley & Sons.

Smith, Frank, J., and Randolph T. Hester. 1982. *Community Goal-Setting.* Stroudsburg, Penn.: Hutchinson, Ross.

Sosin, Michael, and Sharon Caulum. 1983. Advocacy: A Conceptualization for Social Work Practice. *Social Work* 28:12–19.

Spiegel, Allen D., and Herbert H. Hyman. 1978. *Basic Health Planning Methods.* Germantown, Md.: Aspen Systems Corporation.

Staples, Lee. 1984. *Roots to Power: A Manual for Grassroots Organizing.* New York: Praeger.

Steiner, George A. 1979. *Strategic Planning: What Every Manager Must Know.* New York: Free Press.

Stewart, William H. 1976. *Citizen Participation in Public Administration.* Birmingham: Bureau of Public Administration, University of Alabama.

Tait, John L.; Janet Bokemeir; and Janet Bohlen, n.d. *Identifying the Community Power Actors: A Guide for Change Agents.* Ames: Iowa Cooperative Extension Service.

Texas Municipal League. 1975. *Building Citizen Support in Texas Cities.* Austin.

Thompson, Frank J. 1981. *Health Policy and the Bureaucracy: Politics and Implementation.* Cambridge, Mass.: MIT Press.

Tropman, John. 1984. *Policy Management in the Human Services.* New York: Columbia University Press.

Trounstine, Philip J., and Terry Christensen. 1982. *Movers and Shakers: The Study of Community Power.* New York: St. Martin's Press.

U.S. Department of Transportation. 1976. *Effective Citizen Participation in Transportation Planning.* Washington, D.C.: Government Printing Office.

Walker, J. Malcolm. 1983. Limits of Strategic Management in Voluntary Organizations. *Journal of Voluntary Action Research* 12:39–56.

Whitaker, William H., and Jan Flory-Baker. 1982. Organizing Social Action Coalitions: WIC Comes to Wyoming. In *Practical Politics: Social Work and Political Responsibility,* Maryann Mahaffey and John W. Hanks, eds. Silver Spring, Md.: National Association of Social Workers.

Whitaker, William H., and Jan Flory-Baker. 1982. Ragtag Social Workers Take on the Good Old Boys and Elect a State Senator. In *Practical Politics: Social Work and Political Responsibility,* Maryann Mahaffey and John W. Hanks, eds. Silver Spring, Md.: National Association of Social Workers.

Winholz, William G. 1968. Planning and the Public. In *Principles and Practice of Urban Planning,* William I. Goodman and Eric C. Freund, eds. Washington, D.C.: International City Managers' Association.

Wolk, James. 1981. Are Social Workers Politically Active? *Social Work* 26:283–288.

Wortman, Max S. 1981. A Radical Shift from Bureaucracy to Strategic Management in Voluntary Organizations. *Journal of Voluntary Action Research* 10:62–81.

Part III
Future Prospects

14
The Institutional Focus of Planning Theory

Seymour J. Mandelbaum

T he notion that the community of planning theoreticians is adrift or deeply flawed has become (to borrow a phrase from Schön 1983) an "idea in good currency." A series of books and articles and the talk of the corridors at planning education meetings carry the same news: The rational paradigm has collapsed but theorists have not replaced it with a consensual definition of their domain, purpose, or method. Academics have neglected the wisdom, meaning, dilemmas, and possibilities of professional planning practice. Theoreticians no longer speak with practitioners (and certainly they no longer are practitioners). As a result, they cannot speak to practitioners cogently.[1]

This chapter registers a mild dissent from this indictment of planning theoreticians. My arguments has three parts:

1. The conventional account of rationality gained and then rationality lost distorts the history of the field and mistakes the power of its now dominant institutional focus.

2. The most interesting recent statements about individual practitioners lie squarely within this institutional focus.

3. That focus encourages theoreticians to seek a variety of audiences and, ironically, to seem neglectful of professional practice.

Rationality and the Dyadic Image

Theoreticians have been writing for many years about the diverse schools of planning and the confusing lack of either intellectual center or direction in the field. For the most part, the history of confusion is told as a story of rational-

Reprinted by permission from the *Journal of Planning Education and Research* 5:3–9. Copyright © 1985 Association of Collegiate Schools of Planning.

ity invented and then critically reappraised. Once having discovered the limits of the rational method, the story goes, theoreticians did not know quite where to go next. They now seem, as a result, both aimless and (it is sometimes charged) neglectful of their pedagogical role.

Rationality does not play well in that story. Historians have not demonstrated that well-tempered professionals always follow a single or uniquely compelling planning protocol. Theoreticians—catching up with the wisdom of experience—now are attempting to map the contingent relationship between planning tasks and planning processes, between structure and strategy (Bryson and Delbecq 1970; Bryson and Cullen 1984; Christensen 1985; Schendel and Hofer 1979). Contingency theorizing is very promising but is not likely to rescue the idea of a unique instrumental rationality. Fitness will always depend on a metajudgment of the boundaries of the situation of the relationship between ends and means. Even the practical professional may choose unfitting behavior or proposals to fight again on another day or in another arena or, perhaps, simply to insist that it is more important to be virtuous in a community than to be clever (MacIntyre 1984).

Suppose we step outside the conventional narrative that describes the quandry of planning theoreticians in the postrationalist period (Alexander 1984). We are in the midst of an ideational shift, but it is not away from rationality. We are instead turning from the central assumption that the domain of theorizing is defined by a basic division between planners and clients: the client presents the planner with a question, a problem sketch, or a formal brief and receives in return a reply in the form of a study, a plan, or a policy recommendation.

This dyad of planner and client interaction though query and response is a powerful image, generating both important instrumental questions and an appreciation of ethical dilemmas. How, we have all learned to ask, may a planner know a client? What are the responsibilities of an advisor? How may the quality of advice be enhanced?

The questions, answers, appreciations, and sensibilities that flow from the dyadic image define the identity of the professional planner and endow it with meaning. The vital social role of the image explains, I think, its robustness. The image survives despite the threat of a great many experiences that do not fit easily within its frame because it allows professionals to justify themselves and to command resources. The image has been maintained by absorbing criticisms of the narrowness of the technical conceptions of advice giving, allowing some planners to think of themselves within the dyadic relationship as political experts (Baum 1983; Vasu 1979). In landscapes without clients, planners have sustained the image by creating clients in their minds and (occasionally) in the streets, soliciting and inventing briefs where none exists.

The dyadic image operates as what Foucault (1972) called a "discoursive formation"—a common language, a way of talking, a focus of attention. Even within such a formation, there are differences between theorizing and practicing. The theorizing requirements of abstraction, generalization, technical innovation, and criticism inevitably stamp the theorist as an outsider who may influence practitioners but rarely lead them, who may be prestigious but rarely trusted. Education in theory, when it is not overwhelmed by mimetic pressures, attempts with intentional arrogance to bolster students against the socializing influence of practice and to emancipate planners from themselves and the world that is deeply within them.

Every profession that has embedded part of itself within universities has coped with such differences and with the reaction to the arrogance of theorists (Glazer 1974). Each is periodically engaged by cycles of reintegration and reconciliation in which practitioners and some academics call for improved communication between the two communities, movement between academic and practice careers, clinical training for novices, and an appreciation of experiential wisdom.

The current academic talk of the neglect of practice is marked by all the characteristics of such a renewal cycle. There is, however, something new in the current talk. The community of academic planning theoreticians has essentially abandoned the dyadic image employed by practitioners. I suspect that shift confuses practitioners. I know with much greater confidence that it disturbs both their academic colleagues and the theoreticians.

Walking away from a discursive formation is not like leaving a room: one moment you are in and the next you are out. The issues generated by the image of planner and client remain significant even if the dyad is no longer central. Familiar texts and new questioners with old queries, like hooks attaching us to the past, keep pressing planning theoreticians into the familiar mold.

The very openness and fragmentation of a cottage theorizing industry makes it difficult to assert a break with the dyad. The little bank of (often part-time) theoreticians has incorporated great bodies of work into their own: economics to analyze markets as planning processes, systems thinking for powerful models of the guidance role of feedback loops, Marxism and critical theory for insights into both social control and ideology, and so forth, endlessly. Practitioners, observing the voracious appetite of theoreticians for strange gods, must feel neglected. Academic colleagues, observing the scattered pattern of texts and topics in planning theory courses (Klosterman 1981), must wonder about the so-called nonfield and its standards. Most important, it is difficult for even theoreticians to see a new framing image in the great buzz of talk.

Yet for all the diffuseness of the work and the ties to the past, the break with the old discursive formation is there to see. The break does not stem, I think, from a simple accumulation of discrepant experiences, an overwhelming sense that in many situations planning proceeds without planners and without clients. In its origins as a professional ideology, the dyad certainly confronted more anomalies than it does today. The planning profession has succeeded quite remarkably in shaping phenomena so they fit into the dyad. Groups are organized so they can act as clients; governments, so they can be advised by planners.

For theoreticians, the dyadic image cracked because it could not accommodate the challenge of competing ideas. The work of Lindblom (1965) may indeed be central in this intellectual transformation. For the purposes of this argument, however, think of it only as illustrative. The original critique of synoptic rationality and the justification of disjointed and incremental action were easily accommodated into the dyad. In Faludi's (1973) text, for example, disjointed incrementalism is simply one of several professional planning styles.

The lesson of *The Intelligence of Democracy* (Lindblom 1965) is, however, much more insidious. The intelligence lies in a process that allows groups to articulate a wide range of alternatives and then collectively to choose from among them without, however, permitting comprehensive resolutions. The planning process that Lindblom lauded was not a professional style but a major feature of the design of social institutions.

Lindblom is not alone. A comparably insidious emphasis on institutional design rather than professional cognition or procedure appears in the corpus of inquiry on organizational strategy and structure building around and about the work of Chandler (1962), in Williamson's (1975) comparison of the manner in which markets and hierarchies control strategic behavior, and in Foucault's (1972, 1980) and Habermas's (1973, 1979) evaluations of the conditions of public discourse.

Each of these intellectual lines describes a new way of seeing the processes that, in the dyadic image, appear as the work of professional planners. I have labeled this new (but, of course, very old) way of seeing as the "institutional focus" of planning theory. List—to capture the shift in perception—all the familiar cognitive tasks that are required of a planner responding to a client's brief. Then examine the ways in which those tasks are structured and addressed by the design of the organizations and institutions in which the planner's work is located. All institutions define problems, specify constraints, search alternatives, design options, and choose from among them. These roles are embedded in their patterns of interaction. The creation of city polities that can bid for capital but cannot control its movement institutionalizes criteria for public choice. This designed vulnerability rather than the features of professionalized planning dominates the definition and determination of urban outcomes (Mandelbaum 1984; Ashford 1980; Sharpe and Newton 1984). Similarly, it is often said that matrix designs in which authority is ambiguous and responsibility collective encourage the search for alternatives that are suppressed in hierarchical structures (Mintzberg 1979).

Whether or not that is true, the point of vision is the same: the search process is imminent in social relationships.

It is possible to read these institutional analyses within the dyadic image. The professional planner must know about organizational designs, political arrangements, and markets in the same way the architect must understand materials, structures, and user behavior. They are all the substance upon which unique professional planning processes work. Knowledge of substance is, what Harris (1967) has called, theory "in" planning. Propositions about the contingent relationships between strategy and structure become, in this reading of the organizational literature, part of the arsenal of the professional strategic planner. The markets and hierarchies approach informs the judgment of regulative (and deregulative) agencies. The political economy of national and local states guides revolutionary planners or (in another political style) managers of metropolitan planning organizations. Habermas may be arcane but critical theory, once understood, illuminates the communication tasks of ordinary professionals.

This professional reading of the institutionally focused procedural literature exemplifies the cogency and salience of the dyadic image. It is, however, a misreading. Consider, by way of illustration, the institutional issues that face many developing nations. In which domains should they rely on markets to allocate resources, in which on central planning? How would representative institutions shape the articulation of preferences and the processes of collective choice? Is the nation a viable or appropriate arena for development? Is it important to stamp out corruption, or is the auction of offices and policies preferable to alternative decision modes?

Seen through the dyadic image, some of these issues fall away. Corruption, for example, is stigmatized so it is rarely considered as a planning mode. Other issues establish an agenda for technical invention, analysis substituting for prohibited interactions. Central planners seek to simulate the allocation decisions of idealized perfect markets; policy analysts attempt to estimate the similarly idealized interests of a fully informed population. Other issues, finally, devolve into choices in the organization of the differentiated professional role. How close, for example, should the planners be to the strategic apex of the public executive? What should be their relationship to a legislature?

These are important tasks and familiar questions, but somehow they distort the developmental choices by seeing them through the eyes of professional planners. Planning processes are those repeated forms of cognition and interaction through which individuals and groups develop and choose from within their repertoire of behavior. Buying votes with cash is—like cost-benefit analysis or campaigning on the issues—a way of choosing from among alternatives. Stigmatizing corruption does not clarify the relationship between that (ubiquitous) process and its outcomes (Scott 1972).

It is easy to understand the mistake in neglecting a powerful planning mode simply because it does not fit a professional self-image and style. The devolution of procedural choices into problems for technical invention introduces a subtler distortion into the interpretation of the institutional literature, a distortion that is difficult to discern because it is close to our most valued intellectual processes.

Consider, as an example of this distortion, the important role that market failure plays in our widely shared conceptions of public planning. Markets fail, we have learned, when imperfections distort information about consumer preferences. Since real markets rarely, if ever, are perfect and the errors introduced by even small flaws may be large, analysis and public choice must compensate for the unfortunate distortions of the untamed field.

This economist's story of market failure (or, indeed, of market competence) is so familiar that we are tempted to think of it as an ethnographer's account. Hardly! The story is an element in a political program that has sought to narrow and isolate the conception of markets in order to justify, improve, and if necessary, replace them (Polanyi 1944). Ethnographic accounts of markets track complex and interconnected processes of exchange that invest relationships with meaning and justify, under various circumstances, hierarchy, stasis, and tumultuous change. The participants think of exchanges in terms such as *order, equity,* and *right,* which cannot be detached from the socially embedded interactions themselves. In the developing world those terms dominate debates over the uses and limitations of market planning.

The abstruse concepts of consumer preferences and efficiency are attempts to discipline such debates and to provide ways of replacing interaction with analysis. You may think of this attempt as an expression of ideology (Tribe 1972) or, alternatively, as an institutional design that centers on a new class of technical intelligentsia and intellectuals (Gouldner 1979). Both points of view require more—in inquiry and normative justification—than any list of technically rational planning inventions.

Finally, the location of a planning group within an organization and the group's external relationships are certainly matters of institutional design. Nevertheless, reading the institutional literature through the eyes of these locational choices (Walker 1950) is narcissistic. The reading presumes the existence of planners and a distinctive planning unit. In some settings, however, planners are so scattered about and they seem so much to be playing against one another that they cannot be fixed in a distinctive organizational location. In other settings, planning roles are diffused even though only one unit carries a formal planning designation. As a result, it is difficult to track the relationship between the location of that unit and the outcomes of the process of planning. The transaction costs of particular locations are swamped by the larger dynamics of the design of the organization and its field. If you want to understand the relationship between process and outcomes, you have to focus on those dynamics and not simply on the organizational location of formally designated planners.

Is the institutional focus of planning theory appropriate only in the developing world? Virtually everyone who writes about development assumes that current institutional designs are problematic. In the developed world—or, to speak more narrowly, in the United States—the planning profession is, in contrast, well articulated; the economist's language pervades public discourse; the conceptions of technical rationality and optimum decision making are broadly perceived as legitimate; and clients and client organizations abound. In such a world, should not planning theorists work within the dyadic image and the discursive formation that maintains it?

Posing the challenge in this way accepts the notion that planning processes are embedded in the design of institutions but then urges us, as professionals, to take those designs as constraints and work within them. That close, constrained, internal work is adequately framed by the dyadic image.

Institutional design issues are, however, highly salient in the United States. The debate over the intersection of industrial and urban policy largely hinges on rival judgments of institutional dynamics and capacity. There is a good deal of sloganeering in the talk of public/private partnerships to enhance urgan strategic planning, but blow away the fluff and something more remains than a rearrangement of professionals and clients or a new set of technical inventions. The modish fascination with negotiation and environmental mediation is a return to interaction in place of analysis (or at least a shift in their relationship) and demands a search for new designs that encourage resolutions. Working planners rather than just political philosophers find deep issues of federalism in their day-to-day professional choices. City planners—of all people—should be deeply concerned about citizenship and the role of local polities in the national political system.

There is a second reason not to revert to the dyadic image in the United States. Whatever its value to practitioners, the image does not help theoreticians very much. It has been very difficult to establish regular relationships between variations in the behavior of individual planners within institutions and variations in outcomes. There may indeed be such relationships, and they may matter deeply. Until they can be demonstrated publicly, however, they are the stuff of experiential, tacit, and local wisdom, not of formal theorizing. Academic simulations of practice (as in studios) provide an opportunity to explicate and criticize assumptions, but we should not exaggerate the cogency of the exercises, the groundedness of the critique, or the half-life of the remembered lessons. I strongly suspect that criticism on the job is a more effective pedagogical instrument than even the best university studio. (Criticism of practice directed to practitioners at the work site would also contribute mightily to the education of theoreticians).

The Individual Practitioner

A series of recent books and articles has encouraged theoreticians to focus their attention on the ways in which practitioners think about their work, survive in their social settings, solve problems, and grow wiser. This work is very productive because it breaks the grip of our all too common tendency to confuse idealized protocols with actual practice, to denigrate experiential knowledge, and to exaggerate the role of general methods and theory in addressing particular constrained situations.

It would be a mistake, however, to read this literature as a return to the dyadic image. The major prescriptive work, Schön's *The Reflective Practitioner* (1983), sometimes appears to advise individual planners to adopt the open style he describes as Model II as if it were a method of technical rationality comparable to cost-benefit analysis or linear programming. It would, however, be suicidal to be open and error confessing in a den of adversaries — Schön's models describe organizational structures and behavior, not individual cognitive styles. Just as Model I organizations can tame creative participants, so Model II designs can tease innovation from timid souls.

The institutional perspective in Schön's (1983) work goes beyond the individual organization. It would be foolish for an organization to adopt a Model II design if it employed well-understood technologies to address routine tasks in stable environments. The socially interesting issue running through Schön's work is the ecology of interorganizational fields. Do fields have Model II capacities in their behavioral repertoire? Are individual organizations able to shift styles as technologies or environments change (Mintzberg 1984)?

A similar institutional perspective appears in the apparent individual focus of Baum's *Planners and Public Expectations* (1983). Baum would certainly be delighted if more planners understood the political role of their agencies. The force of his argument, however, goes beyond intellectual sophistication or practical shrewdness. Baum's shrewd sophisticates would seek, if I read the text correctly, to match structure and function in a new way, tearing away the mantle of the confusing professional ideology embedded in the dyadic image. That argument may be right or wrong — there are good things to be said for myths and mismatches — but it clearly deals with institutional designs, not individual cognitive styles. Baum's critics who argue that he underestimates the political caginess of planners miss his critique of the planner as political operator and his deep prosthetic intentions.

Finally, consider Peter Hall's *Great Planning Disasters* (1980). Hall ends with rather tame suggestions for improved forecasting and incremental development, suggestions which fit easily into the technical repertoire of the individual planner. The case studies, however, tell a more disturbing story. The core of Hall's argument is that differentiated, professionalized planning encourages the selection of projects that disperse costs and concentrate benefits. That proposition—like Baum's—may be right and may be wrong (and certainly requires further refinement). There is no doubt, however, that it is about institutions and not individuals and that it is a planning theoretic hypothesis virtually begging for research.

The argument would be the same if I had chosen to discuss any of the other theoreticians who have encouraged us to study practitioners and the conditions of practice. Far from urging the imitation of practice, they seek ways to reconstruct institutional relationships outside the frame of the dyadic image of brief and response.

The Neglect of Practice

I have argued to this point that there is a new consensual institutional image of the focus of planning theory and that the force of this consensus is apparent precisely in the new wave of attention to the individual practitioner. This final section weakens that argument, shoving some readers, I fear, back into the quandry from which I have tried to rescue them. The new institutional conception of planning theory has none of the clarity of the dyadic image and cannot justify the profession in the old way.

I have already argued elsewhere that it is impossible to develop a complete general theory of planning. It is simply too hard to create and maintain a uniquely compelling and brief canon of descriptors for planning processes, settings, and outcomes (Mandelbaum 1979). The dyadic image seemed to escape from impossibility by specifying a narrow focus on planners and clients. The institutional perspective enjoys no such tacit constriction of attention. There is no a priori way to specify the appropriate scale or configuration of the institutions subjected to inquiry. Vary the purposes of theorizing and it may be necessary or wise to consider the planning processes of individual organizations, interorganizational fields, professions, cities, communities, nations, polities, clans, markets, hierarchies, societies, clubs, or hybrid combinations of these and other general forms.

Theorists are, of course, not content with a buzz of confusion. The field is rife with efforts at simplification and integration. A quick look at two of them reveals both their generative power and their limits as new consensual frames.

Perhaps the best known synthetic attempts to tame the buzz of diverse theories seek either empirical or normative hierarchies among institutions. If international systems dominate local networks or if the modes of production control those of reproduction, then the analysis of planning processes is simplified. This is the force of the current interest in Marxism (Dear and Scott 1981). In a quite different political style but with the same implications, if only the collective choice processes of cohesive small communities are justifiable, then the differences between large institutions are normatively uninteresting (Friedmann 1979). Again, theorizing is simpler.

The second line seeks an underlying dynamic in every institution. The most widely employed model for integrative positive theorizing is undoubtedly that developed in general systems theory. In the work of Kuhn (1974), for example, quite different institutional forms are subject to a common descriptive language and propositional inventory. General systems theory has, however, had its day and no longer is the source of compelling social insights. The generative power of recent work stems not from the elaboration of the original abstracting impulse but from the convergence on a general critical standard: truthful communication. Williamson's (1975) contrast of markets and hierarchies, for example, rests on an analysis of the ways alternative configurations control lying and other forms of dissimulating behavior.[2] Raiffa (1982) and others have shown that the position of all the participants in partly cooperative games may be enhanced by truth telling and that some negotiating protocols encourage openness. Galbraith (1977) and Mintzberg (1979) focus on the quality of information flows to provide bases for the assessment of organizational designs. Foucault (1972, 1980) and Habermas (1973, 1979) focus on the assessment of societal designs and the distorting effects of domination.

Step inside either the hierarchical or the communication syntheses, and you discover a welter of both internal and external criticism. Has the search for hierarchy—large over small, small over large—become so self-fulfilling that it ignores opportunities for both action and meaning at many scales and in many institutional configurations (Sharpe and Newton 1984; Castells 1983)? Have the lines that separate communication from power become so confused that both truth and domination lose their meaning (Geuss 1981)?

The richness of the argument reveals the grip of impossibility. Planning theoreticians are doomed to argue about the very terms they employ to seek and organize knowledge. This lexical variety is not likely to be tamed by the demands of the users of theory. The dyadic image specified the professional planner as the audience for theorizing. There is no similarly articulated audience for institutionally focused theorizing. Institutional theories speak powerfully to the tasks assumed by professionals and may, indeed, be accused of inflating the norms of professional discourse into criteria for all social encounters (Heller 1982). Nevertheless, institutional theorists also look past the professionals to a variety of both organized and diffuse groups.

Talk of the linkage between strategy and structure must be addressed to men and women at the apex of organizations. Analyses of the uses and limits of markets, the implications of federalist designs, or the conditions of intergroup communication are (or should be) directed to policy communities and broad publics rather than a cadre of planners.

A well-bounded and purposeful audience exercises a disciplining influence on a field. In the absence of such an audience, the community of planning theorists is likely to continue to seem in the eyes of practitioners and academic colleagues both fragmented and neglectful, riddled with great rifts of incommensurable purposes, language, and analytic models. I do not mean, however, to imply that synthesis across these rifts is either unwise or impossible (Ward and Reed 1984). Novices entering professional practice for the first time and experienced practitioners trying to make sense of familiar activities will bring together disparate ideas in ways that illuminate paths of both individual and collective choice. We cannot hope, however, for one all-purpose synthesis that can dominate all the games that will be played against it.

Notes

1. A quite different version of this chapter was presented at the 1983 conference of the Association of Collegiate Schools of Planning. I am grateful to John Forester and Howell Baum who commented at great length on that version. I am responding as much to sessions and informal conversations at ACSP meetings as to published texts. I particularly remember a long late-night discussion in Chicago with Frank Fisher, John Forester, Howell Baum, and Shoukrey Roweis. The published texts include Baum (1983), Schön (1983), Beauregard (1980), Alexander (1984), Forester (1983), Bolan (1980), and de Neufville (1983).

2. I suspect that a great many people started to speak more openly about lying after reading Bok (1978).

References

Alexander, Ernest R. 1984. After Rationality, What? A Review of Responses to Paradigm Breakdown. *Journal of the American Planning Association* 50:62–69.

Ashford, Douglas, ed. 1980. *National Resources and Urban Policy.* New York: Methuen.

Baum, Howell. 1983. *Planners and Public Expectations.* Cambridge, Mass.: Schenkman.

Beauregard, Robert A. 1980. Thinking About Practicing Planning. In *Urban and Regional Planning in an Age of Austerity,* Pierre Clavel, John Forester, and William W. Goldsmith, eds. New York: Pergamon.

Bok, Sissela. 1978. *Lying: Moral Choice in Public and Private Life.* New York: Pantheon Books.

Bolan, Richard S. 1980. The Practitioner as Theorist: The Phenomenology of the Professional Episode. *Journal of the American Planning Association* 46:261–274.

Bryson, John M., and John W. Cullen. 1984. A Contingent Approach to Strategy and Tactics in Formative and Summative Evaluations. *Evaluation and Program Planning* 7:267–290.

Bryson, John M., and Andre L. Delbecq. 1979. A Contingent Approach to Strategy and Tactics in Project Planning. *Journal of the American Planning Association* 45:167–179.

Castells, Manuel. 1983. *The City and the Grassroots: A Cross-Cultural Theory of Urban Social Movements.* Berkeley: University of California Press.

Chandler, Alfred D. 1962. *Strategy and Structure: Chapters in the History of the Industrial Enterprise.* Cambridge, Mass.: MIT Press.

Christensen, Karen S. 1985. Coping with Uncertainty in Planning. *Journal of the American Planning Association* 51:63–73.

Dear, Michael, and Allen J. Scott, eds. 1981. *Urbanization and Urban Planning in Capitalist Society.* New York: Methuen.

de Neufville, Judith Innes. 1983. Planning Theory and Practice: Bridging the Gap. *Journal of Planning Education and Research* 3:35–45.

Faludi, Andreas. 1973. *Planning Theory.* Oxford: Pergamon Press.

Forester, John. 1983. The Geography of Planning Practice. *Environment and Planning: Society and Space* 1:163–180.

Foucault, Michel. 1972. *The Archeology of Knowledge,* A.M. Sheridan Smith, trans. New York: Harper Colophon.

———. 1980. *Power/Knowledge, Selected Interviews and Other Writings, 1972–1977,* Colin Gordon, ed. New York: Pantheon.

Friedmann, John. 1979. *The Good Society.* Cambridge, Mass.: MIT Press.

Galbraith, Jay. 1977. *Organization Design.* Reading, Mass.: Addison-Wesley.

Geuss, Raymond. 1981. *The Idea of A Critical Theory: Habermas and the Frankfurt School.* Cambridge: Cambridge University Press.

Glazer, Nathan. 1974. The Schools of the Minor Professions. *Minerva* 12:346–364.

Gouldner, Alvin W. 1979. *The Future of Intellectuals and the Rise of the New Class.* New York: Seabury Press.

Habermas, Jurgen. 1973. *Theory and Practice,* J. Viertel, trans. Boston: Beacon Press.

———. 1979. *Communication and the Evolution of Society,* E. McCarthy, trans. Boston: Beacon Press.

Hall, Peter. 1980. *Great Planning Disasters.* Berkeley: University of California Press.

Harris, Britton. 1967. The Limits of Science and Humanism in Planning. *Journal of the American Institute of Planners* 33:324–335.

Heller, Agnes. 1982. Habermas and Marxism. In *Habermas: Critical Debates,* John B. Thompson and David Held, eds. Cambridge, Mass.: MIT Press.

Klosterman, Richard E. 1981. Contemporary Planning Theory Education: Results of a Course Survey. *Journal of Planning Education and Research* 1:1–12.

Kuhn, Alfred. 1974. *The Logic of Social Systems: A Unified, Deductive, System-Based Approach to Social Science.* San Francisco: Jossey-Bass.

Lindblom, Charles. 1965. *The Intelligence of Democracy.* New York: Free Press.

MacIntyre, Alasdair. 1984. *After Virtue.* Notre Dame, Ind.: University of Notre Dame Press.

Mandelbaum, Seymour J. 1979. A Complete General Theory of Planning Is Impossible. *Policy Sciences* 11:59–71.

———. 1984. What Is Philadelphia? The City as Polity. *Cities* 1:274–285.

Mintzberg, Henry. 1979. *The Structure of Organizations.* Englewood Cliffs, N.J.: Prentice-Hall.

———. 1984. Power and Organization Life Cycles. *Academy of Management Review* 9:207–224.

Polanyi, Karl. 1944. *The Great Transformation.* New York: Rinehart.

Raiffa, Howard. 1982. *The Art and Science of Negotiation.* Cambridge: Harvard University Press.

Schendel, Dan E., and Charles W. Hofer, eds. 1979. *Strategic Management: A New View of Business Policy and Planning.* Boston: Little, Brown.

Schön, Donald A. 1983. *The Reflective Practitioner: How Professionals Think in Action.* New York: Basic Books.

Scott, James C. 1972. *Comparative Political Corruption.* Englewood Cliffs, N.J.: Prentice-Hall.

Sharpe, L.J., and K. Newton. 1984. *Does Politics Matter? The Determinants of Public Policy.* Oxford: Clarendon Press.

Tribe, Laurence H. 1972. Policy Science: Analysis or Ideology? *Philosophy and Public Affairs* 2:66–110.

Vasu, Michael L. 1979. *Politics and Planning.* Chapel Hill: University of North Carolina Press.

Walker, Robert A. 1950. *The Planning Function in Urban Government.* Chicago: University of Chicago Press.

Ward, Spencer A., and Linda J. Reed, eds. 1984. *Knowledge Structure and Use: Implications for Synthesis and Interpretation.* Philadelphia: Temple University Press.

Williamson, Oliver E. 1975. *Markets and Hierarchies.* New York: Free Press.

15
Toward a New Epistemology of Practice

Donald A. Schön

The Crisis of Confidence in Professional Knowledge

Although our society has become thoroughly dependent on professionals—so much so that the conduct of business, industry, government, education, and everyday life would be unthinkable without them—there are signs of a growing crisis of confidence in the professions. In many well-publicized scandals, professionals have been found to be willing to use their special positions for private gain. Professionally designed solutions to public problems have had unanticipated consequences, sometimes worse than the problems they were intended to solve. The public has shown an increasing readiness to call for external regulation of professional practice. Laypersons have been increasingly disposed to turn to the courts for defense against professional incompetence or venality. The professional's traditional claims to privileged social position and autonomy of practice have come into question as the public has begun to have doubts about professional ethics and expertise (Hughes 1959). And in recent years even the professionals have shown signs of a loss of confidence in professional knowledge.

However, it is not long since 1963 when the editors of *Daedalus* (Lynn 1963, p. 649) introduced a special volume on the professions with the sentence, "Everywhere in American Life the professions are triumphant." They noted the apparently limitless demand for professional services, the shortages of teachers and physicians, the difficulty of coordinating the proliferating technical specializations, the problems of managing the burgeoning mass of technical data. In the further essays that made up the volume, doctors, lawyers, scientists, educators, militarists, and politicians articulated the themes of professional triumph, overload, and growth. There were only two discordant voices. The representative of the clergy complained of declining influence and the "problem of relevance" (Gustafson 1963, p. 743), and the city planner commented ruefully on his profession's lagging understanding of the changing ills of urban areas (Alonso 1963). Yet in less than a decade the discordant notes had become dominant, and the themes of professional triumph had virtually disappeared.

In 1972, a colloquium on professional education at the Massachusetts Institute of Technology (MIT) included representatives of medicine, engineering, architecture, planning, psychiatry, law, divinity, education, and management. These individuals disagreed about many things, but together they shared a profound uneasiness about their professions. They questioned whether professionals would effectively police themselves. They wondered whether professionals were instruments of individual well-being and social reform or mainly interested in the preservation of status and privilege, caught up in the very problems they might have been expected to solve. They expressed doubts about the relevance and remedial power of professional expertise.

It is not difficult to account for this dramatic shift, over a single decade, in the tone of professional self-reflection. Between 1963 and 1972 there had been a disturbing sequence of events, painful for professionals and lay public alike. A professionally instrumented war had been disastrous. Social movements for peace and civil rights had begun to see the professions as elitist servants of established interests. The much-proclaimed shortages of scientists, teachers, and physicians seemed to have evaporated. Professionals seemed powerless to relieve the rapidly shifting crises of the cities. There were scandals of Medicare and, at the end of the decade, Watergate. These events cumulatively created doubts about professional strategies of diagnosis and cure. They revealed the complexity of phenomena with which professionals were concerned. They led to skepticism about the adequacy of professional knowledge, theories, and techniques to cure the deeper causes of societal distress.

Participants in the MIT colloquium shared these sentiments of unease and tried to analyze their predicament. Some of them believed that social change had created problems ill-suited to the traditional division of labor. An engineer observed that "education no longer fits the niche, or the niche no longer fits education." The dean of a medical school spoke of the scope and complexity of a health care system only marginally susceptible to the interventions of the medical profession. The dean of a school of management referred to the puzzle of educating managers for judgment and action under conditions of uncertainty. Others were troubled by an irreducible residue of art in professional practice. The art seemed indispensable even to scientific research, and engineering design seemed resistant to codification. As one participant observed, "If it's invariant and known, it can be taught, but it isn't invariant."

Professional education emphasized problem solving, but the most urgent and intractable issues of professional practice were those of problem finding. "Our interest," as one participant put it, "is not only how to pour the concrete for the highway, but what highway to build? When it comes to designing a ship, the question we have to ask is, 'Which ship makes sense in terms of the problems of transportation?' " And representatives of architecture, planning, social work, and psychiatry spoke of the pluralism of their schools. Different schools held different views of the competencies to be acquired, the problems to be solved, even of the nature of the professions. A professor of psychiatry described his field as a "babble of voices."

Finally, participants called for the liberation of the professions from the tyranny of the university-based professional schools. Everett Hughes (1959), one of the founders of the sociology of the professions, declared that "American universities are products of the late 19th and early 20th centuries. The question is, how do you break them up in some way, at least get some group of young people who are free to them? How do you make them free to do something new and different?"

The years that have passed since the colloquium have tended to reinforce its conclusions. In the 1980s, no profession can celebrate itself in triumphant tones. In spite of the continuing eagerness of the young to embark on relatively secure and remunerative professional careers, professionals still criticize themselves and are criticized for failing both to adapt to a changing social reality and to live up to their own standards of practice. There is widespread recognition of the lack of a framework of purpose within which professionals can play their roles and exercise their skills.

In retrospect, it is not difficult to see why participants in the colloquium should have puzzled over the troubles of their professions. They were becoming aware of the indeterminate zones of practice—the situations of complexity and uncertainty, the cases that require artistry, the task of problem setting, the multiplicity of professional identities—that have since become more visible and problematic. Nevertheless, there is something strange about their unease because professionals in many fields find ways of coping effectively, even wisely, with situations of complexity and uncertainty. If the element of art in professional practice is not invariant, known, and teachable, it does appear learnable. Problem setting is an activity in which some professionals engage with recognizable skill. And students and practitioners do occasionally make thoughtful choices from among the multiple views of professional identity.

Why should a group of eminent professionals have been so troubled by the evidence of indeterminacy in professional practice? It is not that they were unaware of the ways in which some practitioners cope reasonably well with such situations. Indeed, they might have counted themselves among those who do so. It is more likely that they were troubled because they could not readily account for the coping process. Complexity and uncertainty are sometimes dissolved but not by applying specialized knowledge to well-defined tasks. Artistry is not reducible to the exercise of replicable routines. Problem finding has no place in a body of knowledge concerned exclusively with problem solving. To be able to choose among competing paradigms of professional practice, one cannot rely on professional expertise. The professionals were likely disturbed to discover that the competences they were beginning to see as central to professional practice had no place in their underlying model of professional knowledge.

In the following pages, I describe this underlying model and this implicit epistemology of practice, and I outline a fundamental dilemma of practice and teaching to which it leads. I propose that we seek an alternative epistemology of practice grounded in observation and analysis of the artistry competent practitioners sometimes bring to the indeterminate zones of their practice. I describe and illustrate the reflection-in-action essential to professional artistry and suggest some of its implications for professional education.

The Dominant Model of Professional Knowledge

The epistemology of professional practice that dominates most thinking and writing about the professions and that is built into the structure of professional schools and research institutions has been clearly set forth in two essays on professional education. Both essays treat rigorous professional practice as an exercise of technical rationality—that is, as an application of research-based knowledge to the solution of problems of instrumental choice.

Schein (1972, p. 43) proposes a threefold division of professional knowledge:

1. An underlying discipline or basic science component upon which the practice rests or from which it is developed,
2. An applied science or engineering component from which many of the day-to-day diagnostic procedures and problem solutions are derived,
3. A skills and attitudinal component that concerns the performance of services to the client, using the underlying basic and applied knowledge.

Schein views these components as a hierarchy that may be read in terms of application, justification, and status. The application of basic science yields engineering, which in turn provides models, rules, and techniques applicable to the instrumental choices of everyday practice. The performance of services rests on applied science, which in turn rests on the foundation of basic science. In the epistemological pecking order, basic science is highest in methodological rigor and purity, its practitioners superior in status to those who practice applied science, problem solving, or service delivery.

Glazer (1974, p. 363), in a much quoted article, argues that the schools of professions such as education, divinity, social work, and town planning are caught in a hopeless predicament. These so-called minor professions, beguiled by the success of the major professions of law, medicine, and business, have tried to substitute a basis in scientific knowledge for their traditional reliance on experienced practice. In this spirit, they have placed their schools within universities. However, Glazer believes that their aspirations are doomed to failure. The minor professions lack the essential conditions of the major ones:

> Can these fields settle on a fixed form of training, a fixed content of professional knowledge, and follow the models of medicine, law, and business? I suspect now because the discipline of a fixed and unambiguous end in a fixed institutional setting is not given to them. And thus the base of knowledge which is unambiguously indicated as relevant for professional education is also not given.

Glazer and Schein share the epistemology of professional practice that is rooted historically in the positivist philosophy that so powerfully shaped both the modern university and the modern conception of the proper relationship of theory and practice (Habermas 1968; Shils 1978). Rigorous professional practice is conceived as essentially technical. Its rigor depends on the use of replicable techniques derived from scientific research, based on knowledge that is objective, consensual, cumulative, and convergent. In this view, for example, engineering is an application of engineering science; rigorous management depends on the use of management science; and policymaking can become rigorous when it is based on policy science.

Practice can be construed as technical, in this sense, only when certain things are kept clearly separate from one another. Deciding must be kept separate from doing. Rigorous practitioners use their professional knowledge to decide on the means best suited to their ends, with action serving to implement technically sound decisions. Means must be clearly separated from ends. Technical means are variable, appropriate, or inappropriate according to the situation. But the ends of practice must be fixed and unambiguous, like Glazer's examples of profit, health, and success in litigation; otherwise, how is it possible to evolve a base of applicable professional knowledge? Finally, research must be kept separate from practice. Research can yield new knowledge only in the protected setting of the scholar's study or in the carefully controlled environment of a scientific laboratory, whereas the world of practice is notoriously unprotected and uncontrollable.

These tenets of the positivist epistemology of practice are still built into our institutions, even when their inhabitants no longer espouse them. Just as Veblen (1918) propounded almost seventy years ago, the university and the research institute are sheltered from the troublesome world of practice. Research and practice are presumed to be linked by an exchange in which researchers offer theories and techniques applicable to practice problems, and practitioners, in return, give researchers new problems to work on and practical tests of the utility of research results. The normative curriculum of professional education, as Schein (1972) describes it, still follows the hierarchy of professional knowledge. First students are exposed to the relevant basic science, then to the relevant applied science, and finally to a practicum in which they are presumed to learn to apply classroom knowledge to the problems of practice. Medical education offers the prototype for such a curriculum, and its language of diagnosis, cure, laboratory, and clinic have long since diffused to other professions.

From the perspective of this model of professional knowledge, it is not difficult to understand why practitioners should be puzzled by their performance in the indeterminate zones of practice. Their performance does not fit the criteria of technical rationality; it cuts across the dichotomies built into the positivist epistemology of practice. Artistry, for example, is not only in the deciding but also in the doing. When planners or managers convert an uncertain situation into a solvable problem, they construct—as John Dewey pointed out long ago—not only the means to be deployed but also the ends to be achieved. In such problem setting, ends and means are reciprocally determined. And often, in the unstable world of practice, where methods and theories developed in one context are unsuited to another, practitioners function as researchers, inventing the techniques and models appropriate to the situation at hand.

The Dilemma of Rigor or Relevance

For practitioners, educators, and students of the professions, the positivist epistemology of practice contributes to an urgent dilemma of rigor or relevance. The dominant view of professional rigor—the view which prevails in the intellectual climate of the universities and in the institutional arrangements of professional education and research—holds that rigorous practice depends on well-formed problems of instrumental choice to whose solution research-based theory and technique are applicable (Simon 1972). But real world problems do not come well formed. Instead, they tend to present themselves as messy, indeterminate, problematic situations. For example, a civil engineer who worries about what road to build cannot solve the problem by applying locational techniques or decision theory. He or she confronts a complex and ill-defined situation in which geographic, financial, economic, and political factors are usually mixed up together. If this person is to arrive at a well-formed problem, he or she must construct it from the materials of the problematic situation. And the problem of problem setting is not well formed (Rein and Schön 1977).

When practitioners set a problem, they choose what they will treat as the "things" of the situation. They decide what they will attend to and what they will ignore. They name the objects of their attention and frame them in an appreciative context that sets a direction for action. For example, a vague worry about hunger or malnourishment may be framed as a problem of selecting an optimal diet. But situations of malnourishment may also be framed in many different ways. Economists, environmental scientists, nutrition scientists, agronomists, planners, engineers, and political scientists debate the nature of the malnourishment problem, and their discussions have given rise to a multiplicity of problem settings worthy of *Rashomon*. Indeed, the practice of malnourishment planning is largely taken up with the task of constructing the problem to be solved.

When practitioners succeed in converting a problematic situation into a well-formed problem or in resolving a conflict over the proper framing of a practitioner's role in a situation, they engage in a kind of inquiry that cannot be subsumed under a model of technical problem solving; it is through the work of naming and framing that the exercise of technical rationality becomes possible.

Similarly, the artistic processes by which practitioners sometimes make sense of unique cases, and the art they sometimes bring to everyday practice, do not meet the prevailing criteria of rigorous practice. Often, when competent practitioners recognize the pattern of a disease in a maze of symptoms, construct a basis for coherent design in the peculiarities of a building site, or discern an understandable structure in a jumble of materials, they do something for which they cannot give a complete or even a reasonably accurate description. Practitioners often make judgments of quality for which they cannot state adequate criteria, display skills for which they cannot describe procedures or rules.

By defining rigor only in terms of technical rationality, we exclude as nonrigorous much of what competent practitioners do, including the skillful performance of problem solving and judgment on which technical problem solving depends. Indeed, we exclude the most important components of competent practice.

In the varied topography of professional practice, there is a high, hard ground that overlooks a swamp. On the high ground, manageable problems lend themselves to solution through the use of research-based theory and technique. In the swampy lowlands, problems are messy, confusing, and incapable of technical solution. The irony of this situation is that the problems of the high ground tend to be relatively unimportant to individuals or to society at large, however great their technical interest may be, while in the swamp lie the problems of greatest human concern. The practitioner is confronted with a choice. Shall he or she remain on the high ground to solve relatively unimportant problems according to standards of rigor or descend to the swamp of important problems and nonrigorous inquiry?

Consider medicine, engineering, and agronomy, three of Glazer's (1974)

major or near-major professions. These fields contain areas in which problems are clearly defined, goals are relatively fixed, and phenomena lend themselves to categories of available theory and technique. Here, practitioners can
function effectively as technical experts. But when one or more of these conditions is lacking, competent performance is no longer a matter of exclusively
technical expertise. Medical technologies such as kidney dialysis or tomog-
raphy create demands that stretch the nation's willingness to invest in medical
care. How should physicians behave? How should they try to influence or
accommodate health policy? Engineering solutions that seem powerful and
elegant when judged from a relatively narrow perspective may have a wider
range of consequences that degrades the environment, generates unacceptable risk, or puts excessive demands on scarce resources. How should engineers take these factors into account in their designing? When agronomists
recommend efficient methods of soil cultivation that favor the use of large
landholdings, they may undermine the viability of the small family farms on
which peasant economies depend. How should the practice of agronomy take
such considerations into account? These are not problems, properly speaking, but problematic situations from which problems must be constructed. If
practitioners choose to address them, they must approach them through
kinds of inquiries that are, according to the dominant model of technical
rationality, unrigorous.

The doctrine of technical rationality, promulgated and maintained in the
universities and professional schools, infects the young professional in training with a hunger for technique. For example, many students or urban planning are impatient with anything other than hard skills. Students of management often chafe under the discipline of endless case analysis; they want to
learn the techniques and algorithms that they see as the key to high starting
salaries. Yet professionals who tried to confine their practice to the rigorous
applications of research-based technique would find not only that they could
not work on the most important problems but also that they could not practice in the real world at all.

Nearly all professional practitioners experience a version of the dilemma
of rigor or relevance, and they respond to it in one of several ways. Some
choose the swampy lowland, deliberately immersing themselves in confusing
and crucial situations. When asked to describe their methods of inquiry, they
speak of experience, trial and error, intuition or muddling through. When
teachers, social workers, or planners operate in this vein, they tend to be
afflicted with a nagging sense of inferiority in relation to those who present
themselves as models of technical rigor. When physicians or engineers do so,
they tend to be troubled by the discrepancy between the technical rigor of the
hard zones of their practice and the apparent sloppiness of the soft zones.

Practitioners who opt for the high ground confine themselves to a narrowly technical practice and pay a price for doing so. Operations research,

systems analysis, policy analysis, and some management science are examples of practices built around the use of formal, analytic models. In the early years of the development of these professions, there was a climate of optimism about the power of formal models to solve the real world problems. In subsequent decades, however, there was increasing recognition of the limited applicability of formal models, especially in situations of high complexity and uncertainty (Ackoff 1979). Some practitioners have responded by confining themselves to a narrow class of well-formed problems—in inventory control, for example. Some researchers have continued to develop formal models for use in problems of high complexity and uncertainty, quite undeterred by the troubles incurred whenever a serious attempt is made to put such models into practice. They pursue an agenda driven by evolving questions of modeling theory and techniques, increasingly divergent from the contexts of actual practice.

Practitioners may try to cut the situations of practice to fit their models, employing for this purpose one of several procrustean strategies. They may become selectively inattentive to data incongruent with their theories, like the way some educators preserve their confidence in competence testing by ignoring the kinds of competences that such testing fails to detect. Physicians or therapists may use junk categories like patient resistance to explain away the cases in which an indicated treatment fails (Geertz 1973). And social workers may try to make their technical expertise effective by exerting unilateral control over the practice situation by removing unworthy clients from the case rolls.

Those who confine themselves to a limited range of technical problems on the high ground or who cut situations of practice to fit available techniques seek a world in which technical rationality works. Even those who choose the swamp tend to pay homage to prevailing models of rigor. What they know how to do, they have no way of describing as rigorous.

Writers about the professions tend to follow similar paths. Both Glazer (1974) and Schein (1972) recognize the indeterminate zones of professional practice. But Glazer relegates them to the minor professions, of which he despairs. And Schein locates what he calls "divergent" phenomena of uncertainty, complexity, and uniqueness in concrete practice situations while at the same time regarding professional knowledge as increasingly convergent. He thinks convergent knowledge may be applied to divergent practice through the exercise of divergent skills—about which, however, he is able to say very little. If divergent skills were treated in terms of theory or technique, they would belong to convergent professional knowledge; and if they are neither theory nor technique, they cannot be described as knowledge. They function instead as a junk category that serves to protect an underlying model of technical rationality.

However, the epistemology of practice embedded in our universities and research institutions, ingrained in our habits of thought about professional knowledge, and at the root of the dilemma of rigor or relevance, has lost its hold on the field that nurtured it. Among philosophers of science, no one wants any longer to be called a positivist (Bernstein 1976). There is a rebirth of interest in the ancient topics of craft, artistry, and myth, topics whose fate positivism seemed once to have finally sealed. Positivism and the positivist epistemology of practice now seem to rest on a particular view of science, one now largely discredited.

It is time to reconsider the question of professional knowledge. Perhaps there is an epistemology of practice that takes full account of the competence practitioners sometimes display in situations of uncertainty, complexity, and uniqueness. Perhaps there is a way of looking at problem setting and intuitive artistry that presents these activities as susceptible to a kind of rigor that falls outside the boundaries of technical rationality.

Reflection-in-Action

When we go about the spontaneous, intuitive performance of the actions of everyday life, we show ourselves to be knowledgeable in a special way. Often, we cannot say what we know. When we try to describe it, we find ourselves at a loss or we produce inappropriate descriptions. Our knowing is ordinarily tacit, implicit in our patterns of action and in our feel for the stuff with which we are dealing. It seems right to say that our knowing is in our action. And similarly, the workday life of the professional practitioner reveals, in its recognitions, judgments, and skills, a pattern of tacit knowing-in-action.

Once we put technical rationality aside, thereby giving up our view of competent practice as an application of knowledge to instrumental decisions, there is nothing strange about the idea that a kind of knowing is inherent in intelligent action. Common sense admits the category of know-how, and it does not stretch common sense very much to say that the know-how is in the action—that a tightrope walker's know-how, for example, lies in, and is revealed by, the way he or she takes that trip across the wire or that a big league pitcher's know-how is in his way of pitching to a batter's weakness, changing his pace, or distributing his energies over the course of a game. There is nothing in common sense to make us say that know-how consists of rules or plans that we entertain in the mind prior to action. Although we sometimes think before we act, it is true also that in much of the spontaneous behavior of skillful practice we reveal a kind of knowing that does not stem from a prior intellectual operation. As Ryle (1949, p. 32) writes:

What distinguishes sensible from silly operations is not their parentage but their procedure, and this holds no less for intellectual than for practical performances. "Intelligent" cannot be defined in terms of "intellectual" or "knowing *how*" in terms of "knowing *that*"; "thinking what I am doing" does not connote "both thinking what to do and doing it." When I do something intelligently . . . I am doing one thing and not two. My performance has a special procedure or manner, not special antecedents.

Harrison (1978) expresses a similar thought by saying that when someone acts intellectually, he "acts his mind."

Examples of intelligence in action include acts of recognition and judgment, as well as the exercise of ordinary physical skills. Polanyi (1967) writes about our ability to recognize a face in a crowd. The experience of recognition can be immediate and holistic. We simply see, all of a sudden, the face of someone we know. We are aware of no antecedent reasoning, and we are often unable to list the features that distinguish this face from the hundreds of others present in the crowd.

When the thing we recognize is something wrong or something right, then recognition takes the form of judgment. Alexander (1964) calls attention to the innumerable judgments of mismatch—deviations from a tacit norm—that are involved in making a design. And Vickers (1978) notes that not only in artistic judgment but in all our ordinary judgments of quality, we "can recognize and describe deviations from a norm very much more clearly than we can describe the norm itself." A young friend of mine who teaches tennis observes that his students have to be able to feel when they are hitting the ball right, and they have to like that feeling, as compared to the feeling of hitting it wrong; but they need not, and usually cannot, describe either the feeling of hitting it right or what they do to get that feeling. A skilled physician can sometimes recognize a disease or symptom the moment a person walks into his or her office. The act of recognition comes immediately and as a whole; the physician may not be able to say subsequently just what led to that initial judgment.

Polanyi (1967) describes our ordinary tactile appreciation of the surface of materials. If you ask a group of people what they feel when they explore the surface of a table with their hand, they are apt to say that the table feels rough or smooth, sticky or slippery, but are unlikely to say that they feel a certain compression and abrasion of their fingertips—although from this kind of feeling must come the appreciation of the table's surface. Polanyi speaks of perceiving from these fingertip sensations to the qualities of the surface. Similarly, when we use a stick to probe a hidden place, we focus not on the impressions of the stick on our hand but on the qualities of the place that we apprehend through these tacit impressions. To become skillful in the use of a tool is to learn to appreciate, as it were, directly the qualities of materials that we apprehend through the tacit sensations of the tool in our hand.

Barnard (1968) writes of "nonlogical processes" that we cannot express in words as a process of reasoning but evince only by a judgment, decision, or action. A child who has learned to throw a ball makes immediate judgments of distance that he coordinates, tacitly, with the feeling of bodily movement involved in the act of throwing. A high school girl, solving quadratic equations, has learned spontaneously to carry out a program of operations that she cannot describe. A practiced accountant of Barnard's acquaintance could take a balance sheet of considerable complexity and within minutes or even seconds get a significant set of facts from it, although he could not describe in words the recognitions and calculations that entered into his performance. Similarly, we are able to execute spontaneously complex activities such as crawling, walking, riding a bicycle, or juggling, without having to think, in any conscious way, what we are doing, and often without being able to give a verbal description even approximately faithful to our performance.

In spite of their tacit complexity and virtuousity, however, our spontaneous responses to the phenomena of everyday life do not always work. Sometimes our knowing-in-action yields surprises, and we often react to the unexpected by a kind of on-the-spot inquiry that I call reflection-in-action.

Sometimes this process takes the form of ordinary, on-line problem solving. It need not even be associated with a high degree of skill but may consist of an amateur's effort to acquire skill. For example, I recently built a wooden gate. I had made a drawing of it and figured the dimensions but had not reckoned with the problem of keeping the structure square. I began to nail the strapping to the pickets and noticed that the whole thing wobbled. I knew that the structure would become rigid when I nailed in a diagonal piece. But how would I be sure that the structure would be square? I stopped to think. There came to mind a vague memory about diagonals—that in a square, the diagonals are equal. I took a yardstick, intending to measure the diagonals, but found it difficult to make these measurements without disturbing the structure. It occurred to me to use a piece of string. Then it became apparent that I needed precise locations from which to measure the diagonal from corner to corner. After several trials, I decided to locate the center point at each of the corners, hammered a nail at each of the four center points, and used the nails as anchors for the measurement string. It took several moments to figure how to adjust the structure to correct the errors found by measuring, and when I had the diagonals equal, I nailed in the strapping that made the structure rigid.

Here—in an example that must have its analogues in the experience of amateur carpenters the world over—my intuitive way of going about the task led me to a surprise (the discovery of the wobble) that I interpreted as a problem. Stopping to think, I invented procedures to solve the problem, discovered further unpleasant surprises, and made more corrective inventions, including several minor inventions necessary to make the idea of string measurement of diagonals work.

Ordinarily we might call such a process trial and error. But it is not a series of random trials continued until a desired result is produced. The process has a form, an inner logic according to which reflection on the unexpected consequences of one action influences the design of the next one. The moments of such a process may be described as follows:

> In the context of the performance of some task, the performer spontaneously initiates a routine of action that produces an unexpected outcome.
>
> The performer notices the unexpected result that he or she construes as a surprise—an error to be corrected, an anomaly to be made sense of, an opportunity to be exploited.
>
> Surprise triggers reflection, directed both to the surprising outcome and to the knowing-in-action that led to it. It is as though the performer asks, What is this? and at this same time, What understandings and strategies of mine have led me to produce this?
>
> The performer restructures his or her understanding of the situation—his or her framing of what is going on, or the strategy of action he or she has been employing.
>
> On the basis of this restructuring, the performer invents a new strategy of action.
>
> The performer tries out the new action, running an on-the-spot experiment whose results he or she interprets as a solution, an outcome on the whole satisfactory, or else as a new surprise that calls for new reflection and experiment.

In the course of such a process, the performer reflects not only in the sense of thinking about the action undertaken and the result achieved but also in the more precise sense of turning thought back on the knowing-in-action implicit in action. The performer reflects in action in the sense that his or her thinking occurs within the boundaries of what I call an action-present—a stretch of time within which it is still possible to make a difference to the outcomes of action. The following two examples of reflection-in-action are drawn from professional practice.

A designer, hard at work on the design of a school, has been exploring the possible configurations of small classroom units. Having tried a number of these, dissatisfied with the formal results, he decides that these units are too small to do much with. He tries combining the classrooms in L-shaped pairs and discovers that these are formally much more significant and that they have the additional, unexpected, educational advantage of putting grade one next to grade two and grade three next to grade four.

A teacher has a young student, Joey, who disturbs her by insisting that an eclipse of the sun did not take place because "it was snowing and we didn't see it." It occurs to the teacher that Joey does not know that the sun is there, even if he cannot see it, and she asks him, "Where was the sun yesterday?" Joey answers, "I don't know; I didn't see it." Later, it occurs to her that his answer may have reflected not his ignorance of the sun's remaining in the sky but his interpretation of her question. She thinks that he may have read her as asking, "Where in the sky was the sun?" With this in mind, she tries a new question, "What happened to the sun yesterday?" to which Joey answers, "It was in the sky."

In examples such as these, reflection-in-action involves a stop-and-think. It is close to conscious awareness and is easily put into words. Often, however, reflection-in-action is smoothly embedded in performance; there is no stop-and-think, no conscious attention to the process, and no verbalization. In this way, for example, a baseball pitcher adapts his pitching style to the peculiarities of a batter, a tennis player executes split-second variations in play to counter the strategies of her opponent. In such cases, we are close to processes we might recognize as examples of artistry.

When good jazz musicians improvise together, they dispel a feel for the performance. Listening to one another and to themselves, they feel where the music is going and adjust their playing accordingly. They are inventing on line, and they are also responding to surprises provided by the inventions of the others. A figure announced by one performer will be taken up by another, elaborated, and perhaps integrated with a new melody. The collective process of musical invention is not usually undertaken at random, however. It is organized around an underlying structure—a shared schema of meter, melody, and harmony that gives the piece a predictable order. In addition, each musician has ready a repertoire of musical figures that he or she can play, weaving variations of them as the opportunity arises. Improvisation consists of varying, combining, and recombining a set of figures within the schema that gives coherence to the whole performance. As the musicians feel the directions in which the music is developing, out of their interwoven contributions, they make new sense of it and adjust their performances to the sense they make. They are reflecting-in-action on the music they are collectively making, though not in the medium of words.

Their process is like the familiar improvisation of everyday conversation, which does occur in the medium of words. A good conversation is both predictable and unpredictable. The participants may pick up themes suggested by others, developing them through the associations they provoke. Each participant seems to have a readily available repertoire of things to say, around which to develop variations suited to the occasion. Conversation is collective verbal improvisation that tends to fall into conventional routines—for example, the anecdote (with appropriate side comments and reactions) or the debate—and it develops according to a pace and rhythm of interaction that the participants seem, without conscious attention, to work out in common. There also are surprises, in the form of unexpected turns of phrase or directions of development. Participants make on-the-spot responses to surprise, often in conformity to the kind of conversational role they have adopted. Central to the other forms of improvisation, there is a conversational division of labor that gradually establishes itself, often without conscious awareness on the part of those who work it out.

In the on-the-spot improvisation of a musical piece or a conversation, spontaneous reflection-in-action takes the form of a kind of production. The participants are involved in a collective making process. Out of the stuff of this musical performance, or this talk, they make a piece of music, or a conversation—in either case, an artifact that has some degree of order, meaning, development, coherence. Their reflection-in-action becomes a reflective conversation—this time, in a metaphorical sense—with the materials of the situation in which they are engaged. Each person plays his or her evolving role in the collective performance, listens to the things that happen, and responds with new moves that give new directions to the development of the whole. The process is reminiscent of the Eskimo sculptor who patiently carves a reindeer bone, examines the gradually changing shape, and finally exclaims, "Ah, seal!"

It is evident from experience that one can engage in spontaneous reflection-in-action without being able to give a good description of it. A performer who is asked to talk about the reflection and on-the-spot experimentation he or she has just carried out may first give an incomplete or inaccurate description. And by comparing what that person says to what he or she has just done, the performer can often discover this for himself or herself.

It is one thing to engage spontaneously in a performance that involves reflection-in-action, quite another to reflect on reflection-in-action through an act of description, yet another to reflect on the resulting description. Indeed, these several distinct kinds of reflection can play important roles in the process by which an individual learns a new kind of performance. A tennis coach reports his or her use of an exercise in which he or she repeatedly asks his or her students to say where their racket was when they hit the ball; the coach intends to help them get more precisely in touch with what they are doing when they hit the ball so they will know what they were doing when they try to correct their errors. One man used to teach juggling by informing would-be jugglers that they are susceptible to a variety of kinds of bugs—that is, to typical mistakes such as throwing too far forward or overcorrecting an error. He would ask them from time to time to describe the bug they had just enacted.

Professional practitioners, such as physicians, managers, and teachers, also reflect-in-action, but their reflection is a kind particular to the special features of professional practice. *Practice* has a double meaning. A lawyer's practice includes the kinds of activities she carries out, the clients she serves, the cases she is called on to handle. When we speak of practicing the performance, however, we refer to the repetitive yet experimental process by which one learns, for example, to play a musical instrument. The two senses of practice, although quite distinct, relate to one another in an interesting way. Professional practice also includes repetition. A professional is in some measure a specialist. He deals with certain types of situations and techniques, works his way through various cases, and practices his practice. His knowhow tends to increase and confer on him and his clients the benefits of specialization. But specialization can make the professional narrow and parochial, inducing a kind of overlearning and pattern of error to which he becomes selectively inattentive.

Reflection on spontaneous reflection-in-action can serve as a corrective to overlearning. Skillful practitioners who understand the repetitive experiences of a specialized practice may notice and make new sense of phenomena. They may continually engage in a process of reflection, which defies description. Their knowing-in-action may be revealed by their feel for the stuff with which they deal. When they try to say what they know—when they try to put their knowing into the form of knowledge—the formulations are often incongruent with the understanding implicit in the practitioners' patterns of practice.

Conversely, skillful practitioners sometimes respond to a situation by reflecting simultaneously on the situation before them and on the reflection-in-action they spontaneously bring to it. In the midst of action, they are able to turn thought back on itself, criticizing and restructuring the thinking by which they have spontaneously tried to make the situation intelligible to themselves. For example, there are:

> Managers who respond to turbulent situations by constructing and testing a model of the situation and experimenting with alternative strategies for dealing with it;

> Physicians who find that 80 percent of the cases seen in the office are not found in the book, treat each patient as a unique case, construct and test diagnoses, invent and evaluate lines of treatment through on-the-spot experimentation;

> Engineers who discover that they cannot apply their rules-of-thumb to an anomalous or constrained situation and proceed to devise and test theories and procedures unique to the situation at hand;

Lawyers who find new ways to relate a puzzling case to a body of judicial predecent;

Planners who treat plans as tentative programs for inquiry and stay alert to discover unanticipated meanings their interventions may have for those affected by them.

In this last example, consider the cases in which plans and programs have been treated as failures because outcomes fell outside the range of expectations held by designers. In Michigan, social planners, disturbed by migrant workers' habit of taking their children to the fields, instituted a day care service, only to discover that the workers pocketed the money intended for day care and continued to take their children to the fields. The workers apparently placed a higher value on the extra income than on the day care. Designers of the federal housing allowance experiment read as failure the fact that many recipients used part of the funds to paint and patch existing dwellings but allocated the rest to uses that had nothing to do with housing. In Colombia, municipal designers of sites-and-services programs were disappointed to find that many residents used the new structures for income by renting it out to other residents or to commercial establishments. But in each of these cases, failure might be read as success if the planners were to change their images of the interests of their beneficiaries. The planners' intentions seem to have been based on one view of progress, the recipients' on another. Planners capable of reflection-in-action — in this instance, a reflective conversation with the unanticipated outcomes of their moves — might have used the data read as failure to reframe the objectives and expectations associated with programs.

Many such examples of reflection on reflection-in-action occur in uncertain, unique, or value-conflicted zones of practice. Depending on the context and practitioner, such inquiry may take the form of on-the-spot problem solving, theory building, or reappreciation of the problem. When a problem proves resistant to solutions, practitioners may rethink their approach and invent new strategies of action. When they encounter a situation outside the usual range of descriptive categories, they may criticize their initial understandings and construct a new, situation-specific theory of the phenomena before them. When practitioners find themselves stuck, they may decide they have been working on the wrong problem and find a new way of framing it.

The objects of reflection may lie anywhere in the system of understanding and know-how that practitioners bring to their practice. Depending on the centrality of the elements they choose to reconsider, more or less of that system may become vulnerable to change. But, systems of intuitive knowing are conservative, defended, and resistant to change. They tend not to go quietly to their demise, and reflection-in-action often takes on a quality of struggle. In the early hours of the accident at the Three Mile Island nuclear power plant, for example, managers confronted signals that they could only regard as weird, unprecedented, unlike anything they had ever seen before. But they persisted in attempting to assimilate these signals to a situation of normalcy — "not wanting to believe," as one manager put it, that the nuclear core had been uncovered and damaged. Only after twelve hours of fruitless attempts to construe the situation as a minor problem did the manager insist, against the wishes of others in the plant, that "future actions be based on the assumption that the core has been uncovered, the fuel severely damaged."

Many practitioners view themselves as technical experts and find little in practice to occasion reflection. For them, uncertainty is a threat; its admission, a sign of weakness. They become proficient at techniques of selective inattention, the use of junk categories to dismiss anomalous data, procrustean treatment of troublesome situations, all aimed at preserving the constancy of their knowing-in-action. Reflection-in-action, however, is not a rare event. There are practitioners for whom reflection-in-action is central as they develop the artistry of their everyday lives. Such individuals are willing to embrace error, accept confusion, and reflect critically on their unexamined assumptions. Nevertheless, in a world where professionalism is still mainly identified with technical expertise, even these practitioners may feel profoundly uneasy because they cannot describe what they know how to do, justify it as a legitimate form of professional knowledge, increase its scope or quality, or with confidence, help others to learn it.

Conclusion

The study of professional artistry is of critical importance. We should be turning the puzzle of professional knowledge on its head, seeking not only to build up a science applicable to practice but also to reflect on the reflection-in-action already embedded in competent practice. For example, we should be exploring how the on-the-spot experimentation carried out by practicing architects, physicians, engineers, and managers is like, and unlike, the controlled experimentation of laboratory scientists. We should be analyzing the ways in which skilled practitioners build up repertoires of exemplars, images, and strategies of description in terms of what they learn to see as novel, one-of-a-kind phenomena. We should be attentive to differences in the framing of problematic situations and to the rare episodes of frame-reflective discourse in which practitioners sometimes coordinate and transform their conflicting ways of making sense of confusing predicaments. We should investigate the conventions and notations through which practitioners create virtual worlds — as diverse as sketch pads, simulations, role plays, and rehearsals — in which they are able to slow down the pace of action, go back and try again, and reduce the cost and risk of experimentation. In explorations such as these, grounded in collaborative reflection on everyday artistry, we will be pursuing the description of a new epistemology of practice.

We also should investigate how some people learn the kinds and levels of reflection-in-action essential to professional artistry. In apprenticeships and clinical experiences, how are textbook descriptions of symptoms and procedures translated into the acts of recognition and judgment and the readiness for action characteristic of professional competence? How do aspiring practitioners learn to see in the unfamiliar phenomena of practice similarities to the canonical problems they may have learned in the classroom? What are the processes by which some people learn to internalize, criticize, and reproduce the demonstrated competence of acknowledged masters? What is the nature of the complex process we are accustomed to dismiss with the term *imitation?* And what must practitioners know already to learn to construe their practice as a continuing process of reflection-in-action?

As some people learn to reflect-in-action, others learn to help them do so. These rare individuals are not so much teachers as coaches of reflection-in-action. Their artistry consists of an ability to invent on the spot the method peculiarly suited to the difficulties experienced by the student before them. And, just as professional artistry demands a capacity for reflection-in-action, so does the coach's artistry demand a capacity for reflection-in-action on the student's intuitive understanding of the problem at hand, the intervention that might enable the student to become fruitfully confused, or the proposal that might enable her or him to take the next useful step.

The development of forms of professional education conducive to reflection-in-action requires reflection on the artistry of coaching—a kind of reflection very nicely illustrated by the studies of case teaching conducted over the years at the Harvard Business School. If educators hope to contribute to the development of reflective practitioners, they must become adept at such reflection on their particular teaching practice.

In the context of planning education, these questions may lead us to rethink the roles of traditions such as studios, internships, field projects, and case teaching. These teaching vehicles offer opportunities for learning, but it is important to consider the ways in which they are employed as means to provide vehicles for reflection on practice. Students should be asked to perform and to reflect on the frameworks, theories, and strategies they intuitively bring to their performances. Instructors should be asked to teach like coaches, demonstrating their approaches to skillful performance and reflecting with students on their demonstrations. A principal objective should be a reflective practicum in which students are helped to acquire the habits and competences of reflection on their own reflection-in-action.

In exploring such questions, we will be pursuing a new epistemology of practice. Perhaps we will be heeding Hughes's (1959) call for ways of breaking the bonds that have tied the professional schools to the traditions of the late nineteenth century university. Or at least we will be getting some group of young people who are free of those bonds, allowing them to do something new and different.

References

Ackoff, Russell. 1979. The Future of Operational Planning Is Past. *Journal of the Operations Research Society* 30:93–104.

Alexander, Chris. 1964. *Notes Toward the Synthesis of Form.* Cambridge: Harvard University Press.

Alonso, William. 1963. Cites and City Planners. *Daedalus* 92:824–839.

Barnard, Chester. 1968. *The Functions of the Executive.* Cambridge: Harvard University Press.

Bernstein, Richard. 1976. *The Restructuring of Social and Political Theory.* New York: Harcourt, Brace, Jovanovich.

Geertz, Clifford. 1973. *The Interpretation of Cultures.* New York: Basic Books.

Glazer, Nathan. 1974. The Schools of the Minor Professions. *Minerva* 12:346–371.

Gustafson, James. 1963. The Clergy in the United States. *Daedalus* 92:724–744.

Habermas, Jergen. 1968. *Knowledge and Human Interests.* Boston: Beacon Press.

Harrison, Andrew. 1978. *Making and Thinking.* Indianapolis: Hacket.

Hughes, Everett. 1959. The Study of Occupations. In *Sociology Today,* Robert Merton, Leonard Broom, and Leonard S. Cottrell, Jr., eds. New York: Basic Books.

Lynn, Kenneth. 1963. Introduction. *Daedalus* 92:649–654.

Polanyi, Michael. 1967. *The Tacit Dimension.* New York: Doubleday and Co.

Rein, Martin, and Donald A. Schön. 1977. *Problem-Setting in Policy Research.* Lexington, Mass. D.C. Heath and Company.

Ryle, Gilbert. 1949. *The Concept of Mind.* London: Hutcheson.

Schein, Edgar. 1972. *Professional Education.* New York: McGraw-Hill.

Shils, Edward. 1978. The Order of Learning in the United States from 1865 to 1920: The Ascendency of the Universities. *Minerva* 16:171–173.

Simon, Herbert. 1972. *The Science of the Artificial.* Cambridge, Mass.: MIT Press.

Veblen, Thorstein. 1918. *The Higher Learning in America.* New York: Kelley.

Vickers, Geoffrey. 1978. Unpublished memorandum. Cambridge: Massachusetts Institute of Technology.

16
Planning under Freedom: A New Experiment in Democracy

Bertram Gross
Kusum Singh

> There is nothing in the conscious planning of domestic priorities which is inherently incompatible with the freedoms which mean most to the contemporary Englishman or American. . . . A happy and fruitful marriage between freedom and planning can, in short, be arranged.
> —Barbara Wootton, *Freedom Under Planning*

> We have "planners for freedom" who promise us . . . not the freedom of the members of society but the unlimited freedom of the planner to do with society what he pleases.
> —Friedrich Hayek, *The Road to Serfdom*

In most planning—local or national, public or private, civilian or military—a small number of powerholders and experts are free to constrict or expand the freedom of large numbers of people. Maximum feasible participation is too often a ritual involving only illusory changes in the structure of power. As a result, many people are disillusioned with planning. Experience tells them that even well-designed plans are too often transformed into autocratic, bureaucratic, technocratic, or statist controls.

But what about democratic planning? This question reminds us of Mohandas Gandhi's response to a reporter who asked what he thought about Western civilization: "It would be a good idea." If democratic planning were more a reality and less of a rhetorical slogan, and if it were more substantive as well as procedural, it would be a very good idea—as well as a powerful tool in building more civilized societies.

What about planning for freedom? This question goes back to the debate between planners and antiplanners at the end of World War II. Hayek (1944) denounced national economic planning as the road to serfdom and became an international hero among war-rich free enterprisers seeking freedom from government controls and strong unions. Finer (1946) attacked Hayek's views as the road to reaction and called for national planning under law. Wootton

(1945) argued that planning for freedom would free people from the horrors of a postwar depression. Hayek counterattacked by insisting that government planning could lead to freedom only if restricted to planning for competition.

This debate now seems quaintly obsolete. Hayek (1945) clearly failed to face up to the power exercised by free market forces. He avoided any specifics on how to plan for competition in markets controlled by cartels, price leadership, oligopoly, or monopoly. Finer (1946) and Wootton (1945) advocated planning for freedom but relied on formalisms. Neither dealt directly with democratic politics or bottom-up planning. Like Hayek, they viewed freedom too much as license—that is, the power to do as one pleases.

This debate also seems very refreshing. Hayek (1944) helped revive concern about human freedom as an ideal, one that throughout human history has inspired the most sublime philosophies and creeds. Wootton (1945) and Finer (1946) recognized unemployment, poverty, and the business cycle as enemies of freedom. Their American counterparts argued that fuller freedom required wider economic security—a security obtainable under a more democratic capitalism. They convinced President Franklin D. Roosevelt to propose an Economic Bill of Rights (1944) focusing on these rights: employment, decent wages, housing, health care, social security, education, and the protection of competitive businesspeople and farmers. Backed by Roosevelt and then by Harry Truman, they organized support for the 1944–1945 Full Employment Bill first proposed by Truman when he was a senator. This measure heralded comprehensive planning for a full employment society in which enforcement of the right to a job would help make other economic rights more supportable.

Since then, the situation has changed. The right to a job—and even the symbolic word *full*—was stricken from the measure before it became the Employment Act of 1946. The concept of economic rights has faded into the background. In 1974 Representative Augustus Hawkins made an effort to revive the concept through legislation providing for local as well as national full employment planning. But by the time the Hawkins bill became the Full Employment and Balanced Growth Act of 1978, its commitment to human rights and national planning was weakened and the local planning provisions removed. The law's commitment to reducing officially measured unemployment to 4 percent in five years was then evaded by President Jimmy Carter and ignored by President Ronald Reagan. With both real and official unemployment rising to levels that previously would have been viewed as unacceptable, full employment seems to have become what Representative Hawkins considers the highest amount of unemployment that is politically tolerable. The idea of full employment budget as a conceptual tool for economic planning has been lost.

Moreover, comprehensive planning has been largely abandoned in lieu of segmental planning at local and national levels. Single-issue activists rarely discuss economic rights, their connection with civil and political liberties, or the importance of the legislative arena. The machinists' union has proposed a technology bill of right statute but deals with freedom only in attacking free market ideologues (Winpisinger 1983). Many policy analysts and planners have abandoned human freedom as an ideal and seem trapped in a prison of technocratic and bureaucratic language.

Hayek's (1944) spiritual descendants have filled part of the vacuum, as reflected in the free market concepts of Milton Friedman (1981), Michael Novak (1984), or Ronald Reagan (1985). They may have ignored economic rights and have tilted toward freedom for the powerful with too little attention to consequences for others. But they do celebrate freedom as a central ideal and thus strike a responsive chord—even among people who disagree with them on many issues. This is not merely because of their skills as communicators but rather because the message they communicate exalts a version of human freedom above specific issues.

A more democratic version might be based on Cicero's idea that "freedom is participation in power." This idea is inherent in the American Catholic Bishops' new experiment in economic justice—to be conducted through comprehensive planning on behalf of economic rights (Bishops' Pastoral 1984). It has been articulated by thirty-eight legislators, led by Representatives Charles Hayes, Augustus Hawkins, and John Conyers, whose Income and Jobs Action Act aims to develop participatory planning that will "advance the cause of human freedom for all Americans" (Hayes 1985).[1]

These are long-range efforts. The bishops' ideals could not move from pulpit to practice without creative alternatives to single-issue myopia, localism, autocratic leadership and management, bureaucratic perversions, and media manipulation. The Hayes–Hawkins–Conyers legislation could not be enacted or administered without realignments in political and economic power. Both require the maturing of freedom ideals related to moral values to help move the United States toward something much more than freedom under planning—namely, planning under freedom and freedom under law.

Freedom: A Fragile Web

Many people view freedom as a narcissistic or anarchistic right to do what one wants without constraints. "License they mean," as John Milton once wrote, "when they cry liberty." Many planners view freedom as another subject that, like human rights, is often ignored in schools of planning, social work, and public administration.

We share the belief once articulated by Supreme Court Justice Thurgood

Marshall, "My freedom ends where your nose begins." This goes beyond the assumption that the person behind the nose has the right to protection against assault. Marshall's message is that the freedom or any person (any group) is limited by the rights of others. This belief applies even to the rights proclaimed in the U.S. Declaration of Independence: life, liberty, and the pursuit of happiness. Freedom from traffic controls, automobile inspections, or airline regulations, like with liberty for murderers, could mean death for many. The unlimited pursuit of happiness by pollutors, racists, and gangsters would threaten other people's rights to life and liberty. To secure these rights, many responsibilities are woven together with them. Peer groups, organizational watchdogs, or public regulators assume or receive the responsibility to place limits on individual or group behavior. Some of these limits are internalized in individual or corporate conscience. The balance between freedom and control is possible only by some combination of internal and external limits.

Yet the web of rights and responsibilities is fragile. Powerful forces in society usually manage to evade controls and extend their own rights at the expense of those of weaker people. In turn, weaker elements seek countervailing rights (or entitlements) for themselves and new responsibilities and controls on others. Significant progress has been made in establishing certain rights of poor people, minorities, women, children, and the elderly. This progress has been resisted by those who resent limitations on their freedoms. It also has been undermined by the lack of progress in establishing the more general economic rights proposed by President Roosevelt in 1944.

In their new planning bill, Representative Charles Hayes and his cosponsors have reiterated Roosevelt's right to a job in new language as the right to earn a living for all those able and willing to work for pay. In this, they have dropped the emphasis on full-time work and recognized the growing importance of part-time work, flexible hours, and a shorter work year. They also have added the right to an adequate standard of living for those unable to work for pay. This right was missing from the original Roosevelt–Truman and Hawkins–Humphrey proposals. Representative Hayes argues that these two rights could contribute to the balanced growth needed to secure the other economic rights set forth by Roosevelt.

The human rights approach to planning has many potential advantages. It could help appeal to the basic moral values on which more civilized societies would be based, escape the indignities of means tests and bottom-up pleadings for crumbs from powerholders, and provide a broad public interest context for the work of professional specialists and single-issue groups.

But new economic rights involve new responsibilities. Thus, the Hayes approach would expand the federal role in actively promoting more responsibility by local and state governments, employers, labor, and voluntary agencies. It implies that a person's right to a freely chosen opportunity for paid work gives that person the responsibility to earn his or her living rather than just receive unearned income. Above all, it implies that both employees and employers develop more concern, solicitude, and active caring for the rights of others.

Open Politics

"Stay out of politics" is a major slogan of technocratic planners. It also is something of a masquerade. Nonpolitical planners are usually actively involved in behind-the-scenes politics, such as the politics of competing professional specialties or of bureaucratic infighting over public budgets and foundation grants. These planners strengthen their competing positions by inventing new specializations with professional jargon that limits public understanding and creates a closed politics antithetical to democratic practice.

These nonpolitical practitioners work closely with single-issue pressure groups, single-issue coalitions, and other activist counterparts. The activists use persuasion and pressure in lobbying appointed and elected public officials. They come into the open by raising money and campaigning for or against candidates in primaries and elections. But this kind of openness is not conducive to democratic decision making. Like professional specialization, it promotes the submersion of common interests in a welter of special interest maneuvering.

The way out of this situation is not to destroy technical or activist specialization. Nor would it be enough if social scientists were to revive the concept of public interest and if planners were to accept the idea of comprehensive planning for freedom. The essence of a remedy is to bring both kinds of specialists together in broad, multi-interest coalitions. The broadest coalition under the U.S. system is a political party (or party coalition) seeking general control of government. This kind of general control is essential for the kind of planning that integrates special interests into a broad set of common interests—and is capable of following through with concrete action.

On a subject like full employment policy, for example, every single issue is a vital drop in the bucket—but only if there is a bucket. Otherwise, serious efforts may evaporate into air. Or people may be misled into spending valuable energies on Band-Aids, charades, and masquerades.

In a constitutional democracy, the political party or movement is the largest bucket. Whether in power or in opposition, it can contain the precious drops of otherwise isolated actions and theories. As David (1971, p. 308) points out, "party platforms have become important as alternative and partially overlapping national plans on which a substantial degree of execution can reasonably be expected." Although many analysts have supported this national notion, analysis is needed of similar developments at the local level.

Our observations of local politics in Arlington County, Berkeley, Chicago, Detroit, New York, Oakland, Portland, Santa Monica, and Seattle are that primary or election campaigns often present voters with clear choices between competing values orientations. Sometimes an alternative may be offered by a nonpartisan or bipartisan coalition, or opposing alternatives may be presented by adversary groups within one party. In either case, voters have a choice.

Nationally, there often has been too little opportunity for a genuine choice or, when a choice is clear, for a victorious party to follow through on its mandate. The broad alternatives presented by the two major parties have long been blurred by the existence of liberals in the Republican Party and of many more conservatives among the Democrats. Thus, a formal democratic majority in the House or the Senate is often undermined by the de facto majority coalition between the conservative Republicans and Democrats.

In 1946, Paul David, at the Bureau of the Budget, and Bertram Gross, at the Council of Economic Advisers, saw this coalition as a barrier to serious debate over the administration of the Employment Act of 1946. They organized a committee of the American Political Science Association to consider how the two major parties might become more responsible and democratic forces in national policy. The committee offered many reforms aimed at developing a party system that would give voters an open, clear, and enforceable choice (Committee on Political Parties 1950). Considerable progress was made in the next thirty years. The solid South, then an area of Democratic monopoly, became an arena for two-party conflict. The Republican party, formerly populated by many liberals who supported Democratic reforms, became more consistently conservative and committed to the idea that the wealthy are more competent than others to make policy decisions. They have mobilized support for business freedom from strong regulations and from labor unions. In contrast, the Democratic party has deserted the public interest populism of the New Deal and Fair Deal, particularly the goal of defending lower- and middle-class people against vested economic interests.

The Johnson administration rejected full employment planning and budgeting, concentrating on a few worthwhile but insufficient laborpower programs such as job training. The Carter administration used so-called jobs programs, mainly a few worthwhile but temporary, dead-end jobs at substandard wages, as a substitute for full employment policies. After signing the Hawkins–Humphrey Act in 1978, President Carter moved to expand unemployment instead of lowering it—presumably to curb inflation. The aftermath was more unemployment, more inflation, and the gradual abandonment of full employment by the Democrats during the 1980 and 1984 presidential election campaign.

Furthermore, presidential candidate Mondale, in 1984, deserted the Democrats' historical attack on special interests, alienated Reverend Jesse

Jackson's supporters by deemphasizing affirmative action, and affronted Senator Gary Hart's supporters by questioning his call for new ideas. In turn, neither Jackson nor Hart supported enforcement of the Hawkins–Humphrey statute. Freedom from unemployment, poverty, and racism and the predicted downturn in the business cycle received little public emphasis in the Mondale campaign. The retreat on populist principles and on balanced growth created a vacuum quickly filled by incumbent Ronald Reagan's dedication to a special interest version of human freedom and to policies of unbalanced growth as new thinking. Reagan thus branded Mondale as the prisoner of special interests and made Mondale sound more of an echo than a choice. Accordingly, almost half the voting age population stayed away from the polls.

The Income and Jobs Action Act, like the first version of the 1946 and 1978 full employment planning laws, is based on the open politics philosophy of presenting American voters with clear and enforceable alternatives. It would oblige the president every year to present to the Congress and the public a detailed report of full employment intended to make basic rights a reality. It would involve comprehensive planning in local areas throughout the country. The Joint Economic Committee, composed of people from both major parties, would provide the American electorate with a public airing of alternative ways of attaining the act's goals.

The idea of alternatives suggests that there is no one way to make economic rights and full employment at decent wages a reality. Conservative Republicans would emphasize federal incentives for profit-making companies and for investment in high technology. They would promise, as an immediate encouragement to business, higher rates of return on invested capital. Liberal Democrats would give higher priority to meeting the social and economic needs of people. They would offer immediate increases in consumer demand as a basis for capital investment and stabler business profits over the long run. There also are major differences within each party that should be publicized to make voting in elections more a matter of alternative values than of competing personalities.

Inclusive Partnerships

Partnership, in dictionary terms, means "an association of two or more members in a business enterprise." It is the latest fashion in urban planning in New York, San Francisco, Boston, Oakland, and a number of other cities. The typical private-public partnership is often composed of bank and corporate representatives and a few government officials, educators, and community members. But the real power is usually with the large economic operators. Their purpose is to seek social goals through improved incentives for the private sector instead of overreliance on government.

It is possible to share this purpose while pointing out that the alternatives to government include much more than large economic operators. There is no single private sector. The nonincorporated self-employed, small- and medium-sized corporations, and small business partnerships are often excluded from private-public partnerships. Nonprofit organizations of many varieties are usually excluded from top decision making in such groups.

To overcome this weakness, the new Income and Jobs Action Act mandates inclusive partnerships. In addition to government officials, these broadbased groups include "small and large business enterprises; labor organizations and trade unions; the unemployed; non-profit, voluntary and cooperative organizations (including neighborhood, tenant and homeowners' associations and corporations); women; and racial and ethnic minorities.

Moreover, present partnerships often rely on semisecret government handouts. This tendency conflicts with the democratic principle that recipients of public funds should be held openly accountable for their use. In public contracts, this principle is formally observed by detailed specifications for the work to be done, competitive bidding, and administrative monitoring by contract managers. This principle is formally overturned by tax deductions. The billions given away through local, state, and federal tax shelters become legal entitlements powerfully insulated from accountability. Some recipients of these entitlements have no hesitation in financing campaigns against other entitlement programs for middle- and lower-income people.

The remedy offered in the Income and Jobs Action Act is to impose certain conditions on the receipt of federal incentives by larger corporations— namely, on "their performance in living up to well-defined standards of corporate responsibility, including the obligation regularly to certify compliance with laws and regulations governing working conditions, labor relations, affirmative action, environmental protection, taxation, election contributions and bribery at home and abroad."

However, much more specification is needed. Most tax incentives for local real estate and business development should be conditioned on certificates of necessity granted only after public hearings before representative bodies. Entirely apart from lawbreaking, economic performance should also be monitored. This could mean the reduction or removal of incentives in the case of companies like U.S. Steel that use the funds for takeovers and higher executive salaries instead of productive investment. It should also mean expanded incentives for companies that distinguish themselves by contributing to sustainable recovery and full employment.

Panoramic Perspectives

Some people see the United States in terms of the layercake model, with local government as the bottom layer, state government in the middle, and national government at the top. But this model does not operate in practice. Village, town, city, county, regional, state, and national government agencies are intertwined in remarkably complex mazes. Grodzins (1966), a pioneering analyst of U.S. federalism, has suggested that we take the layercake out of our heads and instead think of government as a marble cake. If federal government is the chocolate in the batter, there are large strands and small traces throughout. Thus there is little basis for allocating, say, education or public assistance to local governments and civil rights to the states. There is less basis for assigning overall economic policymaking to the federal government alone.

One way to avoid undue concentration of federal power is to continue the historical process of broadening the domain of the 15,000 town, city, county, and state planning agencies now in existence. When first established, these agencies concentrated on land use, zoning, and building controls. Over time, they added other functions such as public facility planning, capital budgeting, transportation, social services, environmental protection, and economic promotion. Most of these functions became increasingly dependent on state and federal aid. Yet few local governments or their planning advisers have ever attempted to parallel the perspectives provided by the Office of Management and Budget and the Council of Economic Advisers.

Some planning technicians think that local planning has gone as far as it can go. However, others believe that the entire country has a long way to go — and that many local governments are already leading the way. Carnoy, Shearer, and Rumberger (1983) look forward to a new positive role for local planning commissions that includes a creative use of zoning and breaks the hold of business interests over the city planning process. They argue that one way to do this is the local development agreement. Santa Monica, for example, gives private developers the right to build shopping centers, office buildings, industrial development parks, or luxury housing only if the developers, in return, contract to provide middle-income housing, a public park, or day care center or to train a specified number of the locally unemployed for the construction jobs involved. They suggest that "every large- and middle-sized city should have its own development bank and/or public development corporation to engage in entrepreneurial activities."

The Income and Jobs Action Act is more far-reaching. Through it, the members of inclusive partnerships — under the aegis of local government — would cooperate:

(A) to assess unmet needs in their areas, including the need for voluntary leisure, as well for goods and services, adequate income, employment at good wages, and volunteer activities;

(B) to survey the supply of labor reserves and of managerial, professional and technical skills that might be used in meeting such needs;

(C) to analyze the potential for obtaining necessary funds from various combination of private and public sources without undue reliance on Federal funding;

(D) to develop goals for the future (through the year 2,000) of their areas; and

(E) in the light of the activities conducted under subparagraphs (A) through (D), to initiate high priority action projects that attain prompt progress toward such goals both private and public agencies and market and non-market processes.

In all these activities, the act mandates "self-empowerment by people victimized by discrimination in hiring, training, wages, salaries, fringe benefits, or promotion on the basis for prejudice concerning, race, ethnic background, gender, age, religion, station in life, political or sexual orientation, or personal disability." Provisions should also be made for the many problems involved in these efforts to be brought fully into the open at community public forums and aired through newspapers, radio, and television.

No local area is "an island, entire of itself" but rather "a piece of the continent, a part of the main," to paraphrase John Donne. No neighborhood past, present, or future can be understood without seeing it in the context of the whole city. No person who is only street wise can be system smart. No city or state can be understood apart from the nation and world of which it is part. No marble cake can be reduced to single strands of flavor or color.

In all the debates on the scope of national government, there is substantial agreement on the need for positive federal action. The differences center around the type of action. Some favor the expansion of tax entitlements for the rich, military spending, subsidies for U.S. capital in other countries, protection of transnational investments, monitoring of dissidents, or involvement in personal affairs. Others favor more corporatist planning of industrial growth with government subsidies or expansion of social programs and public works. And others support the command economies of pre-industrial societies or see Cuba, China, or the USSR as their models.

We see democratic national planning in the United States departing sharply from each of these formulas. First, the federal government should neither seek the omnipotence of command economies nor allow itself to be reduced to impotence by giant transnational corporations. Second, there is no need for any serious growth in the size of the federal government other than that resulting from population and productivity increases. What is needed instead is a major shift of resources from the from the uncontrolled tax subsidies and the military-industrial complex to activities that meet unmet needs for productive investment and improved social programs.

There is an immediate need to create permanent policies and institutions to foster sustainable recovery from recession or depression in the United

States or any of its areas. Part of this task can be done using measures that require no additional public spending or revenue loss, such as reduced interest rates, lower taxes for lower- and middle-income groups, sharing of voluntary work, elimination of compulsory overtime, or reduction of the weekly working hours on which overtime is based. General policies of this type are found in the Hayes legislation. Equally important would be a provision requiring the president to propose a permanent Works and Services Administration to help finance public and private works and service projects to improve the infrastructure of the United States public works, human services, private industries, and natural resources.

There also is need for action on the global dimensions of U.S. policy. One step would be to enact a low-interest-rate policy to relieve the Federal Reserve system of its present dependence on the monetary fads of short-sighted commercial bankers. This policy would ease the crushing debt burden in Third World countries, reduce the price of overvalued dollars, and promote employment in the export and consumer goods industries. Another step would be a statutory commitment—or a congressional resolution—to support an international economic order based on rising living standards. This step could help reverse the austerity policies now imposed on many countries by the International Monetary Fund and World Bank. U.S. contributions to these international agencies could be made conditional on movement in this direction.

Democratic Managing

Why planning and management? Corporate leaders never ask this question. For them, planning is much more than an exercise in analyzing trends and alternatives. It is an integral part of all managerial processes. Strategic, tactical, and operational planning—both short and long range—are ways to get results, the most important of which are usually more money and power for corporate leaders and their organizations.

Progressive leaders often fail to focus on management. Instead they adopt autocratic managerial styles, think that specialized technical knowledge and a feeling for human relations and politics are sufficient to guide complex undertakings, or believe that a corporation can be democratized merely by placing a few labor, consumer, or government representatives on its board of directors. These may be important conditions, but they are not enough. We believe that democratic planning cannot come to fruition without democratic management. This is as true for nonprofit and voluntary organizations as for profit-seeking corporations and government agencies.

Although democratic management is still in its infancy, a few concepts are becoming clear. It is desirable to reduce unnecessary hierarchy, increase multilevel participation at all decision-making stages, encourage independent labor unions, and promote the free flow of improved information.

Some degree of hierarchy is necessary in any organization, particularly in a complex system; but any amount of hierarchy can foster delusions of grandeur among the higher-ups. These delusions can best be combatted by lateral relations of shared responsibility (sometimes referred to as *heterarchy* or *polyarchy*), by encourgement of counterbalancing hierarchies, and by decentralization of authority (Henderson 1981; Scott and Hart 1979; Thayer 1981). It is important to dispel the myth of a single central planning agency. No representative board, chief executive, or support staff can, by itself, carry out all functions of central planning. A board or executive cannot simply impose the coordination of plans on subordinates. Rather, the functions of each are necessary parts of central guidance clusters. As Follett (1942) proposed, coordination should be "a process of auto-governed activity — the reciprocal relating of all factors."

A popular substitute for genuine democracy is for managers to encourage participation by the managed after the broad decisions have already been made at the top. Others are then encouraged to fight about small details. But this kind of manipulation cannot fool nonmanagers for long. Nor can it bring managers into contact with realities best understood by subordinates. As a result, Follett (1942) urged participation from the start, by arguing that the process of interpenetration of policies must begin while they are still in the formative stage. This approach can broaden the vision and unleash the powers of nonmanagers. It may take time, and it may undermine traditional managerial prerogatives. But over time it can add to organizational effectiveness and efficiency.

Labor unions are strange intruders in any formal organization. As representatives of nonmanagerial employees, they offer a form of industrial democracy that is a profound challenge to autocratic management. The slow and reluctant acceptance of collective bargaining has been an integral part of the historic transformation of earlier capitalism's dark Satanic mills into the modern workplace. It has brought employees from many different organizations together into labor and political movements that have helped strengthen and protect political democracy.

Today, however, some advances of industrial democracy are being reversed. Corporations are learning how to entice some union leaders into helping management keep workers productive. They are replacing employees with machines, conducting drives to bust unions, or moving to areas where labor unions are not tolerated. Some unions adopt the autocratic styles of management. Their officials sometimes prefer weak unions made up of docile locals in contrast with strong unions whose members might threaten to replace the present leadership. The situation worsens when leaders or members allow unions — potentially powerful defenders of poor people, minorities, and women — to be undermined by racism or sexism.

Democratic management means that unions should free themselves from prejudice and oligarchy. They should take the offensive in organizing the unorganized. Instead of concentrating entirely on wages, hours, and working conditions, they should broaden the collective bargaining agenda to include the quality of work, employee training, management development, plans for expansion or contraction, and workplace democracy as a whole.

Information is a source of power, but it rarely flows freely through an organization. Bureaucrats cling tightly to privileged information. Technicians use specialized jargon to keep others from interfering with what they are doing. Formal organizational rules may indirectly foster the falsification of records by those engaged in rule breaking. Information systems may produce huge amounts of useless paper. The annual reports of private corporations or government agencies may mix accurate with distorted information. Budgeting and accounting may be particularly distorted, thus making their democratization a principal priority in democratic management.

One place to start is with government. Program budgeting should be used more widely but with clear descriptions to identify programs. Like most local and state governments, the federal government should have both a capital and an operating budget rather than to group all outlays into one budget. All government agencies should set up capital accounts that bring basic facts on their land, facilities, and inventories into the open. They should develop total impact statements estimating the direct and indirect costs and benefits of each capital and operating program. No agency can do this by itself, however. Good information—whether on the environment, economy, employment, health, or social structure—should be collected by general statistical agencies like the Census Bureau or the Bureau of Labor Statistics.

The social indicator movement of the 1960s was energized by people who sought this kind of information collection. Today, however, economists and statisticians have steered the movement toward traditional definitions and monetary measurements. A reconstructed social indicator movement—rooted in popular politics and oriented toward a more progressive social calculus or social accounting—is needed (Gross 1966). This effort should include the provision of more refined and timely input-output data on the changing relations among economic sectors, as pioneered by Wassily Leontiev. Gould (1979) has pointed out that the test of any true commitment to national planning would be the encouragement of regional input-output studies for all areas of the country.

Representatives Hawkins and Hayes call for a more forthright handling of the government's unemployment data, an approach with implications for input-output calculations. For example, the official government figure for February 1985 was 9.1 million unemployed. However, the government collects but does not widely publicize the fact that an additional 5 million part-time workers are seeking full-time employment and that another 5 million want jobs but are not seeking them. Hawkins and Hayes urge the government to add these figures together and publicize the total sum of 19.1 million. Representative Hayes suggests that this could be done without disturbing the official total. It then would be easier to see how much potential output and government revenue are lost through joblessness and how much output, tax revenue, and deficit reduction would be gained by moving toward full employment.

Bottom-Sideways Communication

"We need bottom-up feedback" is a popular reaction against top-down control by political leaders or agency bureaucrats. But prompt and accurate feedback is not necessarily democratic. Indeed, it can be the essence of undemocratic control. Two-way communication for autocratic control can help elites maintain their privileges at the expense of other people's freedom.

Besides, bottom-up is not necessarily the opposite of top-down. It usually implies a tacit acceptance of verticality—namely, superior-subordinate relationships. In India's campaign for freedom from the British empire, Mohandas Gandhi developed methods of bottom-sideways communication with and among hundreds of millions of illiterate peasants. Once a mass movement was under way, Gandhi's messages up the ladder to the British monarchs were no longer humble petitions from submissive subjects. They had power behind them—power based not only on the Congress party members and various mass organizations but also on wide-ranging networks throughout the country (Singh 1979, 1983a).

In the United States, the nuclear freeze, jobs-with-peace, and neighborhood and tenant movements provide varying examples of bottom-sideways communication. In each, localism is to some extent countered through some sort of national organization. In some of these organizations efforts are made to counter inevitable tendencies toward oligarchy. Many use nonmedia and small media channels instead of relying on the major mass media. This is quite different from the nationwide linkages among U.S. corporate, military, and political elites and from the top-top networking practiced by transnational corporations and the global banking community. It involves fewer elites and more ordinary people.

This kind of lateral communication has one thing in common with the top-top communication of privileged elites and their technocratic aid: an orientation toward developing a common purpose. But the basic purpose (even if more tacit than explicit) is different—namely, to democratize the structure of money and power.

If progress is to be made in attaining this purpose, the immobilizing effects of most mass media must be countered by message systems that mobilize and energize. Theory, rational analysis, and open debate in community forums are necessary. But the great majority of a people can never be brought together at the intellectual or verbal levels alone. Gandhi's personal example of commitment to basic moral values was the message. And this message was reinforced by cultural communion — religious ritual, music, and poetry. In the United States today these factors are rarely to be found outside of churches, synagogues, and mosques. What has happened, one might well ask, to the songs of the earlier civil rights movement? Where is the neighborhood organization, union local, parent-teacher association, or planning commission that opens a meeting with a song or poem? Where, indeed, is the poetry of true freedom? We suspect it has been buried under the dead weight of technocratic professionalism and bureaucratic routine.

The burials may be global in scope. At the United Nations, top-top communication among the representatives of regimes is valuable but a poor substitute for communication among larger numbers of people. In 1975 specialists at the United Nations floated the idea of a new economic order. This idea was followed by super-elite conferences and reports on a new information or communication and then a new technological order (Singh 1983b). A new world order in general is advocated by well-meaning utopians who dream of world government without recognizing the many intermediate steps necessary for such a consummation or who advocate disarmament without considering what economic plans would be needed to replace the stimulus of war, war threats, and military spending.

We believe that no progress toward overcoming these fragmented visions can be made through reliance on top-top communication in the United Nations or other intergovernmental organizations. People-to-people communication is also essential to make the whole world truly kin. This type of communication not only would mean more tourism, more intermarriages, and more educational, cultural, and scientific exchanges but also would require people-to-people forums on a regional and global scale, the transnational organization of labor in its efforts to bargain with transnational capital. Goldman (1983), the historian of the Democratic party, goes as far as to suggest coalitions among national political parties.

A small start in this direction was made in 1984 at a conference, Global Unemployment: Challenge to Policy Makers, at the Friedrich Ebert Foundation in Bonn. Similar work was initiated in 1985 by the University of Stockholm in Sweden; the International Council on Welfare at its conference in Finland; by the Law Centre in Bombay, India; and by the World Future Society in Washington, D.C. With enough preparatory activity of this type, it will be possible by the end of the 1980s or the early 1990s to convene — with popular as well as specialist participation — the first United Nations Conference on Unemployment.

Pincers on Bureaucrats

Public administration and business management literature brims over with constructive proposals for overcoming the deadening aspects of public and private bureaucracies. So do the filing cabinets and waste paper baskets to which such ideas may be unceremoniously consigned. Without support from above and below, good ideas are driven out of circulation—and hopes for freedom from bureaucratic stifling are shattered.

Viable action for bureaucratic reform can emerge only from a social environment with enough antibodies to combat the diseases inherent in bureaucracy and enough vitamins to nourish democratic organizational reform. This kind of environment can be created through an application of what we call the pincer approach to bureaucracy: general guidance and careful monitoring by elected executives and legislators on behalf of people-oriented plans and policies and public interest activism in the form of legislative initiatives and participatory bill drafting as well as the full variety of consultative arrangements.

When these two forces are connected by common values and a popular party or coalition, we have a pincer. Under these conditions, bureaucrats will respond more fully to their consciences and to popular rather than corporate interests. The sense of public responsibility and accountability can then readily sprout and blossom.

Each part of the pincer, of course, needs more elasticity than a stick and more creative vigor than a wet noodle. Executives who try to democratize a subordinate bureaucracy by formal reorganization alone will soon learn the truth in the maxim that "the more things change, the more they remain the same." It is far better to change management styles by setting an example of dedication to efficient service in the public interest.

The normal channels of public activism are more widely used in the United States than any other large country of constitutional capitalism. These channels include voter registration, candidate selection, electioneering, and efforts to influence elected and appointed officials through lobbying, petitioning, and consultation. On occasions these normal channels are more effective when supplemented by typically American actions such as parades, marches, demonstrations, picketing, and other forms of nonviolent activism. Only the more sophisticated of technique-oriented planners recognize this simple truth.

We do not have to go outside the United States to understand this truth. How did American women get the right to vote? Without sit-down strikes in auto and rubber in the 1930s, could the Committee for Industrial Organization (CIO) have organized industrial unions? In the 1950s and 1960s, what kind of civil rights movement would have been born without civil disobedience? One reason why the civil rights movement has declined in recent years is that many leaders have put away their marching shoes. Today, the spirit of Gandhi and Martin Luther King, lives mainly outside the civil rights movements.

Would its revival in the jobs, labor, and civil rights spheres disrupt the social order? Some people view disruption as a way of getting results and say yes. But we view social disruption as the product of violence, militarism, or exploitation. Nonviolent activism or civil disobedience may be nothing less than replacement of that disruption by obedience to higher moral law, to the Constitution, or to statutes that are violated through bureaucratic misinterpretation.

Beyond "Charismacho"

The premise that we need a charismatic leader animates much national politics, where charisma can be bought from professional image makers. It also guides leadership selection in many small groups. But the charismatic leader—by virtue of his presumed superiority or superhuman characteristics—makes his followers dependent on him. This leader expands his feelings of superiority by nurturing the followers' feelings of inferiority. We say "his" because charisma has usually been a form of machismo. When the two come together, we call it "charismacho."

Before the success of their independence struggles, Gandhi and Mao identified themselves as ordinary people. As noncharismatic leaders, they gave millions of others the feeling that they also could do big things. As a substitute for reliance on any one person like Nehru or Chiang, thousands of people became leaders (Singh 1979; Singh and Gross 1983). Later, however, charisma was conferred on both of them. Each was deified—Gandhi against his inclination and Mao by his own scheming—as part of bureaucratic efforts to avoid bottom-sideways mobilization.

Something similar happened with Martin Luther King, Jr. From the first bus boycott in Montgomery, Alabama, to the dramatic events in Selma, Birmingham, and Chicago, King courageously led demonstrations that received wide media attention. But the attention he received, augmented by his powerful oratory, gave the impression of a messiah who could save people by his efforts alone. "Why do they call me the Lord?" he agonized. "I'm no messiah, and I don't have a messiah complex." Oates (1983) argues that this unsought gift of charisma, actively bestowed on a reluctant King by the mass media, divided him from his followers. As a result of this charisma chasm, King did not feel he deserved all the tribute he got. During the 1960s and 1970s an antileadership reaction set in against the hero-macho-charisma model. Some activists revolted against the very idea of leadership, organization, or both.

The world was to be saved rather by the unlead, unorganized spontaneity of the masses.

But more constructive models of multiple leadership and honeycomb (rather than hierarchical) organizational structure have also come into being. In the affinity groups of the antinuclear and antiwar movement at the Greenham Common in England and many places in the United States, there is no one leader, spokesperson, or executive committee. Many decisions are reached by consensus. In the National Coalition Against Domestic Violence, an ethics committee has been developing a cooperative process through which all members can join in combining effective leadership with the empowerment of each group member (Shaw 1982). In some neighborhood and workplace groups, people operate on the principle of leadership rotation where superior-inferior relationships are supplanted by so-called reciprocal superiority and many people can have what John Stuart Mill (1970) called "the pleasure of leading and being led on the path of development." Still more people can synergistically exercise, in the words of Follett (1942), "power *with*" as an alternative to "power *over*"—that is, "a jointly developed power, a coactive, not a coercive power."

These new forms of leadership and organization are often initiated by women seeking alternatives to patriarchy. In some workplaces male and female employees together participate in management decisions on productivity, quality, and technology. Some managers and employees dream about organizations with the capacity to develop responsible leaders and hold them fully accountable for their decisions.

Conclusion

Are all these ideas highly improbable? Perhaps. But the abolition of slavery once appeared mighty improbable. The U.S. Constitution and Bill of Rights were both based on an assumption of slavery as an unchangeable reality. Many decades passed before slaves, defined as three-fifths persons by the Constitution, attained the legal status of full persons. Today, long after the Civil War, freedom from racism is still an ideal.

To plan merely for what presently appears feasible is a recipe for accepting the constraints on freedom imposed by those who mean license when they cry liberty. To plan a new experiment in democracy through locally rooted partnerships in comprehensive planning is different. It is to practice the high morality of caring for ourselves and others at the same time. It is to project the kind of vision that can animate the souls of humankind: freedom based on shared responsibility, the moral strength to resist the false individualism of "anything goes," and the capacity to interweave human values with the complex strands of many experiments in planning under freedom and law.

Note

1. The full statement by Representative Hayes on introducing the Income and Jobs Section Act, including brief highlights and a longer summary, appear in *Congressional Record,* 6 March 1985, pp. H1068–H1078. In addition to Representatives Hayes, Hawkins, and Conyers, the sponsors are Representatives Berman, Boxer, Burton, Dellums, Dymally, Fazio, Mineta, Martinez, and Miller of California; Lehman of Florida; Evans, Collins, Gray, and Savage of Illinois; Perkins of Kentucky; Owens, Rangel, Towns, and Weiss of New York; Kaptur, Traficant, and Stokes of Ohio; Mitchell of Maryland; Crockett and Kildee of Michigan; Clay of Missouri; Kolter and Murphy of Pennsylvania; Frost and Leland of Texas; and Lowry of Washington.

References

Bishops' Pastoral. 1984. Catholic Social Teaching and the U.S. Economy. *Origins* 22:337–383.

Bowles, Samuel, David Gordon, and Thomas Weisskopf. 1983. *Beyond the Wasteland.* New York. Anchor.

Carnoy, Martin, Derek Shearer, and Russell Rumberger. 1983. *A New Social Contract.* New York: Harper & Row.

Committee on Political Parties. 1950. *Toward A More Responsible Two-Party System.* New York: Rinehart.

David, Paul. 1971. Party Platforms as National Plans. *Public Administration Review* 3:303–315.

Finer, Herman. 1946. *Road to Reaction.* London: Dennis Dobson.

Follett, Mary Parker. 1942. Individualism in a Planned Society. In *Dynamic Administration: The Collected Works of Mary Follett,* Henry Metcalf and Lyndall Urwick, eds. New York: Harper & Row.

Friedman, Milton. 1981. *Capitalism and Freedom.* Chicago: University of Chicago Press.

Goldman, Ralph. 1983. *Transnational Parties.* Lanham, Md.: University Press of America.

Gould, Jay. 1979. *Input-Output Data Bases: Uses in Business and Government.* New York: Garland STPM Press.

Grodzins, Morton. 1966. *The American System: A New View of Government in the United States.* Chicago: Rand McNally.

Gross, Bertram. 1966. *The State of the Nation: Social Systems Accounting.* New York: Barnes and Noble.

Hayek, Friedrich. 1944. *The Road to Serfdom.* Chicago: University of Chicago Press.

Henderson, Hazel. 1981. *The Politics of the Solar Age: Alternatives to Economics.* Garden City, N.Y.: Anchor.

Malinowski, Bronislaw. 1944. *Freedom and Civilization.* Bloomington: Indiana University Press.

Mill, John Stuart. 1970. *The Subjection of Women.* Cambridge, Mass.: MIT Press.

Novak, Michael. 1984. *Freedom with Justice.* New York: Harper & Row.

Oates, Stephen B. 1982. *Let the Trumpet Sound: The Life of Martin King, Jr.* New York: Harper & Row.

Reagan, Ronald. 1985. *Inaugural Address.* Washington, D.C.: Government Printing Office.

Scott, William G., and David K. Hart. 1979. *Organizational America.* Boston: Houghton Mifflin.

Shaw, Linda M. 1982. Choosing Leaders—A Cooperative Model. *Aegis* Winter: 57–66.

Singh, Kusum. 1979. Gandhi and Mao as Communicators. *Journal of Communications* 3:94–101.

————. 1983a. Mass Line Communication: Liberation Movements in China and India. In *World Communications: A Handbook,* George Gerbner, ed. New York: Longman.

————. 1983b. People Against Charisma. *Communication* 4:20–25.

————, and Bertram Gross. 1983. 'MacBride': The Results and Response. In *World Communications: A Handbook,* George Gerbner, ed. New York: Longman.

Thayer, Frederick. 1981. *An End to Hierarchy and Competition.* New York: Franklin Watts.

U.S. Congress. House. 1985. *H.R. 1398. The Income and Jobs Action Act.* 99th Cong., 1st sess.

Winpisinger, William. 1983. *Let's Rebuild America.* Washington, D.C.: International Association of Machinists and Aerospace Workers.

Wootton, Barbara. 1945. *Freedom Under Planning.* Chapel Hill: University of North Carolina Press.

Index

Adequacy vs. equity, policy and, 143
Advocacy and political strategy, 205–206
Advocate planners, 184
Aging, coalitions and the, 156, 158, 159
American Institute of Planners (1973)
    Code of Professional Responsibility, 14
American Institute of Planning (AIP), 30
American Planning Association (APA), 45;
    Planning and Women division of, 190
Appalachia, participatory research in,
    128–129, 132, 134, 135

Bargaining, participatory research and, 135
Baum, Howell, 224
Birch, Eugenie, 187
Boston Consulting Group (BCG), 67–68
Bottom-sideways communication, 264–265

Carter administration, 256
Caves, Richard, 68
CDCs. See Community development
    corporations
Chandler, A., 67
Civil rights movement, 266–267
Coalitions, political, 5; ad hoc, 159;
    association, 159; communications
    network for, 162; compatibility of goals
    and, 155; definition, 153; factors that
    create successful, 154, 161–162;
    federation, 159; horizontal, 154–155; in
    human services, 155–161; "Iron
    Triangle," 161; leadership and, 162;
    network, 159, 161; origins, 154; policy
    issue network, 161; political strategy in
    social planning and, 204–205; purpose,
    153–154; resources for, 162; vertical,
    154, 155
Columbia University, feminist advocacy
    planning and, 190
Community development corporations
    (CDCs), 5–6: accomplishment rates,

167–169; factors affecting success of,
    169–174; government programs and,
    166; purpose, 165, 166; roles of
    planners in, 174–178; skills needed for
    working in, 176–178; staff, 170–174;
    types, 166–167
Community planning, participatory research
    and: bargaining and, 135;
    comprehensive rational planning models
    and, 124; examples, 126–130; factors
    affecting outcome of, 131; how
    differences can be handled, 132; phases,
    132–133; planners needed for,
    134–136; power distributions and, 125;
    problems of planning, 123–126;
    purpose, 131, 132–134
Constituencies, developing, 199–200
Conyers, John, 253

David, Paul, 256
Decision process models, strategic planning
    and, 69–70
Democratic planning, 251, 261–264
Demonstration projects, use of, 116

Easy Bay Asian Local Development
    Corporation, 167
Economic recession, effects on social
    planning, 1, 196
Economic rights, 252–253, 257
Employment Act of 1946, 252, 256
Equal Rights Amendment (ERA), 189
Equity vs. adequacy, policy and, 143
Ex ante policy analysis, 110
Experiments, use of, 116
Ex post policy evaluation, 111–112

Failures of programs, views of, 247
Family vs. public contributions in
    programs, 143–144
Feminist advocacy planning, 6; analyzing

Feminist advocacy planning (*continued*)
    urban structure and community process
    and, 185–186; criteria for, 184–185;
    education and research for, 189–191;
    identification as a feminist, 185;
    identifying gender variables, 186–187;
    National Congress of Neighborhood
    Women and, 187–189; New Jersey
    Bergen County League of Women
    Voters and, 188; problems faced by
    women, 181–184; purpose, 184
Freedom, planning under: bureaucratic
    reform and, 266–267; democratic
    planning and, 251, 261–264; economic
    rights and, 252–253, 257; enemies of
    freedom, 252; federal power and,
    258–259, 260–261; feedback and,
    264–265; leadership and, 267–268;
    local planning commissions and, 259;
    partnerships and, 257–258; political
    parties and, 255–256; role of
    government in, 251–252; special interest
    groups and, 255, 257; views of
    freedom, 253–254
Full Employment and Balanced Growth
    Act of 1978, 252
Full Employment Bill, 1944–1945, 252

Gandhi, Mohandas, 251, 264, 267
Goals: coalitions and, 155; planning theory
    and outcomes vs., 15–16; political
    strategy in social planning and, 198;
    organizations and, 140
Greater Philadelphia First Corporation
    (GPFC), 75
Great Planning Disasters, 225
Greenham Common (England), 268
Gross, Bertram, 256

Habermas, J., 17, 55, 56
Hall, Peter, 225
Hart, Gary, 257
Harvard policy model, 66–67
Hawkins, Augustus, 252, 253, 263–264
Hawkins-Humphrey Act of 1978, 256, 257
Hayes, Charles, 253, 254, 263–264
Henderson, Bruce, 67–68
Hennepin County government, 76–78
Homeless, coalitions and the, 156, 159
Housing Act of 1949, 25
Human services, coalitions and, 155–161
Hunter College, feminist advocacy planning
    and, 190

Ideas: how to obtain policy, 141–142;
    ratification of, 142; structure and, 142;
    working guidelines for, 142
Implementation: analysis, 110; definition,
    105; importance, 109; steps, 110–112;
    tips for effective, 112–118; who is
    responsible for, 117–118. *See also*
    Policy analysis
Income and Jobs Action Act, 253, 257,
    258, 259–260
India, participatory research in, 127–128,
    131, 132, 134
Industrial economics models, strategic
    planning and, 68–69
Inquilinos Boricuas En Accion, 167
Intelligence, definition of, 240–241
Intelligence of Democracy, The, 220
"Iron Triangle," 161

Jackson, Rev. Jesse, 256–257
Johnson administration, 256

Kent, T.J., Jr., 47
King, Martin Luther, Jr., 267

Leaders, political strategy in social planning
    and, 202–203
Leadership: coalitions and, 162; planning
    under freedom and, 267–268
Leontiev, Wassily, 263

Malnourishment planning, example of, 237
Mann, Evelyn, 186, 187
Mao, Tse-tung, 267
Marx, Karl, 16, 20
Marshall, Thurgood, 253–254
Massachusetts Institute of Technology
    (MIT), 232
Master Plan approach, 47
Mondale, Walter, 256, 257

National Coalition Against Domestic
    Violence, 268
National Congress of Neighborhood
    Women (NCNW), 187–189
Neighborhood Self-Help Development
    (NSHD), 167
New Jersey Bergen County League of
    Women Voters, 188

Organizational practices, 141
Organizational structure: political strategy
    in social planning and, 201; problems
    with, 145–147

Participatory research. *See* Community
    planning, participatory research and
Partnerships, planning and, 257–258
Philadelphia Investment Portfolio, 73–76
Planners: advocate, 184; and client
    relationships, 218; community
    development corporations and role of,

174–178; differences between political and technical, 27, 33–34, 36; failures and views of, 247; government intervention and, 19–20; hybrid, 30–32, 34, 36, 37; image, 224–225; nonpolitical, 255; participatory research and, 134–136; responsibility, 14, 21; roles, 87, 100–101; as strategists, 87–89; views of society by, 13; women as, 186–187. *See also* Politics, planners and

Planners and Public Expectations, 224

Planning commissions, local, 259

Planning theory: anthropology and, 53; cognitive dissonance and, 44; critical theory and, 55–57; definition, 44–46; domination and power and, 17–18; functional vs. substantive considerations, 15; future research in, 50–51, 57–58; goals vs. outcomes, 15–16; government intervention and, 18–19; historical view, 52; how to teach, 48–57, 58–59; institutional view, 217–224; liberal ideology, 13–16; Master Plan approach, 47; organizational behavior and, 52–53; phenomenology and, 54–55; policy analysis and, 47–48; political economists and, 52; positivism and, 53–54; practice and, 12; problems with field, 48–50; rationality and the dyadic image and, 217–224; theory of justice and, 13–14; utopianism and, 16–18

Policy: definition, 141; how to test, 116; ideas and the transformation process, 141–143; identifying problems and, 113; implementation, 110–111; maintenance, 111, 116–117; monitoring, 111, 116–117; practice and public organizations and, 141; termination, 112; value conflicts and, 143–144; working guidelines for, 142

Policy analysis: alternatives and, 108–109, 113–114; concise information and, 114–115; examples of failed policies, 107; political factors and, 115–116; reasons for failures, 106–108; steps, 110–112. *See also* Implementation

Policy issue network, 161

Policy management, difficulties of public organizations: lack of interest and, 146; organizational structure, 145–147; problem definition, 144–145; public scrutiny and, 146; value conflicts, 143–144

Policy management techniques: importance of decision-making groups, 148–149; importance of ideas, 147; importance of writing skills, 149; staff needed for

implementation, 148; use of policy science, 148

Policy managers: ideas and, 141–143; multiple interests and, 146; pressures on, 146–147; public scrutiny and, 146; role, 5, 140, 141; writing skills, 149

Political coalitions. *See* Coalitions, political

Political factors, policy analysis and, 115–116

Political strategy in social planning, 6; advocacy and, 205–206; citizen participation and, 201–202; coalitions and, 204–205; corporate leaders and, 197; definition, 197; development of constituencies, 199–200; development of leaders for, 202–203; effects of economic growth on, 196; goal setting and, 198; identifying issues, 199; need to educate the public about, 203–204; obstacles to, 206–207; organizational structure and, 201; planners in public agencies and, 197; relationships with influentials, 204; roles of social planning, 196; skills needed for, 198–206; success of, 207–208; use of tactics, 200–201

Politics, planners and, 2–3, 11–12, 16–17, 25–39; ambivalence and, 30–33, 34; concrete or abstract thinking of, 33; future research on, 37–39; the poor and, 26; role orientations and, 29–34; self-perceptions, 28–36; skills and, 34–36; urban renewal and model cities and, 26; what constitutes a political planner, 27, 30

Popper, Karl, 13, 17

Porter, Michael, 68

Portfolio models, strategic planning and, 67–68

Power distributions, community planning and, 125

Practice: convergent knowledge vs. divergent skills, 239; dilemma of rigor or relevance, 236–240; institutional image and, 225–227; meanings for, 246; public's views of, 231; research and, 235–236, 238. *See also* Professions

Prince Political Accounting system, 96–100

Problem definition, 144–145

Professional knowledge, 240–249; reflection-in-action, 242–248

Professionals: public's views of, 231; reflection-in-action and, 246–247; views of themselves, 232–234

Professions, minor, compared with larger, 234–235

Program failure, 106

Public organizations: formulation of ideas,

Public organizations (*continued*)
140; goals and, 140; money and, 139;
organization culture, 139–140; policy
and practice and, 141; policy
management difficulties of, 143–147;
policy management techniques and,
147–149; separation of power in, 145;
steps in transformation process,
141–143; user-provider gap in, 145–146
Public versus family contributions in
programs, 143–144
Public vs. private handling of policy, 143

Ramsey County Nursing Service (RCNS),
71–73
Reagan, Ronald, 252, 257
Reagan administration, 15, 18, 190
Reflection-in-action, 242–248; professional
practitioners and, 246–247
Reflective Practitioner, The, 224
Renigades Housing Movement, Inc., 167
Research and practice, 235–236, 238
Resources: coalitions and, 162; target
groups and, 94–95
Rigorous practice, 236–240
Roosevelt, Franklin D., 252, 254
Rumelt, R., 67

St. Clair-Superior Coalition, 167
Schön, Donald A., 229
Shalala, Donna, 187
Skinner, Joyce, 186
Social Planning. *See* Political strategy in
social planning
Sociological analysis, 13
Spence, Michael, 68
Stakeholder models, strategic planning and,
69
Standard City Planning Enabling Act, 47
Strategic analysis: example, 96–100;
importance, 90–91, 92; planners as
strategists, 87–89; type of information
needed in, 89–91, 92–96; types of
schemes for, 91–92
Strategic planning: by corporate leaders,
197; decision process models and,
69–70; future research and, 79–81;
governments and, 65–66; Harvard

policy model and, 66–67; importance of
analyses in, 90–91, 92; industrial
economics models and, 68–69; portfolio
models and, 67–68; stakeholder models
and, 69; type of information needed in,
89–91, 92–96. *See also* Political strategy
in social planning
Strategic planning, public sector and, 70;
Hennepin County government, 76–78;
Philadelphia Investment Portfolio,
73–76; Ramsey County Nursing Service,
71–73
Strategy, definition, 3, 87
Structure, idea and policy development
and, 142

Target groups, information needed about,
92–96; basic position, 92–93; likelihood
of involvement by, 94; relationships
and, 96; resources, 94–95; specific
concerns, 93–94
Theorizing vs. practicing, 218–219
Theory failure, 106
Three Mile Island, 247–248
Truman, Harry S., 252

United Nations Conference on
Unemployment, 265
U.S. Department of Housing and Urban
Development (HUD), 11–12; women
and planning and, 190
University of California at Los Angeles,
feminist advocacy planning and, 190,
191
Urban General Plan, The, 47
Urban Heights, participatory research in,
129–130, 131, 132, 134, 135
User-provider gap, public organizations
and, 145–146

Value conflicts, policy and, 143–144

Watts Community Labor Action
Committee, 166
Weber, Max, 17

Youth, coalitions and, 158, 159
Youth and family, coalitions and, 158–159

About the Contributors

Barry Checkoway is associate professor of social work at the University of Michigan. He has taught at the University of Pennsylvania, the University of California at Berkeley, and the University of Illinois at Urbana–Champaign. His work on urban social policy planning, citizen participation, and community organization has been published in national and international journals. His edited books include *Citizens and Health Care: Participation and Planning for Social Change* and *The Metropolitan Midwest: Policy Problems and Prospects for Change* (with Carl Patton).

Howell S. Baum teaches social planning and planning theory at the University of Maryland School of Social Work and Community Planning. His previous work on planners and politics is presented in *Planners and Public Expectations*. His current research on the psychological dynamics of planning will be published as *The Invisible Bureaucracy: Problem-Solving in Bureaucratic Organizations*.

L. David Brown is professor and chair of organizational behavior at the Boston University School of Management. He holds an LL.B. and Ph.D. in organizational behavior from Yale University and has authored books and articles on organizational development, conflict management, and planned community change. He also is president of the Institute for Development Research, which works with organizations in Asia, Africa, North America, and South America.

John M. Bryson is associate professor of planning and public affairs in the Hubert H. Humphrey Institute of Public Affairs at the University of Minnesota, where he also serves as associate director of the Strategic Management Research Center. His work on strategic planning, organizational design, and project implementation and evaluation has been published in journals such as *Journal of the American Planning Association, Strategic Management Journal, Academy of Management Review, Policy Studies Journal,* and *Evaluation and Program Planning.*

Judith Innes de Neufville is associate professor of city and regional planning at the University of California at Berkeley and holds a Ph.D. in urban studies and planning from MIT. She is the author of *Social Indicators and Public Policy: Interactive Processes of Design and Application* and editor of *The Land Use Policy Debate in the United States*. She is currently involved in research in local and regional planning processes and their uses of information.

Milan J. Dluhy is associate professor of social work and adjunct associate professor of political science at the University of Michigan, where he specializes in social policy, implementation politics, and urban housing and elderly programs. His publications include *Changing the System: Political Advocacy for Disadvantaged Groups*.

John W. Dyckman is professor of geography and environmental engineering and senior academic advisor in the Center of Metropolitan Planning and Research at The Johns Hopkins University.

R. Edward Freeman is associate professor of strategic management and organization at the University of Minnesota. He previously taught at the Wharton School, where he consulted with a number of private and public sector organizations. His research concentrates on strategic management, business ethics, and decision theory, including his latest book, *Strategic Management: A Stakeholder Approach*.

Bertram Gross is distinguished professor emeritus at Hunter College of the City University of New York and professor of government and economics at Saint Mary's College of California. He served as executive secretary of President Truman's Council of Economic Advisors and has visited many countries as United Nations consultant on planning, development, and management. His books include *The Legislative Struggle, The Hard Money Crusade, Action Under Planning, The State of the Nation: Social Systems Accounting, Organizations and Their Managing, Social Intelligence for America's Future,* and *Friendly Fascism*.

Jerome L. Kaufman is professor and chair of the Department of Urban and Regional Planning at the University of Wisconsin at Madison, where he teaches courses on central city planning, interaction skills, and strategies for effective planning practice. His publications focus on the ethics and values of planners and planning in the United States and Israel. He has served as associate director of the American Society of Planning Officials and has consulted with state and local planning organizations and agencies.

Jacqueline Leavitt is acting associate professor at the Graduate School of Architecture and Urban Planning at the University of California at Los Angeles. She previously taught at Columbia University and helped organize the Planning and Women technical division of the American Planning Association. Her current research deals with tenant behavior in landlord-abandoned buildings in New York City and includes a forthcoming book with Susan Saegert.

Seymour J. Mandelbaum is professor of urban history and director of the doctoral program in city and regional planning at the University of Pennsylvania. His publications include "The Complete General Theory of Planning Is Impossible" in *Policy Sciences*. His current research includes the poetics of policy and planning arguments.

Neil S. Mayer is an economist and senior research associate at The Urban Institute. His research and publications have emphasized community-based organizations, neighborhood revitalization, and urban development, including *Keys to the Growth of Neighborhood Development Organizations* and *Neighborhood Organizations and Community Development: Making Revitalization Work*. He has been active in local government housing, economic development, and land-use planning in Berkeley, California, where he now lives.

Carl V. Patton is professor of urban planning and dean of the School of Architecture and Urban Planning at the University of Wisconsin at Milwaukee. Previously he was head of the Department of Urban and Regional Planning at the University of Illinois, at Urbana–Champaign. He is co-editor with Barry Checkoway of *The Metropolitan Midwest: Policy Problems and Prospects for Change* and co-author with David Sawicki of *Basic Methods of Policy Analysis and Planning*.

William D. Roering is a doctoral student in strategic management and organization at the University of Minnesota. He previously taught management and marketing at St. Cloud State University and consulted with several public and private organizations. His research interests include organizational process, strategic planning, and program implementation.

Donald A. Schön is Ford Professor of Urban Studies and Planning at the Massachusetts Institute of Technology. He is author of *Beyond the Stable State, Theory in Practice* (with Chris Argyris), *Organizational Learning*, and *The Reflective Practitioner: How Professionals Think in Action*.

Kusum Singh is professor of communications at Saint Mary's College of California. She previously was program planner and producer at All-India Radio and faculty member at the Administrative Staff College of India in Hyderaabad. Her publications deal with communication styles of leaders and policy issues in international communication, including "Democratic Planning: The Bottom-Sideways Approach" with Bertram Gross.

John E. Tropman is professor of social work at the University of Michigan, where he specializes in community organization, social planning, public policy, and administration. His several books include *Policy Management in the Human Services, The Essentials of Committee Management,* and *Effective Meetings*. His current interests include social policy and the elderly and the structure and values of social practice.